//
The
Outside Contributor

BY THE SAME AUTHOR

Roaring Boys
This Right Soft Lot
A Cackhanded War
Uncommon Entrance
Sorry, Dad
A Nest of Teachers
Shaky Relations
Lizzie Pye
Donkey Work
A Second Skin

The Outside Contributor

EDWARD BLISHEN

Hamish Hamilton
London

First published in Great Britain 1986
by Hamish Hamilton Ltd
27 Wrights Lane London W8 5TZ

Copyright © by Edward Blishen

British Library Cataloguing in Publication Data

Blishen, Edward
  The outside contributor.
  1. Blishen, Edward—Biography 2. Authors,
  English—20th century—Biography
  3. Radio broadcasters—Great Britain—
  Biography
  I. Title
  828'.91409   PR6052.L57Z/

ISBN 0-241-11949-9

Typeset by Sunrise Setting, Torquay, Devon
Printed in Great Britain by St Edmundsbury Press, Suffolk

*To Alan and Jen & to Mae and Sidney
with love*

Acknowledgements to A.P. Watt Ltd on behalf of Michael B. Yeats and Macmillan London Limited for permission to quote W.B. Yeats's epitaph on himself (from 'Under Ben Bulben') and lines from 'In memory of Eva Gore-Booth and Con Markiewicz.'

PROLOGUE

'Do you shoot snipe?' he asked. No, I said. 'Have you fished Lough Creagh?' I said I had not done that either. 'You know dear Lord Sutton, I am sure.' I was sure, I said, I did not. He seemed undismayed by this stranger's failure to score a single point in his quiz. He thought I'd be amused to know he had once swopped 'artificials' with dear Lord Sutton, and caught a bigger trout than dear Lord Sutton's own record catch. I did not know how to be amused by this, but nodded. We were in the presence of a great rhododendron, growing like a blossoming tent; it was rowdy with bees, and bees anxious to dine on it formed a thunderous jam in all directions. The bog garden smelt as this whole country smelt: sweet, tender, subtle. At my feet our ageing Jack Russell, Sal, expressed her disdain of the occasion. With her, maturity had consisted of a systematic intensification of her impatience with the world. She'd been furious, yesterday, with the attention we'd given to Yeats's grave. Being on holiday with this small dog was like being constantly attended by a dotty maiden aunt. It was what, I thought uncomfortably, by making her our companion, we'd converted her into.

'A pity,' he said, 'about this place. No one to appreciate it.'

It was Saturday morning, and most of the population of this

corner of Ireland seemed to be in the park. As we stood there, numerous persons had paused to speak well of the rhododendron. But I guessed this man was not thinking of people. He was thinking of lords: and especially the most undear lord who had erected the house that used to stand here. 'Adjoining the house,' I'd been reading in a mid-19th century account of the district, 'is a fine conservatory, well-filled with orange trees and other exotics: there are also in the demesne a variety of gardens, shrubberies, flower parterres, pheasantry, laundry-house, gamekeeper's lodge, fishing temple, moat-houses, farmyard, with workshops, stable &c &c.' At this point the historian seemed to think he ought to check any over-excitement felt by a naive reader. 'Such are, however,' he pointed out calmingly, 'but the ordinary acquisitions of a wealthy nobleman's abode.'

This damned man who'd fastened on me as I stood waiting for Kate had probably never forgiven the destruction of the house, and the throwing open of its grounds. I was ready to be sad about the loss of great houses, but felt content that this one should have disappeared. It had been built over a system of tunnels so contrived that, the history said, 'there is no appearance of menial movement near the house.' There had been a wholly successful avoidance of any glimpse of the men, women and children on whose labours had depended the operation of all those banal conveniences of a wealthy nobleman's abode. In a bar in the town Kate, who'd been reading an account of how the lord had dealt with a demand for better treatment from his tenants – among other things he'd made them carry lacerating burdens, shirtless – said it was a good thing he'd gone. There hadn't been a sharp intake of breath; but there was an impression of one. The town seemed unready yet to speak ill of the ghost of its tormentor.

I thought my own tormentor looked like a sour John Logan. A week ago, back home, my one-time maths master (perhaps the worst mathematician in the world) had paid us what he'd promised would become his annual visit. His original home, of course, had been somewhere round here. Would he have admired that tyrannical lord? It was, if you believed him – and he was never more than half-believable –

the crumbling of a great Irish house that had, oh horror, made a teacher of him. At Queen's Grammar School, Barton, nearly fifty years ago, he'd told me – bent over waiting to be beaten for choosing to write a bad poem in a worse maths lesson – that he'd seen me running about the town, little ruffian, and had never expected to have the misfortune to teach me. It was a moment I still hated to remember. I was fairly sure now that he'd said it – to someone who, as it happened, was an incurably mild and diffident townee – because I was a scholarship boy. He'd felt it necessary to knock the town out of any such boy, however short he fell of the raucousness Logan had in mind – and to knock into him . . . what? Well, John Logan and I had talked about these things, lately; and he'd written about them, too, from his rooms in that public school of which he'd become the Mr Chips – or, given his vast Irishness, Mr O'Chips. Together we'd dug up a scene that perhaps had been, by both of us in our different fashions, smoothed into too neat a mound. We'd conducted this dig together into an old heap of memory, and some astonishing things had come out of it.

This decade, being in one's fifties, I thought, was full of diggings of that kind. You'd piled up fifty years of memory and pseudo-memory, impressions faintly true and wholly false: suddenly the quick-stepping heroes and villains of your childhood and youth reappeared, shuffling and bent: things began to fall into place, and often not the place they'd always seemed to occupy.

Sal sniffed at my feet, angrily wishing we were elsewhere, and I thought how she'd had a similar quantity of experience packed into a briefer space. Only yesterday she was racing along the world's beaches, in hopeless but wonderful pursuit of the world's birds. She'd almost flown herself, leaping to snatch them out of the air: only they had that insolent advantage of being winged. Now all the birds might have been as arthritic as she was, and she'd not have bothered to take them. There'd been, for both of us, this pure decline in pace, and need to recalculate the proportions of our memories.

Kate appeared at this moment: who'd have been angry if she'd known I was having these valetudinarian thoughts. I remembered that she'd even frowned a little when I'd reported what Anthony Powell had said on the book programme I presented in a corner of the BBC's external services. He'd just completed the sequence of novels, *A Dance to the Music of Time*, that had taken him twenty-four years: and I'd asked him how his feelings about the writing of them had changed between 1951 and 1975. 'Well,' he said, 'when I began, if I had a character aged fifty, I felt sorry for him. Now, if I have a character aged fifty, I envy him.' It struck me, approaching sixty, that it *had*, after all, and despite one's anger about ageing, been a curiously youthful decade. That is, a sort of parody of youth. If old age involved you in second childhood, your fifties constituted – did they? – a second adolescence.

To my wife, the sour version of John Logan now said, 'My dear lady!', lifted his haughty cloth cap, and moved on. He *was* like Logan! My old teacher called Kate 'Dear lady', kissed her hand, and executed manoeuvres alarming in a seventy-five-year-old in order to open doors for her. In principle Kate deplored all that, and was still worrying over the discovery that in fact she enjoyed it.

I had a sudden vision of Logan performing one of his astonishing old man's scuttles. But then at the public school they still called him 'Monkey', for his being too impatient to wait for the library steps. In search of a book on the top shelf he'd swarm up to it, they said, by way of the others. I had a half-hope that the end might come when he was doing that. It would provide an appropriate epitaph: 'Died climbing the shelves at Savernake in search of a book.'

Kate had kept me waiting under the rhododendron because she'd been writing up her diary. Well, much had happened yesterday, and some of it had not been easy to describe. We'd visited Yeats's grave at Drumcliffe, and picked a buttercup growing on it to press in the pages of the *Collected Poems* my sister had bought for me a great many years earlier, at a cost of 12s 6d. It had replaced the handwritten selection I'd made from the copy in the school library. Kate had gone down the road and picked a bunch of wild flowers to make up for the stolen buttercup. Sal had sniffed and snorted at the poet's resting-place as a mark of her inappeasable impatience. And as we did these small things, under the shape of Ben Bulben, in the breath of a buzzing small ordinary day, we were addressed by those disdainfully icy words in which Yeats abjured all breath:

> Cast a cold eye
> On life, on death.
> Horseman, pass by.

And later we'd found ourselves at Lissadell House.

> The light of evening, Lissadell,
> Great windows open to the south,
> Two girls in silk kimonos, both
> Beautiful, one a gazelle . . .

Every element in those lines, including the caressing name of the house, had years ago prompted the architect in my imagination to construct a long elegance of stone, late-sunlit, in a great greenness of parkland. Instead, this grimly square house, of gloomy stone, like that of Drumcliffe Church: its squareness, as of a box, clutched in a squareness of trees and bushes that made for it outer boxes: of sunlessness, and then of the trees and bushes themselves. It was a blind house: there was no immense view for the great windows to open on . . .

But the wood around it! Here was an interlacing of trees and sunshine: and, when you broke through that, the beach, wide, empty, rocks and seaweed: the long arm of water, silent and sparkling: and the hills towards Sligo. We sat, thoughtful and burning in the heat that came so strangely after Yeats's cold words and the dark cold house; and then, across the sea, on the distant sands that echoed these we were sitting on, I thought I saw two crows. Then I realised that, if they were that size at that distance, they'd be giant birds: and thought it was a single creature, a black dog. But then we heard a thunder of hooves, carried easily by the water, and knew it for a black riderless horse.

I thought of my friend Ben, with whom I'd grown up, and who also loved that poem and the idea of this Irish house with the haunting name: and thought how odd it was he should feel such love, since the poem drew past and present shudderingly together. Ben had said to me recently that he had no nostalgia himself, very little interest in the past, no habit of comparing past with present. In fact, at heart he had some scorn for such habits. One should live *now* – there was no other time to live! I'd been talking about John Logan, and how he'd walked round the changing room at school, carrying his referee's whistle: and with the strap of it flicking out at our naked flanks. 'I guess he was a sadist,' said Ben. 'Do you think he was worth remembering?' Ben was amused by the thought of my diary, kept continuously since 1934. He was amused by the idea of, as he called it, 'hanging on to things.' 'But it's not what I do,' I protested. 'It's simply that I find life is rather like serving as a member of a jury in a very long trial – which is really your own, though it impinges on the trials of all the other people you've known. Everything that happens is evidence, and one day there will be a summing up. I don't want to arrive at that moment without some notes to fall back on.'

Though that wasn't, actually, for me, the whole of it. I was fascinated by life as the outrageous storyteller it was, proposing every day an unlikelihood and immediately piling another on top of it. If you had been watching closely, I wanted to say to Ben, you had seen Ben himself, merely as an example, being transformed in the winking of an eye, a headlong half century, from a particular kind of shy unpractised boy to a particular kind of bold experienced man. Ben had treated me recently to a grand sort of dinner in one of the grand sort of restaurants he'd grown accustomed to: and I remembered (but kept the memory to myself, as a mere instance of my hanging on to things) an occasion when as boys we'd gone to see *Lear*, and Ben had lost half a crown: and, quite failing to turn our dismay into the kind of joke we then favoured, since for both of us half a crown was a fortune, we'd hunted for it, in vain, up and down the dark floor of the Old Vic gallery.

Kate said that riderless horse, after the blind house, had taken the warmth out of the day for her. Perhaps we should go back to where we were staying: even though it meant enduring my cousin Will's latest theories on the origin of the passage tombs.

Well, *there* was an example . . . *there* were two examples of the impossibility of treating life as if it consisted only of the present moment: as if it weren't some unfolding affair in which Exhibit A might turn out to be as important as the latest exhibit, Exhibit X as it might be. First, the passage tombs. We'd gone into the mountains in our little car, Will guiding us, by way of a daunting maze of narrow stony paths: having to turn at fearsome angles on peaty ground, the tyres smoking: and so, to where cairn was raised after cairn, in a great landscape – as far as you could see, a green boniness of hills, and the blue stains of loughs. And so to the cairns themselves, with their low portals. How had I made myself wriggle in, under the great roof stones, and lie with Kate and Will in those low chambers? Claustrophobe, I'd never been anywhere better designed to bring my shrieking horrors upon me: and had never felt further from them. That strange peacefulness! Our hearts slowed: we crouched there, smiling, not speaking. Even Sal turned on her side and was silent.

And, when we came away, Will said they claimed the tombmakers came from Brittany or Iberia: and of course it might not have struck the idiot archaeologists that the traffic was the other way. I said whatever their faults, they must have thought of that one: and they'd have been drawing on investigations in other fields, and . . . But Will had a great need to find that the intellectual establishment was witless, because he'd never come anywhere near to making his way into it, where he belonged: his father, my uncle, having all those sons, and then, unmarrying and marrying more grandly, dispatching them with five pounds in their pockets or nothing at all to colonies and dominions and orphanages. Will took refuge in transcendentalism, in meditative regions of the spirit where there was no archaeologist or other idiot scholar within miles. He was constantly advising me how to transcend a frustrated life, and to raise myself above daily triviality: and

I wondered how he could make this offer when he must know that the world of our comic frustration and of daily triviality was the one I was happy to move in. I loved Will, and was not really unready to listen to him talking of finer and finer nothingnesses in the overgrown garden that his flirtations with Buddha forbade him to trim: but now, as we left the tombs, my head was full of the whiteness of the stone, of that strange stony compactness and tension: the tense peace of the little chamber on the hill in the huge landscape. I wanted neither to speak nor to listen. But then we met a farmer who said, as if it had been yesterday, that the makers of the tombs were all giants and cannibals. He took us over the heather to look down on the site of a Stone Age village, in a slanting field of rock under one great rounded cliff and above another. There'd been vandalism, he said, '*Campers!*' – and the cry had the tone in which he'd cried: '*Giants and cannibals!*' – and he'd pulled down the signs directing people to the tombs.

And I thought of the landscape bound to the past, and of Will bound to the past, too. What did Ben mean when he talked disapprovingly of 'hanging on to things'? If there were no attempt to make sense of such connections, would they not make nonsense of us?

I remembered then that, as it happened, creatures from this landscape, certainly not giants, small meaty men, were at this moment under the foundations of our house at Barley Wood, near London.

In the hot summer of 1976 the clay under the house had shrunk, there'd been a settlement, dismaying cracks. For a time we were eyeball to eyeball with the insurance company: they were inclined to blame trees, which would have meant the fault was all ours. Then an engineer with a reputation established that it was a nearby culvert that was to blame: its hundred-year-old walls were defective, and it had been leaching away a layer of gravel on which our stability depended. And the Irishmen arrived: with a cement mixer, a motor for their drills, a corrugated cabin, assorted hurricane lamps and oildrums and canvases, which they arranged with tasteful unpleasantness on our lawn. If we'd been able to choose our own agents to counter this disaster, we couldn't have done better. They treated the broken house, and its broken owners, with a boisterously cheerful pity: the holes they made were rapid, confident, singing holes. Kate had a dream in which they simply stayed there, underneath us, holding the house up with their shoulders, musically acclaiming their homeland, and longing to hear from their mothers. There'd been a long postal strike in Ireland, and they were cut off from news. We said we were going there, and where exactly we were going, and were given an errand by one of them, whose village would be near at hand. Meanwhile, they drilled, and followed their drills downwards. It was like living in a hollow tooth under treatment, and we were glad to go.

In this land of the best bad weather we'd ever known, such sweet-smelling rain, such delectable winds, storms so desirable that made the world smell of wild garlic, the villages seemed to us strangely ugly. Some were being busily reuglified, and plastic shopfronts in shameless reds and oranges and brutal blues were being installed everywhere. Our Irishman's was a mining village, in the hills, itself being made plastic, and said to have strong links with the IRA. His brother had a fish-and-chip shop lower down, our underpinner told us, but his mother was higher up, and if the shop was closed, anyone would direct us. The shop was closed, indeed, but there was no one to tell us where to go. There was no one to be seen, at all. There was in the air a sensation as of *High Noon*. We made our not unnervous way upwards, and there, at the address we'd been given, most of the village was assembled: looking unconvincingly astonished as we appeared. We thought they'd guessed our errand from our coming in a car with English number plates, and being seen looking checkingly at the name over the fish-and-chip shop, and trying its door. In the depths of the crowd was our underpinner's mother, clearly relieved to know her son was in no worse place than under our house. She was wonderfully like him, but even tougher, and we could easily imagine her plunging beneath our flowerbeds. She said she'd heard this underpinning could be like tying weights to the brim of your hat, it might bring it down over your eyes and damage your nose. But no reason to worry: and, if there was hope of saving the day, we'd been wise to give ourselves into Terry's hands. He was one of thirteen children, not of course all underpinners. At the latest count there were twenty-six grandchildren, which meant it was noisy on Sundays. The rest of the village, accidentally present, smiled, nodded, frowned, and drifted away.

Back from Lissadell, I walked by the evening lake with Will. What astonished me about Ireland was the many varieties of light it offered. Now on the lake a reddish-brown smudge was a boat, and a blue smudge was a fisherman standing in it. There were thick slow waves that turned the shadows of islands into so many heavily-moving bars, vanishing into and emerging from one another. The whole scene was like a collection of optical puzzles. A distant tree would seem suddenly to have been painted in with a quick black stroke, and then as quickly washed out again.

Will was briefly here, as he was briefly everywhere: his childhood had destroyed in him any impulse to permanency. He had, I thought, the restlessly patient face of the grandfather we had in common, whom we knew only from photographs, and who had dropped dead of overwork at forty: vanboy at a department store by day, porter at Billingsgate by night, seven sons and a daughter. Will Have-nothing, Will Seek-nothing! Except that he was hungry for the company of anyone at whom he could direct the gale of ideas blowing perpetually inside him. They were all, really, retorts to other people's ideas: what the injustice of his childhood had left him with being the need to prove the settled world, the world that stayed put , to be wrong in everything.

I said he was obviously, like me, an outside contributor. That was what the BBC called me. I wasn't on the staff. 'We're not on the payroll, Will,' I said, although I knew I *was* on the world's payroll as he wouldn't be. I wanted to stand beside him, and thought that if, for myself, I could make any rough-and-ready sense of things, it would lie in the wish to be seen as one of the outside, not the inside, contributors. And not in the BBC sense, only.

The view of the origin of the passage tombs with which Will was belabouring me now, the charming resignation of his face making room for his unorthodox lecturer's expression of dramatic scorn, was one that seemed to look, not indeed to Brittany or Iberia, but to South America. Without an ounce of evidence, he had flotillas of aboriginal mystics crossing the Atlantic with the express aim of making, of the idiot archaeologists, greater idiots still. It always tired me when Will used the language of scholarship in this fashion to float historical fantasies; but I thought in any final division of men and women into the Wills and the anti-Wills, I'd hope to stand closer to the former than to the latter.

And this decade in which I'd been in my fifties – it was full, wasn't it, of ghosts, repeats of the pattern, chickens coming home to roost: curious confirmation, most of it, that – as with many people, I guessed – it was the position closer to the outside, rather than the other position, that I was drawn to. I didn't want to have Will's grievous sense of exclusion, but I was against being wholly at home – wholly *inside*.

Well, I thought of that rank and remarkable outsider I'd once taught, and who throughout the decade had rung me methodically from far places, at late hours: Gary Bunce.

PART ONE

1

'Eddy?' said the half-past-midnight voice. 'Is that Eddy? It's Gary Bunce again. The bad penny. Remember? Haven't got you out of bed? The fact is, I'm down. Thought of you. Half hour's chat with Mr B will set me up again, I thought. So here I am.'

And there, dammit, he was: in Portsmouth or the Isle of Man or Dundee or, once it had been, on board a ship at sea. He had a voice that stood stiffly but not entirely respectfully to attention, as if it were issuing from a faintly insolent sort of sentry box. I had taught him twenty years earlier, at Stonehill Street: at the time, as I remembered, it was difficult to get much out of him, but soon after leaving school he had chosen me as his confessor, and at intervals I had these politely bullying appeals for my attention, always at unsocial hours and often on spectacularly defective telephone lines. Everything about him enraged me, and nothing so much as the cunning (as it seemed to me) with which he made the expression of rage impossible.

'The trouble is, Eddy,' he was saying, 'that I seem to have chosen the wrong job again.'

Take the way he called me Eddy, a form of my name I detested. The theory, if there was one, must be that it would put me at my ease: but its never having been agreed or even discussed between us – its quality as of someone reducing someone else to absurdity at a stroke – the feeling I had that it was a device for pinning me to the spot: each superficially friendly 'Eddy' having an edge to it as of someone being forbidden to hang up – all these things made me want to hop with fury, and at the same time forbade me to hop. There was, after all, the possibility, small though it was, that Gary Bunce's needs were real. I'd have had no answer to the suggestion that his manner was, simply, sensationally unfortunate.

'Can you imagine that, Eddy?' In my sleepy misery I'd heard nothing for some minutes. 'I mean, Stonehill Street was bad enough. That staff room. I know you won't mind my saying this, Eddy, but I never understood how you put up with it. All those boring people in that little room. But this canteen . . .'

Over the years a pattern had emerged. Most of Bunce's calls were signals of his determination to throw up yet another job, on any of a variety of grounds for disgust, but not to do so until he'd somehow made me responsible for his failure to persist with it. An unsatisfactory canteen seemed his slenderest reason yet for moving on. But as I thought this, staring out of the window at the sensibly sleeping night beyond, he shifted to more familiar territory.

'I'm afraid I hit the boss,' he said. 'You know me, I'm afraid.' As in all his references to his behaviour at school, he managed to make repentance sound remarkably like the reverse. 'I hit him rather hard.'

There was a hoarse silence from the Scilly Isles or wherever it was.

Then he asked: 'Have you ever hit the boss, Eddy?'

I had for a wild moment a vision of beating, perhaps about the head, a senior employee of the BBC. It might be a good thing to do. It was easy to think of Bunce as a not unfamiliar product of Stonehill Street, loosely hostile: but more than once I'd discerned, in the unallowable conduct of my old pupils, some element of good sense. It would cause astonishment in Bush House, but perhaps the occasional sideswipe . . .

It occurred to me, as Bunce's voice retreated backwards down the phone and became mingled for the moment with a deep bass bellow, that, if I were to embark on this interesting change of personality, I had more immediate targets than my friends in the external services. At the moment it would not be unpleasing to blacken an eye or two in BBC television.

We'd been out that day (which was why an after-midnight call was particularly unwelcome) filming for my interview with the novelist, Conrad Wick. He was a Canadian who had brought an unusual eye to bear on one of the great London markets. His latest novel made of the traffic in fruit and vegetables a symbol of general decay, and it had been thought necessary not so much to rub the point in as to pummel it home by having a major part of the interview conducted in Covent Garden. It was a bitterly cold and windy day, and every lorry capable of transporting foodstuffs from whatever corner of the kingdom had contrived to reach the market at much the same time. Amid a snarling of gears and shouts of alarm, with the air full of potato dust and flying orange wrappers, I put my elaborate but delicate questions to Conrad, and he gave his elaborate but delicate answers. It was as if medieval philosophers had disputed in Billingsgate. I knew, as we worked, what asses we would look when it was transmitted. Actually, when in his novel Conrad sketched in a mess of abandoned tomatoes in a gutter, it did make your spine tingle, more than a little. He had the gift of juxtaposing everyday things, they could be profoundly ordinary, so that each made the others amazing. That is, for the lightning moment in which you read his book. Many books, I'd come to think, provided a sort of temporary excitement of weather, a storm: it was like other excitements – real enough: but it might be a weather entirely confined to the book. I liked Conrad, enjoyed reading him, but could not imagine re-reading him. Anyway, what he could do in words with a mess of tomatoes in the gutter had no resemblance to what television could do with the same image. Conrad and I had frozen while the producer gave his nervous attention for an hour to the photographing of tomatoes, supposedly thrown away, in fact most carefully arranged and rearranged. After which he'd decided that he wanted many shots of Conrad and me, feigning to talk, standing at this and that angle to the tomatoes. We smiled, frowned, spread our hands. These were 'noddies', the shots with which an editor was free to support the general notion that, if the camera lingered for a second too long on a talking face, the nation would abandon television and return to radio. I hated noddies whenever I saw them, and spent much of my time as a televiewer attempting – and failing – to match them with the words ostensibly being uttered. They never matched. I did not understand how a producer could ever imagine they would. We all have a tremendously well-developed instinct as to what gestures go with what statements. I knew as Conrad and I grew chillier and chillier in a Covent Garden becoming noisier and noisier that we were producing noddies that would drive viewers like myself up the wall. It is all much worse when you are very cold. Conrad and I were providing frigid noddies – as well as noddies with potato dust in the eye. It would be horrible. A reasonable novelist, and an earnest interviewer, would be transformed into posturing and smirking idiots. The true stars of the occasion would be the tomatoes, the only participants not accompanied by agents or buttressed by contracts.

'It's a joke, Eddy,' said Gary Bunce, reversing his backward movement down the telephone line and advancing upon my ear with horrifying suddenness. 'It's a fantastic joke.'

'It?' I murmured.

'Life,' Gary howled. 'Life. You said so in the classroom. Round about 1955. I took it to heart.'

'Goodnight, Gary,' I said: and hung up. I was resigned to keeping him happy, to the extent of an inconvenient phone call every six months: but I would not encourage him to fantasise about the effect I'd had on his life by way of some casual remark made out of exhaustion twenty years earlier.

I slipped back between sheets gone cold, thinking of Jack Seed.

I was going to see Jack soon, in his unimaginable garden flat in unlikely Bondi in improbable Sydney. That was, of course, in a continent in whose reality I'd had no real belief, as a place to live in as distinct from a geographical proposition, since I'd first heard of it in a classroom at Barley Road, c 1926.

I'd taught Jack, too, at Stonehill Street. Recently he'd informed me by letter that his amazing transformation into a teacher was about to be capped by his astounding decision to teach Asian and Pacific history. And this, he said, was a strict result of something very thrilling I'd said one afternoon about Japan.

It must have been one of those Friday afternoons when a teacher's grasp on reality falters and he makes things up. At the time I'd known next to nothing about Japan. If I'd said anything about it, it must have been hopeless invention. But Jack, one of the liveliest and most promising creatures I'd ever taught, had taken it, in Gary's appalling phrase, to heart. My casual moment of fatigue had led Jack to mug up on Java, and give his grave attention to Samoa. I had never been so conscious that a teacher, more than most, may shape other people's lives by inadvertencies. His very yawns may, for others, be decisive.

Now that I was in my fifties I found that much of life was a roost for one's half-forgotten pigeons to return to. How extraordinary, I thought, trying to smuggle myself back to sleep, the way life filled with ghosts. Beside me in the bed, my wife Kate: a solid woman, but a ghost, too. Only the other night, as she turned thoughtfully in the light of a lamp, her mind busy with some domesticity – care, I guessed, for one son or other – I'd caught in the fifty-odd-year-old character of the movement the Kate I'd first encountered, a quarter of a century earlier. She wasn't large now, but then she'd been slimness itself, lightness itself, a dancing creature, as I'd always thought. In the early days of our acquaintance, she'd taken me often to Cecil Sharp House, home of what today might hideously be called ethnic dancing, where I extended the list of dances I was baffled by to include the mazurka, the polka, and a dance in which you go ducking between your own legs while your arms are heartily twisted by your partners on both sides. For some dances, they called out instructions: which, as far as I was concerned, might have been knitting instructions. I knitted and purled my heedless legs, and wondered if Kate might turn out to be available for marriage only to competent square-dancers. When I thought now how important to her view of ideal humanity was the knowledge of which leg to put before – or it might be behind or alongside or at some impracticable angle to – the other, I realised that one might gratefully sum up life in such a sentence as: Nevertheless, dancing is not everything.

Ghosts! Well, recently I'd met one from Barley Road Elementary School itself.

2

It was Jimmy Soper. Like me, he'd always lived in Barton. Not a large town: but you could part in 1930, when I went to the grammar school and he didn't, and only effectively meet again somewhere about 1971. He belonged to a world that it made me dizzy to know I'd once been part of: in which Chester Conklin and Charlie Chaplin and Harold Lloyd, leaping or lumbering across the coarse treasured pages of *Kinema Fun*, were as real as Fred Wicks, Jack Withers, Bernard Slow and Jimmy Soper himself, who formed not so much the gang I belonged to as the little mob in whose wake I travelled. As they went whirling through the streets, I whirled with them. What I remembered was no specific occurrence, only this sense of rapid howling motion – our going, whooping, through our own quarter of the town. Of each of them I retained not so much a physical image as a feeling for what his spirit amounted to: so that Fred Wicks, in a red way – did he have red cheeks? – was squeakily abusive, the one given to shouting at tramps, and Jack Withers was grey and heavily sober and mostly amazed, and so on. And Jimmy Soper, whose face had always remained clearest in my mind, had been very small, trim, self-deprecatory, and his hair was laid flat. The rest of us had heads either bristly or unkempt, but Jimmy's hair was always arranged in two flat wing-cases, held perfectly in place with some shining sort of oil. And, now that I met him again, he was as small, as crisp and tidy, as unpushing, and as flat of hair, as he'd been nearly fifty years before.

Oh goodness, I said, as we stood in the Saturday morning entrance to Barton market (behind us, I noticed, Fred, who'd been a stallholder as long as I could remember, had branched out into toilet rolls: GIVE YOUR BUM A TREAT FOR 20P he'd scrawled on cardboard), weren't those . . . happy days, in a way, all that warm foolish excitement, all that tearing about? I told him of John Logan saying in my first year at Queen's that he recognised me as one of those he'd seen speeding noisily through the High Street, part of that tousled comet of boys, and he'd never thought he'd have the distasteful task of teaching me. Jimmy smiled, a faint orderly smile, as if he saw the master's point of view. Surely, he said, I didn't remember those days or attach any importance to them? I saw that his word for us, as we had been, would be the same as Logan's: ruffians. I'd gone a long way since then, he said, clearly thinking that our common memories were, for me, those of a false beginning, and that I could only wish to disown them. I looked at his small face, which absurdly over the interval since our childhood had gathered a greying moustache, and didn't know how to tell him with what dizzy affection I thought of those old times, and of him. At least, I said, he'd come to dinner some evening, wouldn't he, and we could, among other things, talk of Barley Road? And to my astonishment, and grief, he shook his head, firmly. No, he said. No. He thought our ways of life must be quite different. It wouldn't do. Thank you, but it certainly wouldn't do. His small neat face was polite but firm, and I recalled that part of the memory I had of his spirit as a child was a memory of obstinacy. In our noisy adventures he had always been the one who did what he said he'd do, and never did what he'd said he wouldn't.

3

'After all,' Jimmy had said, as if reminding me of a good reason why I was in no position to be loosely friendly, 'you're often on the radio.'

Locally this very ordinary accomplishment tended to be regarded either as Jimmy regarded it, as a cause why I should think of myself as a person of virtual unapproachability, or as evidence of my being a conceited ass who'd probably done a number of shady things in order to achieve a prominence much better deserved by others: including a man who, when I entered a local pub, would say loudly to his companion: 'They have *anyone* on Radio Four nowadays!'

The curious thing was that most of what I did in radio was not to be heard at all in Barton: or, indeed, in the British Isles. The programme for which I went weekly to Bush House had begun as a programme about books – recorded and copied here, the patter went, and taken as tapes by thirty or so broadcasting authorities round the world for use on their domestic air. It embraced briefly a general arts programme, and then settled down to a weekly half hour of books alone. It was a matter of interviews, not reviews: and as the years went by I began to feel, having interviewed so many, as we felt in the Barley Road playground long ago, setting out to amass more conkers or cigarette cards than anyone else in the world. At the rate of two or so a week, I was, in this curious fashion, harvesting a hundred or more of my fellow writers a year. And the special pleasure of it, for me, arose from what didn't really make sense about it.

From the beginning, and not out of virtue, but because I couldn't see the point of doing otherwise, I read the books. I took it for granted that you couldn't talk to a writer, of all people, about work of his, or hers, that you hadn't read. I was early shocked by the number who said: 'You've *read* my book!' They said it in a wide spread of intonations of very great astonishment. The common experience being that of interview by persons who'd glanced at the blurb, or been fed with a digest by a secretary.

Well, I'd known that sort of thing myself. My friend Rufus and I had once shared the dismay of it. We were interviewed about a book we'd written together, *The Submarine God*, based on the Greek myths. It was at a startling hour, before breakfast, and we were received by an interviewer in his shirt sleeves, a creature of the night. It was always possible to feel that broadcasting at unsocial hours was self-addressing: a great many wearily bright men and women being involved in the pretence that the nation was not soundly and sensibly snoring. So, to begin with, Rufus and I felt we were noisy persons unkindly raising their voices in the national dormitory.

The interviewer, in between smiles and early morning murmurs, turned the pages of *The Submarine God* desperately, as it seemed to us, in the manner of someone who'd never seen a book before, let alone our book. He professed himself chiefly concerned with the effect of such a book on children: appearing to believe that it was addressed to babes-in-arms, and that the vast uneasinesses of mythical narrative were sensational inventions of Rufus's and mine. Owing to the prevalence in the myths of powerful events, the illustrations, by our friend William, were . . . powerful. The interviewer suggested that these, too, were cruelly unsuitable for the kindergarten. We'd barely managed to propose that there was a singular shortage of the milder sorts of myth, Rupert Zeus, Aphrodite-the-Pooh, and that we'd aimed rather above the heads of the recently born, when the interviewer, throwing the nation a jocularity that seemed to contain an apology for interviewing persons one would grapple with if one saw them anywhere near a nursery, brought the experience to an end. Of one thing we were certain, as we withdrew bruised into the dewy early morning blankness of

Upper Regent Street: he had not read the book. Reading the book had not been considered a relevant activity. Rufus and I linked arms and imagined our elder colleague, Homer, subjected to such baffling interrogation, so early in some Aegean day. And we vowed never to be put into this posture again, knowing we'd unfailingly accept any invitation to be so: almost any publicity for a book being welcome. But we were, all the same, scarred, and ruefully dismal. It would have made so much better sense to talk about the book as it was, instead of the interviewer's idle guess at it.

And I remember being in a radio station from which seamless patter was broadcast by a disc jockey and interviewer who'd been doing it, they said, for fifteen years. There was a strong suggestion that during this period he had never left the studio. I was goodnaturedly but absent-mindedly welcomed by the producer and various companions of his, who were peering into the studio through an observation window and making shorthand comments of a wearily derisive kind about the person being interviewed: as it might be, No. 133 for the day, I being No. 134. Then it was my turn: able to imagine the wearily derisive remarks that would be made about me.

The interviewer interrupted a disc to announce that I was with him. 'This gentleman,' he said, 'has written a book which I understand is the second in a series of autobiographies in which he describes how he rose from being a schoolmaster to being a broadcaster. And I understand he says that, in broadcasting, people look for controversial characters to take part so as to create a bit of excitement.'

One could clearly become a simple source of corrigenda. No, not the second in an autobiographical series: no, not an account of an ascent from schoolmaster to broadcaster, nor any inclination to think such a movement could be described in such terms. And actually no, nowhere in the book or elsewhere at any time had I ever said or dreamed of saying that broadcasting favoured contention at the expense of everything else.

I muttered an amazement or two.

He understood, he said then in a tone of inattentive

affability, that I ran a great daily programme about books, universally broadcast. 'So how,' he asked, 'is reading in the world compared with, say . . .' he wanted to be precise ' . . . ten years ago?'

I murmured helplessly. I had, after all these years, no problem in talking on radio: except when confronted with questions that God himself could not have answered.

'And so . . . what about lace?' he cried. I thought he'd lost track, understandably, never very obviously having had it: he thought I was in textiles. 'Shirley Conran,' he said. Ah, *Lace!* 'I haven't read it,' I said. 'And that,' he said, sounding like a man who'd just enjoyed the most satisfactory four minutes of his life, 'was . . . ' He hunted for my name. On my way out, I passed No. 135, on his way in. To the producer and his friends I said he'd nearly thrown me with that question about broadcasting always seeking controversy: but no one was listening, and I realised that it was unlikely any of them had been listening to the interview itself. 'Goodbye,' I said, but no one knew I was going. So I made a face, which no one noticed, and left. At the reception desk by the front door a cleaner was sitting, holding her fatigued mop as if it had been a lance. 'Ta, love,' she called. 'Thanks for coming.'

I had none of the gifts of such interviewers, and it didn't occur to me to dispense with reading. I read furiously and happily: they said it would be for three months. The years went by. I was reading at least two books a week, making notes as I went. The problem of holding a book in your head as you read it had always bothered me: as reviewer, and now as interviewer. I copied out what seemed important sentences and passages: and reading through these when I'd finished was a needed reminder of the course and shape of the book. I had more questions always than made sense for an interview that would be cut down to four and a half minutes. But a way to travel through those questions would emerge from the encounter with a writer. And he'd know at once that I'd read him. I don't think I've ever known an easier approach to people's goodwill than obviously to have read their books.

But of course it didn't, over so many years, make much sense at all. My investment of time in each interview was likely to be huge. I was happy, but irritated, too: longing to read more books of my own choice, or simply to read a book without making notes as I went.

I thought wistfully of how it must feel to have no questions at all to ask a writer.

Freelances, producers and others working in the department read the other books and conducted the other interviews. It made me aware how each of us put his or her own stamp on that curious exercise. I tended, for a long time, to take several words to climb aboard a sentence: revising what I had to say as I went along, as if talking were writing. 'You're always knee-deep in crumpled balls of paper,' Rufus had said once about an address I'd given. My producers, most of whose working lives were spent at an editing machine, cutting, shaping and condensing, could remove some of my hesitations and second and third thoughts with their razor blades: they could not always reduce the effect of murmuring diffidence or sudden, as it seemed to me absurd, excitement. It took me many years to mind less about my own voice and manner. Some deep disease of bashfulness made listening to myself – as I had to do as the week's interviews were put together, as I wrote the narrations that connected them, and as we recorded the entire programme – a comical dismay. It didn't help that other people thought I sounded well enough, most of the time. They couldn't hear my voice as I did: off-the-peg from Queen's Grammar School, with more than a touch of John Logan about it. No wonder, I'd think at my most distressed moments, Jimmy Soper didn't want to come to dinner.

But then Jill was a perfectly sensible and acceptable woman, one of the department's producers: and *her* interviews sounded like pillow talk. It was simply that she had a caressing and coaxing habit of voice: but, once you'd made a little scene in your head out of those accidentally lewd intonations and huskinesses, it was hard to listen to her without laughter. 'What was the germ of the book?' she'd ask some fearless explorer. It was about as much as anyone could manage to say whilst nibbling an interviewee's ear. Their legs stirred together as he said, fearfully (for men who'd defied deserts often turned pale in the presence of a microphone), that, er, it was, um – well, really to go back a bit – in 1934, as of course, er, a pretty small child, he'd – er – 'And you are the first ever to find a way through,' she'd sigh, face downwards on his breast. 'She's off mike,' someone groaned once, as the tape revolved. 'Still on him, by the sound of it,' said an impudent secretary.

With Harry, an interview turned into an event in a police station. The author had been brought in, caught red-handed whilst publishing a novel, and now, bruised as the result of an unfortunate scuffle with his captors, was face to face with the Chief Inspector. Harry's questions were cool and deadly. 'You have this central character . . .' he'd say: and there was nothing left for the author but to confess: Yes, he *had* this central character: but it had been lent to him in a pub by a man whose name he'd never known. 'And at what point did you realise that this second thread was necessary to the story?' No good the author pretending there was no second thread: 'Haven't seen a second thread for years! Honest!' Though even a second thread was not so fatal to an author's case as an umpteenth book. 'This is your *sixteenth* novel?' Madness for a scribbler ever to hope to conceal his past record from the Inspector. He'd written novels before. A hardened and impenitent novelist. Take him away. 'Sir Angus Wilson,' I'd say, 'talking about his new book . . .' But my voice was drowned – so I thought, trying to sound grave – by the groans and curses of the great man as he was dragged down to the cells.

And, interviewed by Millie, a writer was in the presence of the headmistress. Silly boy, foolish girl, playing about with words! Millie had often spoken about this at assembly. It made her tired; but they went on composing their little books, thinking you wouldn't notice. 'Why did you want to write on this theme?' Millie was as much amused as tired. Well, she'd heard all the excuses so often! Interviewees opened up to Millie, misled by her genial voice, the amusing use of the lorgnettes – the pleasant wink of silver from the cupboard where the school's athletic cups were displayed: but that was always fatal. 'So what I don't understand, Count Tolstoy,' I'd imagine Millie saying if our programme had been at a rather different time in a rather different place, 'is why you had to – well, that's really what you did, isn't it? – why you had to push Anna Karenina under the train!' A hundred lines were in prospect, at least: *I must be kinder to my heroines*.

4

It was some time in the mid-1970s that John Logan came back into my life.

At Queen's he'd at first been an all-purpose teacher, misinstructing us in mathematics (which he simply did not understand) substituting for absent Latinists (his Latin being hit-and-miss, and confused with faintly remembered Greek). His true skill was in games.

I think now how inappropriately doleful the sound of the word 'games' is in my ear, still, as a result of what Queen's made of them. Games were promoted as a means by which ruffians could be turned into gentlemen; and boys otherwise likely to give themselves largely to sex and tobacco, into boys morally austere if not forbidding. John Logan was somewhere near the heart of this enterprise. He was Irish, a dandy, a snob: in a stodgy venture, this attempt to use Rugger and cricket as aids to social upwardness, he was the one who danced, was prankish. In the school corridors, among trudging teachers, he was always in step with some subliminal minuet. His snobbery was enormous, transparent, and a point of origin for lively lessons that took the place of mathematics whenever his pose as a suitable teacher of this subject became too exhausting for him. Then he would display, or lead up to the display of, the Athlone ring.

First he would offer an account of the Logans. They, he'd inform his audience of twelve-year-olds, had been moderately rich. He'd affect to reconsider that word 'moderately', and then agree with himself that it *was* the word. Most of us were immoderately poor, and were fascinated by this glimpse of a sort of sliding scale of wealth. 'Rich' was to us a natural superlative, and it was amazing to think it might ever be modified, or associated with dissatisfaction. Well, John Logan would explain: this was after 1914, when they'd lost their French, German and Russian interests. They'd also suffered loss in their Anglo-Irish interests during the Great War and the Irish Revolution: and were obliged to rely almost entirely on South America. I see still the vivid picture that flashed up in my mind following this statement: the battered but still breezy Logans, in some great crumbling Irish house, gazing across the Atlantic towards their unspecified saviours in Argentina or Chile – ranchers, I supposed, goldminers, that sort of thing. But we knew, said John Logan, what happened in that wretched continent. Political upheaval: everywhere, abrogation of the law. ('Abrogation, Morton? Abrogation, anybody? My dear chaps, why not ask? Am I so forbidding?' There'd been a spasm of unease: he *was* supposed to be teaching). Between 1920 and 1924, the Logans had lost the lot.

'Our Via Dolorosa, chaps!' I think he was always on the point of challenging us to say what the Via Dolorosa was, but never did: if we were to be lifted out of the sordid world we'd sprung from, we must learn to take grand phrases on trust, unexplained. It was here, as he brought to a climax his account of the decline and fall of the Logans (which to us sounded curiously like their rise and triumph: well, how splendid to have 'interests' to lose, and to be able to blame an entire continent for one's failures of fortune!), that he'd display the ring on his finger. 'The arms of Athlone! There being a connection! Which didn't, however, save your excellent master and Lord of Games from an usher's life!' John Logan would sigh enormously: and a bell would end the lesson. 'An usher's life, Morton!' We'd file past him to the door. For such an occasion as this he'd take the games master's whistle from round his neck and, with the strap, whip us with amiable hurtfulness as we skipped past. 'An usher's life, eh, Blishen?

Woe, woe, *woe*!' And a sting on the back of the leg.

The Logans taking their revenge for whatever a Via Dolorosa was.

He had much to do with an aspect of school life that played, in another form, with ideas of class difference: that (one felt) submerged, powerful subject in the timetable. It revolved round nakedness. When in the early 1930s we moved to new buildings from buildings deeper in the town that had been partly Elizabethan and largely Victorian, we had for the first time baths and showers for use after games: and most of us exhibited an enormous dread of being seen without our clothes. It was, of course, lower middle-class prudery . . . stemming from lack of experience. Among those who didn't suffer from it was my friend Andrew Bell, who was a paying pupil and seemed to have a positive appetite for throwing his clothes off. I felt it as yet another of those crushing differences about which one could do nothing, and which condemned most of us to be for ever inferior. Andrew danced at shrieking ease under the cold shower and Podge Smith, a vast ugly boy from East Barton, ran up to me in a corridor, snickering: 'I've just seen Andy Bell's cock!' Though I thought that would not be an uninteresting spectacle, still I was humiliated by Podge's dreadful excitement. For a long time I thought of John Logan, who was in charge of the changing rooms, as a tyrannical opponent of modesty. One was sentenced to nakedness. 'Let me see you under the cold shower!' An unspeakable command. More affably: 'Off with your lendings!' *That*, in my view, was an example of the elegance in which those I thought of as the upper classes wrapped their natural cruelty. Mr Miller, one of our masters, was said to have gone to lodge in a house owned by Miss Pym, who'd arrived temporarily on the staff in the Great War and had never left. 'Scandal in the village!' John Logan cried, flicking me with his whistle-strap. It seemed to me unbearably witty. Such wit was absent from my own kind. Another of those sudden pains: if only *our* people had been witty, too. Never had my mother and father uttered a single line in that style, and they never would do so. I added this hopeless longing for witty parents to my grotesque long-standing desire that my mother were some sort of poet (out of the Cockney Twilight, I guess), and played a harp. I wanted her to sit in our darkened living room, her fingers wandering over the strings. Sometimes I'd wound myself by imagining how monstrously she'd have giggled, if she'd ever known of this ambition of mine.

In any case, she'd have thought I meant the jew's harp.

After he'd left Barton, John Logan had had a famous career as a pioneer of new forms of PE. He'd ended up at Savernake, where he seemed to have established himself even more stylishly than at Queen's as the Irish gentleman charmingly resigned to teaching. He'd got in touch because of something I'd written about Queen's. I'd said its snobberies had prevented it from being useful to first-generation grammar schoolboys like my friend Ben and myself. Well, for me it had been vital that it should win over my father, who had come very rapidly to the conclusion that the school sought to make a mock of him by way of his son. It stuffed the boy's head with ideas not quantifiable in terms of incomes, pensions and general steadiness of occupation. When I began to keep my diary it was to my father as if I'd been commanded to do so by Percy Chew, the headmaster: who in fact would have strongly disapproved of it. 'Your trouble, Blishen. Writing too personally. Too much I, I, I! Count the I's in Charles Lamb, count the I's in Charles Lamb!' (Percy Chew said nothing merely once.) I had begun to count the first person pronouns in Charles Lamb, and the level was high. 'All decent scholarship, gentlemen, is impersonal. If you follow the example given here, you will rarely use the first person, and then only with apologies. Always the mark of the second-rater – always the mark of the second rater. Much used, you'll find, by that piffling blackguard, Shelley!' Even at fifteen I could see there was something odd about the notion that personal testimony, opinion and observation could, or should, be excluded from the general heap of human witness.

Of my parents, Percy Chew said: 'Let's see, Blishen – your *people*! Your father's a minor official of some kind? Your mother – I can't recall your mother – '

My mother, on any school occasion, set out quite desperately to be unrecallable. The grammar school startled her and set her a problem: which was that much that it did tempted her to giggle. Gowns and mortarboards made her want to slap her knees – except that she was always too careful of my reputation actually to do this. If she might have made any impact at all on such a man as Percy Chew, it would have been as a small flustered woman who was clearly forbidding herself to slap her knees: the cause of her desire to do so being his MA hood and the black square that, on top of his large round head, suggested some kind of macabre geometrical joke.

Worse than this, Percy Chew spoke to my father, on their rare encounters, as if he was indeed a minor official of some indistinct kind, notoriously married to a woman no one could remember. 'The boy has distinct gifts, distinct gifts,' Percy would declare, 'but serious problems, serious problems too: we have a long way to go if we are to make a scholar of him, as I think you will agree.' My father had no idea what was involved in making a scholar of me: had he known what Percy Chew had in mind (he thought I might just possibly be of value, heavily supervised, as a junior member of staff in one of our less important museums), he would have been explosively indignant. It was Percy Chew's refusal to speak to the man my father clearly was – someone with the most limited experience of the educational scene, to whom the very idea of there being such a thing as scholarship was unfamiliar – that ruined such hopes as I had of getting to a university.

It was Percy Chew's snobbery, crowning the general snobbery of the place, that, as I thought, made Queen's such a disastrous establishment. Well, Williams, our English teacher, saw my friend Ben as the most brilliant schoolboy he had ever known. 'Born into the purple,' Williams would declare, 'Ben Fletcher would be in the House of Commons at twenty-four: in the Cabinet at thirty.' That might have been overstating it, rather: but there was no doubt about my friend's sparkling gifts – and no doubt whatever that Percy Chew appeared to have overlooked them in the light of some such view as the following: that though Blishen's mother was unrecallable, but known to be a respectable housewife, Ben's mother was a charwoman: Ben's father, a railwayman, having died when Ben was a small child. It seemed clear that, even if Williams exaggerated a little, it was generally true that Ben was an astonishing schoolboy of great promise: and that, as my hope of university vanished because Percy Chew wouldn't talk to the man my father actually was, but maintained his mortarboarded pomp throughout their contacts, so Ben's brilliance had lacked a champion because his mother was a charwoman, and his father didn't exist.

John Logan wrote to say he was deeply disturbed by this view of Queen's; it haunted him, and kept him awake at night: and yes, he'd gladly call and talk on his next tour of friends in Barton.

5

To Percy Chew, now retired, I was a figure out of melodrama. Feeling temperate, he'd call me 'one of the levellers-down and sour grapes people': at less benign moments I was 'one of the Judases who betrayed the grammar school'. I wondered what he'd make of our son Tom, who'd also gone to Queen's, but after it had been betrayed.

After university Tom had been in street theatre, working largely among children, and was now a porter in a hospital in Salford. We went to spend with him what turned out to be a strangely beautiful weekend.

Not much of the Salford of L. S. Lowry and Walter Greenwood remained: there were these last stretches of red brick terrace at the foot of tower blocks, or stranded in wastes left by the demolishers. They were occupied largely by families described by officials as problem families – and by Tom and his friends. In No. 7 East Street the brickwork exuded ancient stenches, and offered pneumonia: it had been calculated, said Tom, that every brick contained a pint of water, the whole of Salford, including the churches, having been built of porous brick. We had Tom's bedroom which he'd painted in various blues: dark blue ceiling, paler blue chimney breast. The bed was a double mattress on the floor. We lay there with flames dancing in the grate, with Tom on a cushion near the fire, talking to us. It was an extraordinary moment, as we all agreed. For Kate and me, a fire in a bedroom, something we'd not known since days of deeply happy illness during childhood. For us all, the pleasant oddity of parents stowed on the floor, a son as host. I remembered Jack Seed, my old pupil whom I was to see soon in Sydney, writing about a visit to England, and how he'd taken his father and mother to a restaurant of a kind outside their experience: and how astonishing it was to find his elders cowering under his wing. 'Almost as odd,' Jack wrote, 'as it will be to act as host to an old teacher.' They were nice, I thought, these reversals, or amusingly drastic rearrangements, of familiar relationships.

And children visited. Two small boys, playing a game Tom had invented for them, or they for Tom: you picked a Scrabble letter and said: 'Something in your house beginning with an L?' Geoff was quick with that one: 'Leak.' 'Something in the street with an F?' 'Folkswagen,' said Steve. We went walking, through the companionable remains of the old Salford, skirting the savagely unhappy highrise towers. 'See,' said Steve, as we passed into Fawcett Street. 'Fawk-it Street!'

I found I could hardly grasp Salford – couldn't understand how it ever came to be created, how anyone had persuaded himself that human beings might be sacrificed to this blackness, this dirt, this bitter discomfort. Or, today, to this rump of the old squalor and baleful body of the new.

A few doors down in East Street was Tom's friend Naruddin: in his mid-seventies, Indian, sitting in what little space there was in a tiny crammed room in which the television flickered perpetually. He cackled his woe as to the loss of sexual pleasure. 'Used to be midnight . . . now is always half-past six.' I thought of a recent visit I'd paid to the old writer, Frank Swinnerton, and how it had led to the discovery of obscene limericks, written for his own relief by Arnold Bennett. Everywhere, the hungry human body. Naruddin, who concealed nothing, made no secret of his dismay at physical failure. 'No tickey-tack,' he declared, with a flash of still-white teeth. The image gave him some consolation: he came back to it several times during our visit. And when we went: 'I love Tommy . . . Nice to meet you, sir.'

Tom arm-in-arm with Kate, he in the long overcoat, style of a Jarrow marcher of the thirties, that he'd bought for fifty pee. Catching them up (Naruddin had detained me to make sure I'd understood how awful it was to be terminally limp), I imagined for a moment a horror at the scene that would have been greater than Percy Chew's: my father's. He'd have been appalled to see his grandson so dressed, in such a setting. 'And you wonder why I didn't want *you* to go to university!' So much social advance rejected! 'Your grandfather hadn't two pennies to rub together, but he'd never have been seen in a coat like that!' In the next house, children, father, sick mother, in another tiny room, an encampment, shared with a budgerigar. The father begged us not to hurry away: 'Twenty friends are better than one.' The children were bright: Tom worried about their future, at this baffled end of the social scene.

Kate's love for her son, always great, was greater still after that weekend. He had turned his back on the comfortable world, and had made himself a useful companion to his neighbours, helping to sort things out when officialdom spoke to them in the foreign language of forms, demands, requisitions, assessments. Tom himself said the element of charade could never be forgotten: he *could* come home to Barley Wood at any time, he *had* his degree, escape was easy. But he was drawn, anyway, to these victims, so often so valiant, of a cruelly competitive society. Their sense of humour, in many respects, was his.

He wrote to tell us of a comment on our visit, a gloss on all the ambiguities of the situation: not what Percy Chew would have said, but close to what he might have felt. 'Jimmy next door said how nice he thought you were: the only thing he couldn't understand, how come they'd got a cunt like me for a son. "They should have a bank accountant for a son," he said, "and look what they've got – *a fucking hippy*!"'

Such different forms taken by the business of being young! I thought back to my teens: under my father, who knew no way of using his power except by being powerful – who never let me go: and when he died still thought of me as a piece of himself that had gone spinning out of control, becoming insubordinate somewhere about 1936 and remaining insubordinate thereafter. Embarking on impermissible occupations, marrying without consent a woman of perniciously independent character, adopting an alien style of parenthood! Add Percy Chew, who thought I showed every sign of becoming the sort of person Queen's was committed to nipping in the bud: 'The type of young man,' I'd recorded him word for word at an apoplectic sixth form moment, 'going back on the creeds he's been brought up to hold, not because he disbelieves them, but simply because he has been disappointed and hasn't the forbearance or backbone to make the best of things.' At the funeral of Em Williams, my old English teacher's widow, I'd caught his glare across the church, and thought with astonishment of the words that, at that sad moment, were undoubtedly roaring in his head: 'None of that sense of continued loyalty to their school all decent chaps should have . . . Down-leveller! Judas!'

And add John Logan, come to that. As Percy Chew had set out to make us wretched about having a free thought of any kind, so John Logan had brought an institutional glower to bear on our sexual natures. On the edge of PE, which aimed to teach the body that its ultimate felicity lay in a neatly executed handstand, was all that sexual plumbing: which had to be referred to as glancingly and discouragingly as possible. John Logan had even described the new changing rooms, the baths and showers, as instruments for instructing us in the boring banality of the human shape! Could that prancing Irishman have been as sexually null as he sought to make his pupils?

When he left Queen's the parting present he chose was a

two-volume textbook entitled *Adolescence*.

By then he had forgotten I'd ever been a howling townee. I'd won the school poetry prize with an interminable poem about Christopher Columbus. (I remember my mother affirming in her unpractised hand that it was my unaided work, though my dear non-harpist would never have known if I'd cobbled it together out of the most famous lines in English poetry). I'd also acted in the school play, and Logan had found ingenious means of writing me out of Rugger and cricket, on the grounds that I was being instead some sort of poetic and thespian athlete. Percy Chew had not been convinced by this: he regretted that I'd been chosen to play Richard II in *Richard of Bordeaux*. 'The wrong king! the wrong king! May confirm . . . have to say . . . a certain tendency to spinelessness! Henry the Five – now that would have been better for this particular fellow, eh, Williams?' The English master, at our elbows, grinning his complex Welsh grin ('Ignore the Great Man, Edward, if you can!'), and patching together some rapid theory about playing a softie being a pointer to the need to make a toughie of oneself.

I thought then that I had no friends but Celts, Williams and Logan: but shrank from the vision of Logan, from his study of *Adolescence* Vol. I and *Adolescence* Vol. II, becoming more and more coldly expert in the wonderful and terrible disgraces that had me in their grip.

Well, these differences in ways of being young! Now, in the 1970s, a generation that had always worn suits was handing over to a generation that had never worn them. At times I'd catch sight of some BBC elder in conversation with Mike Wallace. There's no doubt the elder thought Mike a politically restive sloven, and Mike thought the elder a product of a world that didn't know it was dead. The truth is that they were both men whose appearance was based on the stiffest and squarest grounds of principle. Mike was casually intelligent, couldn't conceal the fact of his upper middle class background, spoke in a voice that none of his efforts at untidy utterance could plausibly roughen: and wore what he said his parents regarded as the ultimate scourings of an Oxfam shop. 'We are, you know,' he told me, 'a generation, perhaps the first, that's able to dress exactly as it wishes. Anything goes!' I looked – through the eyes of someone who in his time had been viewed askance by his father, Percy Chew and John Logan for a tendency not to comb his hair – at his statutory jeans, obligatory wide belt, necessary open-necked shirt . . . and must have raised my eyebrows: for Mike said, 'I know it's difficult for your generation to accept. It is an entirely new situation, you see.'

I didn't quarrel with him about it. This was clearly always the ultimate in fashion, believing yourself to be beyond fashion.

Of course, there is astonishment when your children prove to be capable of living lives of their own. At the bottom of every parent's soul there's something that feels this foolish surprise, accompanied by twinges of resentment. Like much that lies around in the soul, these things have to be shrugged off, monstrous absurdities: but I saw that my father, who never in his life shrugged off a cause of offence, however faint, must have furiously objected to my independent existence. Here I was, making this shallow claim to be my own man! Here I was, attended by this other unconvincing adult, Kate! To my father I was never more than a child. I was for ever the hysteric caught, c 1936, between the view he had of my future, as a careful civil servant with his eye fixed on a secure retirement, and the view that Williams had, which was that I might become some sort of writer.

As the years piled up, it seemed to me a deeply urgent thing – no matter for mild domestic advice – that fathers and mothers should let their children go. The very core of the relationship: for as long as needed, until the onset of adulthood, as wise a protective love as possible: thereafter, as real a stepping aside as could be managed. How I'd writhed in the chains into which my own father had converted the bond between us! There is no limiting the risks to which the living are subject: there is not much the best advice can do. You must rely on your trust of the creature you have helped to shape, and such affection as has arisen between you. Your best hope is in the end to be a friend consulted as other friends are, though with the special value that follows from your having known each other so long, and being parts of the same family web.

To make preremptory attempts to give orders to the young when they have taken up their position in the circus ring of their own temperaments, beginning to make sense of a sudden riot of clowns, lions and trapeze artists, is merely to add to the young ringmaster's perplexities.

6

I wondered what Percy Chew, who thought literature had come to a halt with Kipling, would have made of my interview with Frank Swinnerton.

It was in snow that I went to see this old man, aged 94, who wanted to be called Swinny, and had found himself able at last to write about his friend Arnold Bennett. Couldn't do it while Bennett's widow was alive. Dreadful woman. Had to say so. There he was in his Surrey cottage, with his deaf and smiling wife, a sweet withered apple of a woman, this man who'd lived on the edge of enormously famous friends, himself a sort of literary suburb. He'd outlived them all, and in the warmth of his cottage, so close to his century, he could be felt to relish his survival. They'd always be better-known, but he'd always be longer-lived. It was a mischievous turnip of a face, a little white beard, and you could see in it the cruelty Bennett had found there (it was Swinnerton who triumphantly reported that perception), and the kindness. I'd thought of him as a gnome of literature, before it struck me that it was among gnomes that you might expect this marriage of malice and benevolence. He asked suddenly if I'd like to see some letters he had of Bennett's, notebooks, bits and pieces. I said of course, and he put his wellingtons on and crossed the yard behind the cottage to a barn where these important literary relics had been stored. They'd been given to him on Bennett's death (he said on his return hugging a large cardboard box) by Bennett's secretary, who'd wanted to save them from the widow. 'She'd have burnt them.' I picked up a notebook and turned its pages. Here were notes on misers: it was clearly the notebook he'd been keeping when writing *Riceyman Steps*. I picked up another and found in its neat pages the shape of a limerick: and was reminded of a passage in his journals where Bennett says he'd spent the afternoon writing indecent verse in order to relieve his feelings. 'There was,' I could just about read – and I read it aloud – 'an old Bey of Algeria . . . ' The second and third lines defeated me, but not the fourth. 'But a cunt is a cunt,' I read. 'I've never come across that,' said Swinnerton, who seemed to have been altogether incurious about these remains. Was he leaving them to the British Museum? The gnome grinned. Didn't know what to do with them.

And I realised that only he and my producer and I (Mrs S continuing to smile deafly), out of the whole population, knew that this line, affirming the genitalness of genitals, was by Arnold Bennett.

7

One of the problems of being in your fifties – and why it was curiously pleasant to have John Logan on stage again – was that you lost control over your cast of characters. Old close friends had drifted away, or you'd simply lost sight of them. They moved a mile, and might have vanished. I began to think that one of the pleasures offered by the theatre was that it enabled us to follow someone's story to the end . In real life, most of the people who'd known Macbeth intimately in his youth – always round at the Macbeths for such small banquets as were on offer from young subalterns – would ten years after the events at Dunsinane have said: 'Talking of feeling guilty about not keeping in touch – do you ever hear from the Cawdors? . . . Dead? Great Scott! No, how did *that* happen?'

Late in Act III, I met again a major fellow-actor from Act I sc. vii: Kate having become the centre of a small event known as hysterectomy. Some of the things that happened to you had curious names. A perfectly good word, that, without which medicine would be at a loss: but offering a strangely academic account of a human experience. Wasn't it, I thought, as with careful cheerfulness Kate assembled her going-to-hospital kit, an extra reason why illness is so dismal, and hospitalisation worse: because we find ourselves suddenly in a forest of deeply unsympathetic, unyieldingly technical words. Everything we do, the liveliest of our acts, could be described in such a vocabulary: we have been able to prevent that happening in most fields, but illness is not among them. Kate had already suffered from the spiky world of the medical dictionary. She'd had two years or so of the cruel pain that follows when something goes wrong with the admirable but fallible spine (which Percy Chew thought I lacked). During an early examination at Barton General Hospital she'd listened to a discussion of her case between the specialist and his attendant students. To Kate's horror, it seemed they were talking of multiple sclerosis. Dismissed, she cried: 'But please tell me what is wrong with me! *Is* it multiple sclerosis?' The specialist made an astonished face. 'Certainly not. It's a scoliosis. Merely a scoliosis.' 'And what,' Kate found herself needing to ask, '*is* a scoliosis?' More astonished still, faced with such unaccountable curiosity, the specialist explained that it was a lateral curvature of the spine. He then, Kate still looking dizzy, explained that it was a failure of the spine to be perfectly straight. Kate's spine was leaning to the left.

Hysterectomy, though it was another chilly term, was quickly converted into a hospital ward in which half a dozen fellow-sufferers were transformed by their fate into wonderful melancholy bawds. This great vague rearrangement of the seat of their liveliest experiences made them at once woebegone and wicked. They had an attendant mob of husbands, who'd appear at visiting hours sheepish and alarmed: and wonder, I think, why half the beds in the ward seemed to be nudging each other and giggling. The fact was, said Kate, that the character of each husband had been revealed and discussed, in terms to which the discussion was naturally led by the nature of the imminent operation. After the first unthrilling hospital meals, this band of husbands was commissioned to smuggle in foodstuff of a more acceptable kind. They managed, somehow, to do this long after visiting hours were over, by means of a sort of daring raid: and the ward, said Kate, smelled like a fish-and-chip shop. It was all vinegar.

Lively, funny, boring – and, said Kate sadly, another of those socially divided occasions: because – with the greatest good-humour, since in other and important terms there was clearly nothing aloof about her – she was taken to be some other sort of creature altogether, taking an unfamiliar newspaper, not given to chatter about her husband's erotic foibles: and lacking eagerness for fish-and-chips at midnight.

But there was one more unbawdlike lady in the ward: and she turned out to be the wife of my old friend Jim Hackett.

Not that 'friend' is an adequate word for what Jim had been for me, over thirty years earlier. Then he was a linotype operator on the *Crawley Hill Standard*, where (as I saw it) I'd been marking time before my hope of realising myself as a fusion of all those writers Percy Chew most condemned was foiled by the destruction of civilisation, which H. G. Wells had prophesied and Adolf Hitler clearly had in hand. Jim, self-taught and a man of radical good sense, would sit in his bower in the printery, his fingers delicately moving over the keyboard of his machine – gleaming metal lines of amazingly mortal prose, some mine, falling into place as he worked – and would listen understandingly to my account of my latest nineteen-year-old agony. 'My dear fellow,' he'd say, as the universe collapsed around me – my father impossible, my passionate affair with Tess Grayson developing hideous symptoms of the coarsest sort of farce – 'take it easy. You'll hardly believe it, but the future stretches in front of you! Oh yes, I know about Hitler, and agree with you. But you know, even given the fools and villains who govern us, civilisation isn't to be brought to an end as easily as all that! Well, last night I was reading *A Tale of Two Cities*. . .' Jim read Dickens serially, and among the roots of his belief in the durability of a self-destructive humanity was his failure to imagine a world in which, somewhere or other, someone wouldn't be reading *David Copperfield*. The thought of Jim had always been, for me, a reminder not only of my astonished youth, but also of the immense supportive power that lay in literature. W. H. Auden had said a poem, and I guess he might have meant any work of literature, had changed nothing. How could he know? From the demonstration literature provides of the attempt to understand human experience, and of the enormous pleasure that may be had from the attempt, innumerable people drew strength and purpose: and if it had been intense in youth, and diluted in bewildered maturity and age, still it might at any time shape this or that vital response. Supported by Dickens, Jim had supported me, and I had always been grateful for it.

Now he was a small, shrunken, unhappy man. May's ordeal in hospital seemed to cause in him more than sorrow for the discomforts she might endure, the shock to the transformed body, however safe the transformation.

'My dear fellow,' he said, the form of address taking me back to the astonishingly different world of 1939, 'it's strange that we should be reunited for such a reason. You see, May . . .'

We went to a number of pubs, after hospital visits, before Jim completed this confidence. Their not having children, he said, had always been a grief to them; but I'd not believe it, perhaps, seeing he was over seventy, if he said he'd only recently understood why there could be no child. Or perhaps he'd always been in a position to understand, but had only lately allowed himself to do so. Many years ago, he remembered, the doctor had called for some reason, some distress of May's, and after that had been dealt with she'd said there was another trouble she'd like to discuss, but she'd be glad to do it in Jim's absence. And Jim, in those distant days finding the occasion explained by some such phrase as 'a woman's thing', had left the room. And they'd never had a child. And now, as May had the womb removed that had had no hope of an occupant, everything had fallen into place for him – or he'd been able, old fool that he was, to tell himself what he already knew.

And what he knew, I thought, as we stared at each other over our pints of beer, was not only that May had had some cause of sterility (though, as I thought, it might have been Jim's, but they'd never have inquired), but that behind that had lain a sterility even greater: her inability ever to talk to Jim about this matter so close to them both. This damnable shyness!

A shyness, I thought, that Percy Chew and even that cavalier John Logan might have taught to this or that old schoolfellow of mine, in the name of self-control and in the midst of the general attempt to ensure that the manners of Barley Road (Jimmy Soper and I and others whooping through the town) did not contaminate the decent ambitions embodied by Queen's.

And I thought of Fred Jenkins, met often in our favourite local pub, who'd known my Cornish grandmother ('Difficult lady') and been in the Boys' Brigade with my uncle Will ('Wonderful on the cornet'), whose wife had slowly lost her wits. 'Oh shut up!' Fred would mutter when, in the Sunday pub, her madness took over in its mild fashion. 'Ho ho ho ho!' she'd cry, about nothing that was going on outside her: a response to some helpless wretched inner joke. A man of immense courtesy, Fred, a chauffeur largely to doctors: but obliged to offer this rebuke because no one's courtesy is absolute, and he wished he could bring Winnie to the pub without these occasional very loud chortlings. Then she had to go, she had to go into a local psychiatric hospital, there was no alternative: and there on his visits the decent trim Fred had discovered that a half-witted woman who'd clearly never recover could be treated as (brought up in East Barton among horses) he said a horse would never be treated. He'd grown up in a world where you found a refuge for old horses, in which they were treated with very great decency: and here he was, in a world where a woman whose wits had snapped or worn away was treated as if she were less important than a horse. Those weren't her glasses! he cried. Well, they said, they collected glasses at the end of a day, and redistributed them the next morning, and it wasn't always possible to get it right. And those weren't her teeth! Much the same answer. And on some visits he'd realised that she'd fouled herself, and no one had done anything about it. Distraught, this fastidious man had cried: 'But she is still my wife!' Kate drove him back and forth to the hospital, and with particular pleasure to the meeting of the governors he had caused to be summoned: he would not endure it, said Fred, who'd once (as chauffeur) driven my grandmother's doctor into a ditch. ('The old fool said I was out in the middle of the road! Did he apologise? He did *not*!') After the meeting, the governors promised things would be different. Would they have been? We never knew, for soon afterwards Winnie's misery came to an end.

I thought, listening to my early mentor, Jim, talking about the reticence that had made an insidious nonsense of his marriage, of Fred, whose marriage had suffered this obscene climax. Oh God! I had lived only fifty years or so, but the spread of sensitivities within that short span had been both cruel and confused.

What, as one always had to ask oneself, was happening *now*?

How suddenly one's healthy mate could be turned into a green unconscious thing! I leaned over Kate, sensing that in some deeply subliminal fashion she was addressing me. Her parched lips moved. Some assertion of despair or devotion, perhaps. All was well, I knew, but I'd be glad when all looked well, too.

Yes, she said on my next visit. 'I was trying to speak to you. But from so far away. You see, you kept leaning over me. I was trying to say, "Your hair is tickling my nose."'

And then, with her lewd friends, and becoming increasingly lewd herself, she moved to the hospital's convalescent unit. Once (before anything was ever called a unit) it had been the local isolation hospital: the dread of being sent there had hung over all our childhoods. Now the grounds were full of women exposing their wounded laps, as they had been recommended to do, to the summer sun. A great comedy of alleged overlookings and furtive spyings, a few real perhaps, but most happily imagined: nightdresses tugged down in flurries of delighted indignation . . . The gardener was seen as an indecent monster, who planted trees in order to peer out from behind them: he was raucously deplored and adored.

And a young doctor from the gynaecological department, an Australian, came to see that things were going well. Kate had had amazing luck: her surgeon having favoured a bikini cut, an incision running across the belly that in healing would merge with such natural wrinkles as a belly has: a bikini could be worn without embarrassment. Kate's scar vanished almost at once. For the doctor she raised her nightdress: he made his inspection, and murmured: 'They don't come better than that!'

It was just possible (said Kate, now deeply affected by the general bawdry), that he was referring to her operation scar.

She had asked this medical admirer about the problems of making love, given such a severe modification of the machinery. It would be fine in the end, he said – but a husband, or lover, or both, might at first find it a little like driving at great speed into a cul-de-sac.

The advice was of no use to me, as I pointed out: since I was a non-driver.

8

'Well, lovely lady . . .' said John Logan.

Kate, as she told me afterwards, couldn't remember ever being addressed before in this ridiculous fashion, and noted uneasily that she liked it. This was going to be an odd evening, I thought, as my old teacher made himself ganglingly at home on our far too modern couch. We'd wrenched him out of all his contexts, surely. I imagined how he'd not be caring for our pine ceiling, and wouldn't approve of a single picture on our walls.

He'd come off the train crumpled, carrying an ancient case secured with string. His hat was of some exhausted tweed: impossible to guess its original character – it formed now a sort of limp bonnet. He had, of course, I thought, made a distinction out of being seedy. Fifty years earlier, Barley Wood would have seen nothing odd in him. But now, I noticed, one or two of my neighbours, the human equivalents of our pine ceiling, looked at us sharply.

I took the case cautiously into my grasp. 'My dear!' John Logan cried. 'It's less likely to burst than appears.' And then, as we approached the modest square box in which Kate and I lived: 'So this is the family estate!'

As we entered the house and Kate greeted him, she and I realised together that she'd forgotten to remove her pelvic model from a surface in what Logan would have been horrified to learn was called a utility room. This transparent plastic representation of the female pelvis looked like nothing so much as a sort of permissive moneybox. It caused unease even in visitors without gynaecological knowledge, and in my view made sexual connection seem either impossible or horribly dangerous. Kate used it when she talked about sex in schools. 'I married a sex educator,' I'd said at dinner recently. 'Who didn't?' a guest had cried. Logan grunted as he looked at it, but we thought it best to say nothing.

He'd been visiting in Barton, he said: and was as usual dashed by the town's decline. 'Used to be charming! Fine shops, fine service! Now it's formless! Dreadful shops! No service! Seedy, rundown houses! Remember, excellent lady, dear former pupil, what it was like in the thirties?'

Yes, yes, we remembered that.

I thought sometimes I would actually swoon when I recalled the Barton of my childhood – as it was on a late Saturday afternoon in winter, the lights coming on, every shop having an individual face. There was Foster's, the greengrocers. Tom Foster had been briefly in Fred Karno's theatrical company, a friend of Charlie Chaplin's: and he'd turned to greengrocery as if it were a logical alternative to working on the stage. And his shop was a theatre: on a corner site, it was always a marvel of fruit and vegetables beautifully disposed, one huge still life, and on those late Saturday afternoons blazing with light. It was a brilliant amazement of oranges and apples and cabbages and cucumbers and bananas. And Tom Foster would be there in his fustian apron and his flat cap, directing the drama of the great exchange of fruit and greenstuff for cash. In Foster's, it was possible to think of money, all that copper and silver, as another form of greengrocery. I had that feeling about the pennies my mother offered that lay in knowing that every one of them was memorable to her. Fifty years later she'd recall in detail what things cost then: a stick of celery, a pound of tomatoes, half a dozen oranges. She had her own favourites among the five Foster daughters, all of them with hair of this or that degree of redness. The reddest of all was the sourest: I myself had a helpless aching love for the sweetest, in whom red verged on gold. They wore aprons of a strong green colour; and amid all that shouting, those cheerfulnesses tossed from well-known shoppers to well-known shop-people, and back again, that metallic sound of weights being thrown into scales, that thunder of potatoes being poured into emptying bins, the Foster girls were easy goddesses, never submerged: sweating slightly – oh, the effect of sweat on the golden arms of my favourite! – and able to return any remark made by any customer in any mood. Among my reasons for loving them, myself so shy, was admiration at their never failing to know what to say. Triumphantly giving a twist to the corners of their brown paper bags, each bearing a diagonal shout of TOM FOSTER THE BEST FRUIT AND VEGETABLES, they were the presiding geniuses of Saturday evening Barton.

But geniuses of other kinds there were all the way along the street. Not a shopkeeper from one end to the other but was a legend in his own lifetime. Did I most love going with my father into Samuel's, the oil shop, where old Mr Samuel, and several young Mr Samuels, and a number of Samuels barely out of the nursery, all wore aprons smelling of paraffin, in a cavern full of oil drums and great bottles containing thick greennesses and thick brownnesses: or going with my mother into Mr Boulter's (remember the step down, that could give you a sickening jolt if forgotten), a tiny womb of a shop in which everything was crowdedly to be viewed, from braces in boxes to bow-ties exhibited as if they were butterflies? Or was my best moment on those wonderful evenings that in which I stared into the window of Towney's, newsagents, in which, from one of those displays of absolutely everything that were a characteristic of shops of the day, I could make my choice of a comic, or more ambitiously a *Magnet* or a *Gem*, or at a moment of rare affluence a paperback Edgar Wallace, before ever I entered tinkling into the print-smelling shop where Mrs Towney, so fat she wisely never moved from a central position behind the counter, and ancient nimble Mr Towney, who did all the darting here and there for this or that literary object, smiled at their familiar customers, entering at familiar hours and making familiar requests.

Or Friday's, the butchers, where my mother was on such good terms with all the blood-boultered Mr Fridays, father and three sons, and (watched by her already ink-boultered child, who sought words for yet more sets of shopkeeping arms, the immense Friday limbs, which I could imagine them quite equably chopping off, weighing and wrapping if requested to do so by such an esteemed customer as surely my mother was), would purchase nothing until a Mr Friday (any Mr Friday), in reply to the question: Is that a really nice bit of breast? had replied that there was no other phrase for it: it was a *really* nice bit of breast! She was looking for something *really* nice, my mother would explain, and Fred or Charlie Friday would infallibly assure her that she'd found it. In my mother, total trust in that score or so of her most intimate friends, the shopkeepers of Barton, existed alongside total distrust. They had to win her every time: but never failed to do so, overriding her unease with their replies to her commonest questions: yes, a lovely bit of breast, the ripest of apples, the crispest of celery, the most hardwearing of underpants, the best cut of the best imaginable bacon.

Well, obviously, I almost swooned, thinking of Barton as it then was, because it was the background to my brief experience of immortality – or ammortality, if there were such a word: that moment when Death and his lieutenant, Change, have no existence for us. The notion of the Miss Fosters being ever anything but round-armed and variously red of hair: or of the Fridays being doomed to disappearance by way of a process far less pleasant than was offered by their chopping blocks – there was no such idea. Everything was forever.

But even that perfectly good explanation of my dizzying love for Barton High Street , c 1929 (I thought as John Logan sighed over its disappearance), doesn't cover it all. Today its shops pass from hand to hand with desperate rapidity. At any moment, seven or eight doomed carpet shops compete for trade in a district already manically carpeted. In April, shopfitters move in to provide a spanking new environment for the purchase of far-out clothes: and, the venture having proved either too far-out, or not far-out enough, they are back again in December, gutting and replacing: here's a new (and equally doomed) environment for the sale of window-blinds. The old line of the street, in which shop grew into shop in a neighbourliness of appearance that rested on none of them attempting frenetically to be unlike the others (and so, as happens now, creating a common effect of frenzy), has long since gone. Nasty plastic façades make their brief and excessive assertions. The big 120-year-old clock on a bracket outside Cleggs the drapers stopped in 1967, and they threw it away. (Cleggs had been replaced by a shop offering baths of a shape eminently suitable for human beings who happened to be octagonal in construction.) They tore out and threw away the shop window of Friday's the butchers, before turning it into a hopeless bistro, succeeded by a transient carpet shop, followed by a momentary health food shop, which itself gave way to a purely temporary ill-health food shop specialising in pasta, which Barton proved to be cool about. The old shop window was mid-19th century: handsome and, as Foster's was an auditorium for greengrocery, an auditorium for meat. Gone!

I love the memory of the old High Street because it was slow to change, made shopping a daily adventure for my mother, was as romantic on a Saturday evening as if it had been some kind of commercial Bohemia. But I know, of course, that there are children to whom in its present embodiment it is deathless, and who c 2040 will remember, swooningly, the elbows of the girls at the swarming cashdesks of the supermarkets.

Of course, said John Logan, Percy Chew had been a frightful lower-middle-class snob. Abrasive, offensive, ridiculous! Though it must be said he had the courage of his own absurdity. He turned up to his first Founders Day in topper and tails, and found no one else in a uniform so out of scale with that modest grammar school. But, having made the mistake, he persisted with it stubbornly for the next thirty years.

What he, John Logan, had to suggest was that Percy Chew had found the school in a state perhaps best summarised by saying that no one felt in a position to compel boys to turn up for games. Oh, very well, he could see I was unmoved, and in rare cases, of course, there might be an acceptable bias in favour of the other sports of literature and music, ha! But reflect that it was also a school where Rugger was not played if it rained! Oh, very well, again: then think of the staff Percy Chew had found himself required to work with. Remember dreadful Knotty, of whom someone had said that his qualification (an external pass degree in classics, from London University), amounted to a certificate of ignorance in his best subject. Think of old Haddock, who could hardly make it from the staffroom to his classroom, and was certainly never punctual. Well, there you are: that was the time (he'd not heard *that* story before, Good God!) when a boy might indeed be taken down into the cellars under Haddock's classroom by his classmates and have his trousers removed and carefully lost. And Haddock would trudge in a quarter of an hour late and proceed with the case on the grounds that the boy had insolently chosen to attend Haddock's class in his underpants. ('Good God again! Did that really happen?' John Logan permitted himself an additional quarter inch of sherry. Had to watch his blood pressure. If I told any more stories like that one, the combination of alcohol and anecdote might do for him. 'What headlines, dear lady! OLD SCHOOLMASTER DROPS DEAD IN BARLEY WOOD LIVING ROOM AFTER LISTENING TO REVELATIONS FROM FORMER PUPIL!') Consider Miss Dipper, who'd been recruited to the staff in the Great War, no one could establish on what grounds – 'Damn it,' said John Logan, 'she had no professional qualifications at all, poor old monster, and . . . what are you suggesting? . . . as a plaything for the masters of the day – ? Good God, imagine Miss Dipper and old Haddock! – Dear lady, you must find this deeply offensive! *Not?* Oh, good! Poor old darling, Miss Dipper, I never knew her wear stockings without a hole in them. Down-gyved, always!'

And Percy Chew had taken on this gruesome collection of academic tramps, with a bit of a leavening here and there – 'I'd come myself the year before,' said John Logan, deciding to be entirely reckless with our sherry, 'and brought with me my private and public school experience which made me demand the games equipment needed to do the job even at a low level' – and, by his unsparing devotion to it, had turned a sleepily dying school into a vibrantly promising one. 'My dear, I wish I had the impression that I was convincing you.'

But, of course, I *was* convinced that Percy had converted a slumbrous establishment into one nervously awake. But he'd done it by pretending that we were what we were not. 'Gentlemen!' he'd cry, and then observe that from any definition he could provide of a gentleman, we were horrifying deviants. Once it was: 'Do try to remember, Blishen, that what was good enough for the elementary school is not good enough for a fellow from Queen's!' I'd been wearing my cap at an angle I favoured, it being the angle at which my favourite characters in maritime fiction wore the caps in which they went down with their ships. My argument, I said, smiling at the ancient Irishman who seemed to have come to terms with our couch, was that the kiss of life Percy had given the school had many of the qualities of a kiss of death. Well, it wasn't only that he had this insufferable view of the ideal human being, a puffed up fellow in topper and tails, and that he thought he could raise the school only by being socially offensive to Ben's mother and mine – to the whole idea of such people as they were, ill-designed to be the parents of fellows and gentlemen – but it was also his attitude to (for example) literature. What about the gulf between the books John Logan lent us from his large personal library, and the attitude to books barked out by Percy Chew in the sixth form room! Logan had lent me Aldous Huxley, Graham Greene, Housman, Hardy: in Percy Chew's view, subversives to a man. 'Housman and Hardy, gentlemen – malcontents, pettifogging snivellers!' He equated them all with modernity, which was simply a term for unrest and disorder. Take D. H. Lawrence: a simple case of a working class boy educated altogether too suddenly. He had failed, and one would expect it, to take methodically on board the difficult cargo of European civilisation. Instead, in a dreadfully unscholarly fashion ('Unscholarly, gentlemen, *unscholarly!* Don't let this happen to you! Don't let this happen to you!'), he'd held forth on practically everything that caught his distempered eye. 'Do NOT read Lawrence on the Etruscans, gentlemen!' (Lots of gentlemen, who had had no such intention, making a careful note to avoid this folly.) 'On the whole, gentlemen, do not read Lawrence on ANYTHING! Friend Blishen, take particular note!' Morally, Lawrence was worse than Shelley, 'a tupenny ha'penny blackguard.' 'For some reason, much is being written about him and his life! Shun it, gentlemen, shun it! The sweepings of salacity! The sweepings of salacity! What did you say, Blishen?' Blishen unable to reveal what he'd whispered to Andrew Bell, which was that the Sweepings of Salacity was obviously a minor Ethiopian prince. Of Aldous Huxley, Percy Chew was even more dismissive than of Lawrence. This was largely because, though Lawrence could be faulted for taking an essentially state-based education too seriously, and supposing it gave him the right to make statements on subjects reserved for scholars, his offence was much smaller than that of an Old Etonian who'd made mischievous use of an education not only incomparable but costly.

'It isn't that Percy Chew had such opinions,' I said, 'although they seem curious ones for a man with some claim to have been educated. It's that he presented them so noisily and fiercely and wholly without discussion to classes of growing boys!' I was drinking whisky faster than John Logan was drinking sherry. OLD SCHOOLMASTER, the headline might read, *AND* FORMER PUPIL DROP DEAD . . .

'Yes, yes, that fearful North London suburban snobbery!' I grinned affectionately at him: how snobbish were his animadversions on Percy Chew's snobbery! 'And , often, so revoltingly expressed! But I had no idea he was so disagreeably dogmatic about literature in the classroom! But then . . .'

But then, he had worked so hard for the school, so devotedly, and games had become indisputably compulsory! 'And, of course, he did appoint excellent men like Willy Williams.'

Kate announced that dinner was close at hand. 'Ah,' said John Logan. 'Decorations, I imagine, and evening dress?' And then: 'You loved Willy, I know, as I did. Dear man! But he was, of course, quite the most appalling skinflint I've ever known.'

Imagine, I thought, if Romeo or Hamlet had lived . . . and had become men chiefly known for their meanness. Or for being tedious. Williams, the chief brightness of my schooldays, had turned, with time, into a bore.

John Logan had loved him, no doubt about that, as I had loved him. But about my love hung still the splendours of my childhood. He had been twenty-four when he arrived at Queen's, a smiling wit: and he'd died at sixty-six, and that had been a year ago. Time made little sense.

It was Williams who had breathed into us his own awe of Shakespeare, his own passion for words and for the relationship of words with reality. He had been a faintly older contemporary of Dylan Thomas, and had once told me that the famous phrase 'the rub of flesh' was not originally Dylan's, but his. He had given it to Dylan, on request. The story was that they were in some shop in Swansea, Dylan perhaps buying cigarettes, Williams certainly buying them (they had, in accumulation, killed him), and Dylan had said: 'Willy, can I have that phrase of yours?' And (as, an awestruck youngster, I reconstructed the incident), Williams had replied: 'Of course, Dylan! Have it, have it! Couldn't be in better hands!' And it was Williams who made war against my father's bitter refusal to consider the possibility that I might go to university. It had been a poor sort of war, I now thought, in execution: though splendid enough in theory. Much had hung once on Williams coming to talk to my father: who'd demonstrated his own angry readiness to be persuaded by lighting a fire in our front room, an act normally reserved for Christmas. But Williams had, quite simply, forgotten to come. I forgave him that, readily, and even belligerently, thinking a man with so busy a head had a right to such forgetfulness. Everything was forgiveable to the man who'd invite me round to his digs and play Chopin to me: who'd tell me about his love affairs, which I'd think of as taking place in Verona or Venice, in terms of soliloquies and poems pinned to tree-trunks; and read to me from Grigson's periodical, *New Verse*: and lend me perilous copies of red-bound books from the Left Book Club. I left one of these last once on a sixth form windowsill: Williams swooped on it and hid it under his jacket with a cry of: 'Edward! Edward! do you want to get me the sack!' If Percy Chew had discovered that Williams was lending out such insurrectionary matter – which, if given its head, might have meant that even persistent Rugger and sustained cricket could not preserve a boy from socialism and other envious theories – it might well have led to dismissal.

Oh, I'd loved and admired Williams, deeply. As the years passed, I'd realised he wasn't the avant garde figure of my imagination. He was a not uncommon human being: born in a nest of gifts, himself gifted but with no persistence at all. Young, and a teacher, he exhilarated: and in middle age, grown cunning in the protection of his own failure, he became a bore, a sadly tedious man. I knew *that*, having been bored by him: but not easily believing it, because he *was* Williams, and one of the great excitements of my childhood.

And now John Logan said, as we ate, that Williams was

doomed by a failure to organise, a distaste for sustained work. 'Wanted to write, but could never bring himself to sit down to the hard chore of writing.' I remembered the letters he'd written to me from Swansea, during school holidays: to an unhappy fourteen-year-old, letters of encouragement. As to being sacked, he'd once written, 'I wouldn't give a Barton damn (and that's pretty cheap) whether the pedagogue-in-chief' (oh, what a relief to have Percy Chew so characterised!) 'kicked me out tomorrow – I could earn my living with my pen, as indeed I hope to do in the future. I have no intention of stagnating in an atmosphere of standard times' (the school, partly steered by John Logan, had gone mad on athletics), 'games committee decisions' (it was not a letter I could ever read to my present guest, even after a lapse of forty years) 'parents' meetings and the other fal-de-lals of modern education.'

'What a pity!' said John Logan. 'Dear lady, you knew him too – what a waste! But poor Em! Poor Em Williams! What a cross she had to bear! But she loved him, she loved the mess he made of things – the only thing she couldn't love was his meanness. She had to hand over her earnings, when she taught – and in return he kept her disgracefully short of clothes – *poor* Em! And every item of household expenditure gone through with a toothcomb! I went abroad with them twice – oh the accounts and complications! – revealing, fearful!'

Before he went to bed, valiantly almost refusing every sort of nightcap ('A little Madeira? – but why *should* you have it? – and it's much more Savernake than Barley Wood! A very little sherry, then'), John Logan said I'd lighted up a corner of Percy Chew he'd always found dark and beyond his understanding. *Of course*, his impulse had been to encourage boys of a certain social respectability, those who had achieved gentlemanliness, and whose parents had made at least a gesture in the direction of such an achievement for themselves. 'My dear, I see this is true, and it makes me sick and angry.'

We hadn't come together, I thought, with any appetite for the destruction of illusions: certainly with no wish to play games with dead bones. But we'd been intensely involved once, as boy and man, in a small but significant corner of the English educational and social scene: and neither had ceased worrying at his memories, trying to get it right. Not in order to erect pillories or award laurels, but because you'd feel (and, surely, be) such a fool, resting your view of the world on a false assessment of the past.

The sad end of Williams' career didn't make nonsense of its brilliant and generous beginning. I was only sorry to have learned that he was miserly. But God knew of any of us – the most displeasing defect might be related to the most remarkable virtue! Williams would always be the most extraordinarily generous skinflint I'd ever known.

As for me, I felt wretched about sending my old Irish guest to bed, suddenly certain as he clearly was that the heroic Percy Chew, in making of Queen's a school of model dignity, had proceeded by a course fatuously off the mark in respect of Thomas Hardy, D. H. Lawrence, A. E. Housman and Anton Chekhov (over coffee I'd quoted Percy Chew on the last – 'Always examining his own rather unlovely inside'): and depending on a severe view of the boys in his charge – that they might, or might not, exhibit symptoms of conformity, of definitely or not being likely to become Lawrence or Hardy: and that the general sympathy of the school, or absence of it, which could lead for a boy to one sort of future or quite another, might depend very much on whether one displayed elements of the gentleman, or no such elements.

But we grinned at each other as the evening ended. 'Despite the appearance of my luggage,' said John Logan, 'I wish to assure you that an emergency in the middle of the night will find me clothed in nightwear which, though of some antiquity, will not cause your neighbours to exclaim with horror.' I thought he might at any moment mention the Athlone ring. He saw my eye going to it, on his finger. 'I believe I might have said quite enough about that, forty years ago,' he said, before pretending not to be appalled by our open-treaded staircase.

9

It often astonished me to be passing through the portals (it was too modest a word for them) of Bush House. I'd find myself thinking back to a game I used to play as a solitary child somewhere about 1924. With such books as we had in the house I'd make grand spaces for my imagination to occupy. Here was a sort of palace space: and here a sort of castle space. Bush was a mixture of such spaces. In a sense, I'd feel I'd constructed it myself, in much that old fashion, on the floor of the room in East Barton we let out to lodgers: it was a toy designed to make the passage of time interesting. For the Bush House lifts I had a strange affection. Uneasy cages, in which the world packed itself. If the Tower of Babel had ever got as far as having lifts, they'd have been like these. Languages were shed at each floor. *There* went a mumble in some African tongue, and *there* a prickly exchange in Polish. Asia had business on the fifth. Tiny persons from China were replaced with gawks from Scandinavia.

Penelope, producing *The World This Morning*, said she'd heard me speaking of next week to my own producer, and she didn't want to hear such talk again. She would direct her worst ill-humour at any presenter who looked beyond the immediate moment. In this business, she said, 'Next week does not exist.' She laughed at herself as she said it, having the habit of viewing her own opinions as she did those of others: the probability of their being absurd was a strong one. 'But, Penelope,' I said, 'one of the characteristics of literature is that it spreads itself a bit, in time. It's a bit elastic, you see.' I wasn't going to be too earnest with Penelope. She could score sixes off the most presentable of earnestnesses. 'I think I heard you say literature,' she said now, delighted. The word 'literature', like the idea of there being a week to follow this one, represented an attempt at grandeur foolishly out of place in this setting. 'Not everything can be called current affairs,' I said. 'Prove it,' said Penelope. She looked like a tiger that found pouncing a little too easy. 'Of course,' she said, 'you're an appalling highbrow.'

I hadn't heard the term since my father had last applied it to me, shortly before he died. He'd used it steadily as a sort of conversational knock-out blow from the 1930s onwards. He would certainly have agreed with Penelope that no human concern had more than a week's reach. The occupation of highbrows was the absurd one of attempting to persuade the rest of mankind (who, luckily, included a hard core of sensible realists like my father) to take a longer view. Thus almost the whole apparatus of schools: most of the further sorts of education: and my own appalling habit of purchasing and, having purchased, retaining books. 'Penelope, you are like no one so much as my father,' I cried. She bent on me one of her dark and amused frowns. 'I hope there are some differences,' she said, making a snake of her hips as, certainly, my father had never made a snake of his.

Penelope had been my producer for some months, and brought to bear on the programme her horror of anything she could identify as heaviness. An item of almost any seriousness was heavy. Anything that lasted over three minutes was well on the way to becoming heavy. Intrinsically, books were heavy, and demanded all of Penelope's considerable competence if she was to create out of them her preferred sort of programme. That was one composed of very rapid, bright, shallow items. Not only her skill but her temperament made her a natural producer of magazine programmes: and one entirely of her making was like some sunlit brook. It chattered briefly, you trailed the tips of your fingers in it: and it was gone. Everywhere she detected pretension – together with those solemn infatuations to which, she held, her fellow-producers were prone. There was one of them who, as Penelope briskly understood his outlook, admired all continentals for being continental – and vivacious. 'Imagine that!' Penelope would cry. 'I mean – *vivacious!*' She spoke as if this flew in the face of a generally accepted view that all continentals were leaden. 'And *Africans!*' she'd cry. 'He thinks they're fascinating! They're *not* fascinating. I mean, they're simply not!' She had a warm, disabused laugh. 'I mean, they just *aren't!*'

I enjoyed, for a term, being Penelope's victim. Her determined lightness of spirit was bracing. She was almost totally straight: being less than honest only when it came to the matter of my narrations. I introduced each interview with the briefest and liveliest account of writer and book I could manage; but for Penelope I was never brief enough. Her trick was to approve the narrations when written, but to urge substantial cuts as we made our recording. 'I think they can do without that, don't you?' she'd cry, her pen already busy with erasures. Studio time was vanishing: it was, as Penelope cheerfully knew, no moment for debate. 'I mean, all they probably want to know is how to pronounce the name of this wretched poet the book's about. That's all *I*'m interested in, really. Is it Yeets or Yates? I've never known.' My schooners with their canvas carefully set for rapid progress flashed into harbour reduced to sailboards. '*They* don't want to be told too much, you know,' Penelope would say as she accompanied her drastically pruned presenter out of the studio. 'Anyway, they'll have forgotten it all five minutes later.'

The variety of producers was as great as the variety of interviewers. There was Alan, who thought of the programme as a worldwide Oxbridge tutorial. He was glad if I treated my narration as a sort of academic armchair: and, whereas Penelope was capable of regarding a mere mention of an author's birthdate as an intolerably pretentious detail, Alan would nod approvingly at some esoteric reference likely to be picked up by one per cent of our audience. Like all my producers, he had considerable professional skills, and could make an extremely acceptable programme in the spirit in which he chose to clothe it. It was simply that Alan's programmes were clothed in tweeds and academic gown, while Penelope's dashed anxiously in and then quickly out of view in their underpants. Josh, on the other hand, had a passion for compensating for the hopelessly verbal character of radio by smuggling in, as often as possible, tremendous amounts of music and sound effects. It was what really interested him: and sometimes, fondly but firmly, I would shrink away when writing a narration from any reference that, however obliquely, might be taken as a cue for music. It meant, roughly speaking, that I would never allude to the possibility of some day in the future being fine, or to cuckoos, or to sorcerers or their apprentices. 'This is his ninth book' might lead to a snatch of the Choral Symphony. The trouble being that, after vast amounts of playing things over on gramophones and timing and retiming them, it would turn out as often as not that the programme was too long, and something must go. An agitated last-minute review in the recording studio made it clear that there was one dispensable element only: the carefully chosen and elaborately excerpted music.

Josh was followed by Stella, who had no time for what she described as 'aural kitsch'. Under her care, the programme wore sensible suiting: and the sailboard became a trim yacht, with one or two clever devices for ensuring that it got from start to finish in exactly 28 minutes 30 seconds.

Being an outside contributor was, I'd think, rather like being a star occasionally permitted to wander inside the solar system. As you made your little journey, in and out, you slowly realised that the other stars were moving in fixed patterns, and that much of their interest was in the character (majestic or not) of those patterns. There were, in the BBC sky, suns and satellites and planets and comets. It was dazzling to be a sub-stellar visitor, but wonderful to slip away again. I'd skip up Kingsway, thinking of that vast movement continuing behind me: with the occasional explosion of some over-brilliant sun, and the despair of a star that found itself in some particularly dispiriting orbit.

It could have odd effects, working year after year in broadcasting as an *inside* contributor. You could find yourself assessing the affairs of the world in terms of a stream of the celebrated – their importance real or momentary – who did what they did, achieved what they achieved, primarily in order to provide broadcast items. In a mild-mannered radio producer, unfailingly polite, there might be a hidden coil of impatience and distaste, resting on a feeling that, in the end, it was he who had the ascendancy: since he could hope to be there, still mildly producing, when this year's crop of celebrities had been superseded by the next.

But was it beginning to happen to me, too – the *outside* contributor? Were my fellow-writers threatening to merge into a single writer?

'For God's sake,' said one of the most industrious of them, as he sat opposite me for interview, 'tell me what my book is about. I've written three since then.'

Please show tickets. BOLLOCKS.

As I waited for the train on Barley Wood station on any Bush House day, I'd notice that this remained the statement made by the gate leading to the booking office. The first part, the adjuration, was the work of British Rail: the latter part, the retort, was anonymous. Nowadays any official declaration pasted up or painted in the station was likely to be challenged in this fashion: and other verbal or graphic features were subject to vigorous editing by aerosol. As we stood waiting for one of our rarely punctual trains, I was often surprised by the selective blindness affected by my polite neighbours. The verbal environment was of the sort once reserved for the walls of urinals. 'Damned awful weather for gardening,' someone would cry, outstaring a suggestion that he should commit on himself a difficult sexual outrage. I was talking once of the same subject, the weather, to a neat-voiced lady who was either well-known to me or not known at all (the cast of the soap opera that was my life had simply become too large), when I realised we were both staring at a picturesque assertion, surely not scrawled up by any of the city-going suits along the platform (but how could one be sure?) as to an informal occasion involving more than one member of the royal family.

This distraught decade! In a world in which history had begun to explode, the armies of disgust and dismay had moved in with spraygun and complex forms of neglect, and the solid environment had begun to crumble. The muttering on the walls was our own muttering, however respectable we sought to be. It was curious, I thought, the part played by the replacement of the old money by the new. How incredulous Miss Baker would have been had she known that one of the foundations that she'd taken care should underlie our existence when we left Barley Road, its duodecimal intricacies enforcing heed of any and every farthing, was being replaced by a currency based on the more rapid and wantonly smoother system known to us then as HTU: Hundreds Tens and Units. It may have had little effect on inflation: but it provided inflation with what it needed, a bewildering change of costume. At the first warning that it was planned, Miss Baker would have marched us into the playground and then returned to make her position clear to the authorities. It was simply not on! I'd thought on my meeting with him of mentioning this vision to Jimmy Soper, who'd been at my side when we mastered the skill of it: £3.19s.5^{3}/$_{4}$d × 17. But I imagined I'd find that Jimmy was a traitor to that old training as he was to our one-time wild and wonderful use of the back streets of Barton.

Under the great dismays, the small ones. The replacement in London, for example, of conveniences with inconveniences. Anyone knowing the city had never needed to suffer serious discomfort. Relief was a street or two away, at most. Now in emergencies I appealed to the old map in my head, to the memory of this or that wrought-iron entrance to this or that deeply welcome arrangement of Victorian ceramics, and remembered that here, there, everywhere, the final padlock had been placed in position.

It was a long smallness of decays and collapses. On a train between Plymouth and London I found myself lunching with a man who'd unwillingly been to Devon to interview for a job. He was a meat technologist: and explained to me the latest state of the art, and how he'd been working, in America, on devices for creating meat out of what was not, and never had been, meat. He had loved working in America: such drive, such confidence, such certainty that one must push the invention of meat as far as it could be pushed, and beyond. He was in his late thirties, but a boy, I thought: believing that the only question to be asked of technological advance was whether it was practical. If it had proved possible to turn the entire world into a vast lamb chop, he'd have been in favour, I think, on the general grounds that he liked to be associated with what was brisk and bold and within the grasp of enterprise. He did not like Britain. It was not brisk: it was not bold: it now barely feigned to be enterprising. Far from turning the world into a lamb chop, it was lax in the skills of refrigeration, and of some kind of super-refrigeration that he tried to explain to me, his eyes bright. He wanted to go back to America. So did his young daughters. But his wife could bear to live only here: thus his miserable journey to Plymouth. His wife loved England, and that was that. I liked him: he did not understand his wife's attachment to this land of the inferior refrigerator, the crumbling pavement, the vanishing loo and the unpunctual train, but he was obscurely moved by it. I said he was one of nature's Americans, perhaps; and he was pleased. He said of my obvious suggestion that Britain was in the trough into which nations fall when they lose empires that he'd not thought of that before. Yes, yes. He did not ask what I did. I suspect he knew that I was helplessly English, in favour of hesitancy, much given to the question mark. I felt I could have told him of Miss Baker's deep commitment to that item of punctuation. Her feeling for it might have been caused by its baroque quality – she taught it more as a matter of Art than of English. Or perhaps the special attention she gave it arose from knowing that when a child at Barley Road began freely to use it the scholarship to the grammar school was in sight. Those who got there did so, in the end, on the strength of a handful of sophistications: of which the question mark was one of the most prominent.

As the decade gathered way, in a general atmosphere of declining and falling: and prices rose: and governments gave displays of helplessness, and there were ominous displays by fascist groups of a willingness to be obscenely helpful: and as I wondered why none among our leaders seemed to address himself, or herself, to the fears, and also to the courage, of the people: so I felt an increasing uncertainty about my ability to carry a burden of my own. Well, it was the sort of burden we all carry: until I made my way into my fifties I hadn't understood how inordinate it could seem. It was simply the weight of consciousness, day after day: of so much remembered, so much forgotten: of all the unresolved elements in existence – which really, as time went on, did seem to be much like being in the middle of several hundred detective novels with no hope of ever knowing the solution to any of them. Add the pressure of wondering about the natures even of those one knew best. People one had known all or most of one's life grew not less, but oppressively more, mysterious. My old simple notions of John Logan, or Percy Chew, or of my old English teacher Williams, simply wouldn't do. And new evidence continued to pour in.

I'd be relieved when the weather made it difficult to do anything but delight in being around. The moment in spring when the bare ugly garden of a week earlier was awash with green. Big bright blowing days. Days when the light was such that everything seemed to have rather more than three dimensions. Days when the sea exploded with trapped sunlight: and Kate and I were two furnaces, embracing.

Or among children: visiting schools, to talk about writing. To the school where, after my first visit, a small boy had written an entire book called *Crumpit the Mouse: 7 Chapters of Thrill*. Or another, for deeply handicapped children, in which Anthony, given to falling asleep, was accompanied everywhere by Sue, his official nudger.

It was to talk about children's literature, and its relationship to folklore, that I was to go to Sydney, and meet again my old pupil, Jack Seed.

Gary Bunce was plainly calling from mid-ocean. 'You are on a ship', I challenged him, reckless with fatigue. It was just after two o'clock in the morning. 'You recognised the chuckle of my friend the purser,' said Gary. 'No,' I said. 'It was some immense sense of distance, and your being in some sort of desert. Sand or water. I thought it was water.' 'Actually,' said Gary. 'The purser isn't my friend. I hit him rather hard – on the nose – earlier today.' 'Oh God,' I said. 'I tell you what,' said the remote crackling voice of this other old pupil of mine. 'Avoid Australia. It was when we put in there that I realised I hated the purser.' 'You advise me to avoid Australia?' I cried. 'Eddy, that's exactly what I do advise.'

'I'm going there next week,' I said, yawning with triumph, and hung up.

PART TWO

1

It is extremely odd, I thought, to be about to fly to Australia. Almost any other destination would be less unlikely. All my life Australia had stood for the idea of whatever was absolutely remote. How unchanged, really, one's childish view of the world remained! Miss Baker, at Barley Road, had pointed to Australia on the cracked varnish of the map she'd unrolled on the wall. When she did that, c 1929, it was as if we were holding our breath, wondering if Captain Cook would ever get there. Was it Miss Baker's teaching, or something in the air of 1929, that made us feel cartography was still tentative?

Anyway, there was this raw red nugget of land: distinguished, by its being hopelessly lost down there, from the British Isles, which were safely found up here. About Australia and suchlike classroom fantasies the small scholars of Barley Road reserved judgement. When it came to plausibility, the clowning pages of *Kinema Fun* had the edge.

And now I proposed to hop there in twenty-four hours. Though, of course, once you arrived at the airport you realised that 'hop' was too active a word. The journey was an extension of the airport. I would enter a fragment of Heathrow and very much later would leave it to enter a virtually identical airport, alleged to be 12,000 miles away. Less a flight than a conjuring trick.

Kate, looking downcast, said I wasn't to be downcast, and must not wish myself home again. And then I was inside this bulky container, and the clock and the calendar fell apart. By the time I had attempted, and failed, to make myself comfortable, we were above the most immense beach in the world, with ribs of what might have been rock, and wandering bleached snakeskins that were . . . appeared to be but might not have been . . . river-beds. How ignorant I was of this world of which I was a creature! There was not down there the faintest mark of human existence. I slept, and was then above a brown land, patched with cultivation and ownership, but *very* brown. It was as England might look if it had been swept by fire. Then, suddenly, complete desert: after which the land for half an hour or so was upholstered in suede, profoundly and rather beautifully stained. Exquisite defilements, I thought, in the midst of that imprisoned jocosity that builds up among long-distance travellers by air, and fell asleep into one of the cracks that had opened up in the jerrybuilt structure that time turned out to be. And when I was startled out of sleep again, nipped by the sudden closure of the crack I'd fallen into, a sequence of intricate abstract marquetry brought us to India.

My first glimpse. I remembered the Barley Road view of the continent: Clive, elephants, palaces, tea. Below was Bombay: a city of tall cement-grey blocks of flats, you thought, until you saw that in and out of those and far beyond them spread the rusty fungus of corrugated-iron roofing. India was rusty corrugated-iron. As we landed, I saw a man going to the edge of field, alongside the runway, and squatting down to shit. The heaped hovels resembled the tumble of red shale on a cliff I knew in Cornwall. Then we were in the air again, and India appeared generally a sort of greenish-grey. We bumped through a monsoon. Time was shattered beyond repair. I had a sensation of having become rapidly bearded, and of having read two novels, or perhaps one novel twice. I observed wryly that I had made notes as I read, though certainly Jane Austen was not to be interviewed. Singapore, they said, in thirty-five minutes, would be hot and sticky. And here it was. The blocks of flats seemed transparent with blue light, and beyond them were ship-shapes of light. Once again 350 trembling tons of us descended through someone else's black hugeness of air. The captain had not misled us: Singapore was hot and sticky. The airport offered watches, cameras, radios: radios, cameras, watches. Then I was witness to yet another demonstration of safety procedures. The drawback for me, I thought with enormous weariness, was that I could be certain of understanding and correctly following such procedures only after a twelve-week course at an evening class, with regular refreshers.

I couldn't be sure if I'd been asleep, or what the distinction between sleep and wakefulness amounted to. But I seemed now to be involved in dawn over Australia. Along the horizon, a burning band. We had really come to the margins of the world. I was feebly surprised to observe that the surface of Australia was one of wrinkled mud. But, thank God, no: it was cloud. It was a continent of cloud.

The last moments of the flight were, after all, tremendous. There, laid out on a great dish at what for me was the end of the world, was Sydney, a puzzle of land and water with a puzzle of mist added. It was early morning. The mists were so low that the shadows of trees were cast within them: inside the pale skin of mist, these shadows like splinters. The great machine descended, totally silent, and the Harbour Bridge appeared, a little bloom of the earliest sunshine above it, a silhouette with its feet standing in a fume of silver: as if, in a corner of this first presentation of itself, the city had signed its name.

'Edward!' cried strangers, and made it possible for me almost at once to faint into a bed in, as far as I could make out, a teachers' training college.

2

And almost at once woke me again, a hollow thing, and took me to see the city. It seemed to be Sunday: and sunny: and my fellow sightseers, German, Japanese and American, having at first struck me as being out of my range altogether – most were high-flying academic figures in this world of children's literature in which I was an improvising artisan – appeared very easy to be with: especially Mae Gloucester Graham, from California, who was certainly the world's smallest professor, whose Chair might have been in something like Mischief. It wasn't at this stage much more than a half-stifled chuckle at a solemn moment, but I thought she was likely to be an ally. She was small, she told me later – not that she thought it much of an explanation – because she was the last child of an ageing father, who'd once said to her, as a rough token of his regret, that that was all that he'd had left in him. Much of her work was among children: and many of them, it seemed, wouldn't settle until they'd confirmed that here was a professor they could, however slightly, tower over. Sydney towered over her, that afternoon. A big-boned city. We were, I was later to discover, on the sneakily silent side of the harbour, as one of Sydney's novelists has called it, the posher suburbs. Bondi and Jack Seed lay over there – on another, rowdier bank. Meanwhile, here was a barbecue: in a garden that had the Bridge virtually in it, a sort of excessive piece of trelliswork. Light up there held that great suspension of metal in its brilliant grip, and traffic could be seen pouring over it, a highway in the air. It was colder than I'd been prepared for. I have no great love of barbecues, seeing them as contrivances for cooking meat with the greatest possible inefficiency and requiring it to be eaten in the greatest possible discomfort. I was glad of Mae's company. At one point she held my hand, and I was grateful: being suddenly aware of having come too far too suddenly, and bringing with me perhaps the cruellest cold I'd ever had.

Someone gave me a cough preventive that turned my tongue black and left my cough where it was: I had an experience of stunned and broken sleep. In the middle of what might carelessly have been called the night I read Samuel Beckett in a paperback taken from a cupboard in my study bedroom. I thought of the girl teacher-in-training who had taken the stunning dismay of this comedy on board as part of her preparation for the classroom. Jack Seed had written about the pupils she'd perhaps be teaching. 'I find the children rather apathetic, I must say. When they reach eighteen or so they develop a fanatical interest in football, but this soon calms down to a dull appreciation of beer.' When I opened another cupboard in this room in which I was wide awake when asleep, and asleep when wide awake, a model fell on my head. I thought how odd it was to come so far to be mildly injured by a representation (luckily, in light wood) of the Globe Theatre.

And Jack, I remembered, had told me of a note given him by an ambiguously penitent child: 'I'm sorry I called you a bullwanker.'

Later, I seemed to be dreaming of an old friend, the producer of the amateur dramatic company Kate and I had belonged to. In the dream he was hostile to Beckett, but his condemnatory quotations appeared to come from Shakespeare. I was struck by the thought that he had been dead now, poor man, for some years. 'But you are *dead*!' I cried, as if clinching an argument: and he turned from me and I saw that, under the thin hair on the back of his head, his head itself was dissolving, it was turning to sand, the sand was blowing into my eyes.

It was, somehow, morning, presumably the next morning, and I was sitting with my fellow-pundits in a plaza somewhere in the city, listening to the Minister for Immigration and

Ethnic Affairs: who said he wouldn't offer any comment on the contribution children's literature might make to intercultural understanding, since this was the theme of the conference: he'd merely say what a thoroughly good thing it was that these almost unbearably knowledgeable persons had come from all over the world to stimulate and . . . It began to rain, and my attention, which had held painfully for five minutes, snapped and scattered. And, with Mae and a tender Japanese who made picture books for the very young in which the things of the nursery were given the mistiest elegance, I coughed my way to the Opera House.

John Betjeman was always influencing my view of buildings. I never crossed Westminster Bridge without thinking of his neo-Wordsworthian line, inspired by the erection of the Shell Centre: 'Earth has not anything to show more square.' So now as I approached the Sydney Opera House for the first time I caught his murmur: 'A rugby scrum of nuns.' And it was, it was! and for a moment there was nothing to be heard but a holy panting, and the scrum half's cry of: 'Coming in *left*, sisters!' Then the joke dispersed and there was this beautiful toy made of sea-shells, which looked at once huger and tinier than expected. I'd seen it before, in specimens of their craft created by Victorian Blishens, stonemasons all: blocks of liverish marble with shells cemented to the top surfaces. On grandmotherly and great-auntish mantelpieces there'd stood small harbingers of this intricate construction, in which now we were to have lunch. Reached, it was all vistas and prows and beaks, and views as if from the bridges of giant ships: the water of the harbour raced past it, busy with small boats.

The Harbour made my heart leap. It was beautiful in itself, but also for the way it played with the city, put hurrying water between suburb and suburb; made the great metal stride of the Bridge necessary: made Sydney as much a thing of the sea as a thing of the land. I was still dizzy with love of it when we sat in the great hall of the University, which was a reduction of some great hall in Britain, and the conference was opened, with a swishing of academic gowns. I thought how odd such occasions were: opportunities ruthlessly taken for persons to torment other persons with speeches of elaborately-wrought banality delivered at a pitch just too low to be picked up easily by the human ear. I filled the time by thinking about Mae being so small. If she'd been another American of the same forename she'd have had to cry: 'Come *down* and see me some time!' Suppose she ever said to me: 'I am at your feet!' 'That's something you can't help,' I'd reply. If . . . The great hall sighed with release: the last speech in favour of people understanding each other, and firmly against people getting each other wrong, came to an end.

Suddenly, silently at my side, as the audience dispersed, was a small man whose face, astonishingly familiar, was packaged in a beard with which I had no acquaintance at all. 'Sir doesn't know me,' said a voice that had given me agreeable trouble in classrooms 12,000 miles away. 'It is not Jack Seed, I suppose,' I said. 'No, I don't suppose it is,' said the small man. 'I do apologise.' 'But even if you aren't Jack Seed,' I said, 'it's a good imitation.' 'Sir hasn't changed much,' said Jack.

I thought, as I shook his hand, that he hadn't changed at all. The beard was a disguise he'd have been perfectly capable of sporting twenty years earlier in the library at Stonehill Street. The essence of him had always lain in the teasing use of his eyes. He'd say something preposterous, or tell a wild lie, and the eyes would steady themselves spectacularly: such a gravity as could lead only to a spill, though not necessarily there and then, into laughter. This was Jack's main trick – comedy brought about by establishing earnestness and then causing it to collapse – and in employing it he'd managed to be the best example I'd ever known of the pupil, the instructed person, as comedian. Though it has to be said that about his eyes when earnest there was at times a glinting fixity that suggested that the comic habit rested on something less easygoing. As it happened, one of his grandmothers had positively been murdered, by a lodger, for her quarrelsome insistence on her own immoderate opinion. There seemed in Jack's background to be two strands: the angry refusal to modify a point of view, intolerable enough now and then to lead to mayhem, and the gentle capacity to dismantle such obstinacy. Jack came from the dismantling side of the family; but as his lady, Cor, told me later in my visit, he was splashed with his grandmother just a little.

'You really would like to come and stay with us after the conference?' he asked now. 'Of course!' 'You're *sure*?' Jack looked across at a sparkling knot of ladies, senior members of the organisation. 'I expect *some* might think you ought to stay in a classier part of Sydney. Do they look as if they'd fallen off Christmas trees, would you say? Pretty tiaras.' The ladies weren't wearing tiaras: but there was a twinkling elegant illusion of such ornaments. 'I want to come if you want me to come.' 'We'd love you to come,' said Jack. 'And we'll show you as much of the city as we can. And take you to a restaurant or two.'

I remembered what he'd written about a girl who'd tried to bring him down from his teacherly pedestal - about two inches high, he said, and dwindling daily – by way of sexual challenges. One morning he'd found that she'd dropped on his desk what he recognised as a diagram of the female genitalia. What should he do? He concluded it might be best to pretend he thought it was a map of Sydney. 'I pointed to a particularly interesting curly bit and said, 'There are some very good restaurants there!' She said, "My God, you *are* filthy!"'

'I look forward to the restaurants,' I said. 'And to seeing more of the city.' That afternoon we'd been taken to the top of a towering shopping complex and from its galleries had looked out over the scene. More intestinal than genital: stomachs and colons of water, livers and kidneys of land. A wonderful confusion of the two elements, with multiple wanderings of one into the other. Jack had written: 'I hope you'll love it as I do. Most of all I love the way the light reacts with the water.' The light formed virtually a third element, the great scattered and elaborately connected stretches of water being mirrors, that threw light up and across, made suburbs of light that seemed now airier, now more substantial than the suburbs themselves.

But at this moment I had to prepare to give, tomorrow, the

opening address, under the stipulated title: *The Impulse to Story*.

3

I drank whisky: I had a shower: I coughed as if a brass band had been trapped in my throat. I perhaps showered again. I then . . . fell awake must be the phrase for it. I'd obviously lost the trick of sleep altogether, and thought there was nothing for it but to read through my speech . . .

I felt strongly affected by meeting Jack again. If I was to talk about what made us tell stories, I could throw my speech away, of course, and talk simply about Stonehill Street: about teaching Jack: Jack's letters from round the world ('H and I plan to ride to Naples on my motorbike this year. Most people laugh at this point . . . He tells me he wants to go to Australia, and if this happens I might go with him for the ride'); Jack teaching; this reunion. It astonished me, the way life made stories. The impulse to story seemed to me to lie in the obsessive need to discover the shape, some shape, in the dishevelment of the actual. Well, I seemed to have said that in my speech. 'The writer, the storyteller, is haunted, I think, by two things: by an immense awareness of the incoherence of life, and an awareness equally acute of life's coherence. It is all over the place and it is all so shapely.'

And then, of course, I began talking about Rufus.

The fact was that Rufus was the most remarkable maker of stories I ever hoped to know. When he and I worked on two books based on the Greek myths, we'd brought together, I thought, two different – yet somehow similar – responses to that paradox about life being a muddle, and forming such powerful patterns. 'Rufus,' I proposed to tell my audience next day, 'works on the shape and drive and sequence of a story with the obsessive exactitude of a watchmaker. Time and again when we worked together I was ready to declare that some narrative twist or turn was good enough; but Rufus was not ready to declare that. He was still at his work of slightly shifting the angles. And, when we'd gone through this curious experience of working together, we found we'd come to apparently contrary conclusions. I'd learned, I thought, how to turn the screw of narrative a few turns tighter. Rufus thought he'd learned to relax in the matter of narrative . . . or to be less neurotically distrustful of relaxation in storytelling.

'I must tell you here,' I proposed to say, 'that when Rufus rings me up, at home, and reveals after a minute or so of gossip that what he has really rung about is the condition of his current story . . . when he does that, and I listen, with admiration and pleasure as I always do, then he says, at the end of his reading, with an unvarying note of anguish and anxiety: Does it move? Does it keep going? Does it go to sleep? Rufus's natural fear as a writer is that his narrative has lost speed, has become stuck in the mud. His compulsion is to keep it moving. Now, that's the compulsion of all storytellers. But in Rufus's case the compulsion focuses in the first place on narrative. I mean, on the idea he has of the marvellous machine that a story may be, and should be. In my case, the compulsion focuses on . . . oh, character, atmosphere, some elements so airy they are not the obvious ingredient of story: that is, of story as a sequence of events. I don't mean that I don't care about narrative and that Rufus doesn't care about the other things. But that's the difference in the way the compulsion focuses. What a storyteller must have, it seems to me, is some such obsession, however focused, with *shape* and *speed* and *movement*.

'Now, what sparks Rufus off, *his* impulse to story, is the challenge of producing an object of artful fiction, an invention, that carries inside itself his feelings about actual events and experiences in his own life. What sparks me off is the challenge of using the exact happenings of my life and, with the minimum of alteration, turning them into a kind of true fiction. And I'm talking about how I do it, and how Rufus does it, and how different the two approaches to storytelling are, not out of any sense of self-importance on my behalf or his, but because here *are* two different approaches: different in the focus of the nervous compulsion, the drive, the impulse: different in the form that our characteristic stories take – pure invention on Rufus's part: on mine, false fiction, or false autobiography, or whatever the term is.

'The differences only point up the similarities. The impulse to story in both cases – and I quote us simply as examples of impulsive and compulsive storytellers – consists in the need to respond to a challenge: and the challenge is one that lies in the simultaneous shapelessness and shapefulness of life.'

Yes, I thought, yes. It was true of what I felt: and of what I believed to be the general human need to make sense of one's life as a story. In Australia, of course – and this is what I now knew lay behind the choice of theme for the conference – there was a war of storytellers. That's to say, the aborigines had made their own kind of sense out of the experience of living, in the way they did, on that immense stage: and now came the white men, with their own long history as storytellers, but easily (and properly) feeling that their stories barely belonged here. D. H. Lawrence (to Percy Chew, that inflated elementary schoolboy) had observed that the white man had a nervous hold only on the fringe of the great Australian landmass. The subtle European tradition of story had barely so considerable a hold. It belonged in so far as it provided an account of the white experience in that enormous island: but, further back, the imagination that had laid hold of the land was that of the aborigines.

It mattered most to children, whose view of the world could not be rooted in a date so recent as 1788: and there'd been what I found uneasy attempts to marry, for them, the aboriginal and European imaginations. The truth was that, in relation to Australia, the products of the first were deep-rooted, spontaneous, had always been there: and of the other, were anxiously sensitive recent inventions.

I thought as I tried in vain to rediscover the secret of sleep that I wasn't sure the marriage of stories could occur any more easily than true marriage between the peoples concerned. All I was certain of was that, for children, folk tales and myths and great legends were an essential food. 'I believe,' I meant to say tomorrow, 'that after working with such stories as the Greek myths – as anyone's myths – it is so much more difficult ever again to be trivial. I don't mean that children who hear and work with such stories become immensely serious, solemn: I do mean that the great weight of these stories, their great size, gives one for ever a sense of respect for the quality of the human destiny. The fact is we are living in a magnificent drama; and what surely every storyteller sets out to do is to transmit a sense of the true and natural drama in which everyone of us is alive.'

Meanwhile, in my present corner of that drama (in which I'd pieced together a picture of the usual occupant of this room: given to making booby traps of models of the Globe theatre, she combined an interest in Samuel Beckett with a passion for Richard Gordon, and either possessed the largest straw hat in the world or carried her shopping in an immense basket without handles), I must clearly learn to exist without sleep, and to rise above the fact that the brass band in my chest had been joined by a wind octet – both clarinet and bassoon being appallingly out of tune.

It was, as it turned out, very much about that uneasiness . . . the conference. The general white Australian uneasiness, that followed from the truth that the great original stories of the continent were not *their* stories: and the particular uneasiness of writers, who feared that attempts to marry the cultures would end in guilty whimsy. After the careworn talk given by a children's writer who'd tried more intently than any, and who'd cried that she thought she was too bold, too bold, an aboriginal poet in the audience called out that she could be bolder still: and she was greatly moved. It was all, I thought, on the very edge of an enormous unhappiness, not to be resolved by conferences: but it was a pleasure to be among so many storytellers.

Of whom Mae Gloucester Graham was outstanding. In a tiny tent of a frock, in a particular American drone, she told stories rivetingly: as if a bassoon had had the eloquence of a flute. What I liked about her was that she was serious about children's literature to the point of gravity, but could be tumbled into a laugh with a look, a word. There was some solemnity in the air, of a folklorist kind, and it was a relief to trip over a joke, and to acknowledge an absurdity. Jack Seed attended a session, and in the coffee-drinking throng afterwards reminded me that the impertinent group to which he had belonged at Stonehill Street had detected some resemblances between me and Jacques Tati's Monsieur Hulot. I illustrated the point with an Hulotesque step or two, and a folklorist said afterwards: 'Couldn't help noticing you and young Mr Seed obviously trying out the steps of some old English dance.'

Gales blew in my chest: one night, at 3 a.m., I read my ghostly hostess's copy of David Storey's *Life Class*. A few more nights and I'd be in a position to write all her essays and sit for all her exams. I caught myself, round about the same hour, wearing what I'd decided was her straw hat, and thought of conference madness. It had struck Rufus and me once, in Canada. The first symptom being an attempt, in the middle of another sleepless night, to take photographs by the flashes of a thunderstorm, though we'd known it wasn't possible; and that, if it had been possible, the results – incandescent images of university buildings indistinguishable from cardboard boxes – would have been fit only for burning. I'd thought of Rufus during some of the sessions of storytelling. It was what he was always alarmed about, at such gatherings: a masterly narrator wholly dependent on his fountain-pen and typewriter, and on the slow creation of sentences thought and re-thought, he feared he might be required to improvise in public whilst seated in a tepee or igloo. He had warned me when in Australia to keep miles between any campfire and myself. During that visit to Canada he'd said, with deep satisfaction: 'As authors you and I would have been drummed out of every Indian tribe in North America.' He had developed such an animus against the folktale that he would have regarded being scalped for his stories as the local equivalent of being well reviewed.

Some of us talked at a township on the edge of Sydney. There was a monstrous town hall, and a monstrous mayor, both out of scale with their setting: the town hall a palace, the mayor a physically enormous man with an air of extravagant power. Ghengis Khan would have recognised a greater than himself. After we'd talked, we were conducted to the Mayor's Parlour, which might have been renamed the Mayor's Hangar. Receding into the distance in all directions, it was filled with vast couches, armchairs designed for men and women of improbable size, and occasional tables that would have dwarfed most regular tables. The mayor was an affable man, who'd given thought to the literary character of the occasion: asking Mae bluntly how she managed to read so much without doing herself a mischief. He'd made when young the discovery that, for him, reading and good health were incompatible. Nevertheless, he'd certainly read a book or two, and on some other occasion might be able to recall a title. He'd done most things in his time, but he'd be honest: remembering titles wasn't a knack of his. He supposed even Mae, asked suddenly for the name of a book, might flounder. Mae, who at a moment's notice could have stood in for the British Library catalogue, assented pleasantly and refused the offer of a mayoral cigar almost as large as herself. To me the mayor said, looking down the length of the Parlour with its meagre present population of bookish persons: 'I'd like you to see this place when it's being properly used! It hums! It *hums!*'

What nothing had prepared me for was a characteristic of at least this corner of a corner of Australia: a beauty that sprang from the foliage, on the whole, being darker than the trunks of the trees. Here, so much was silver: everywhere, the silver of living trees, the silver bones of dead ones.

And on a hot Sunday, when I was on my way to the Blue Mountains, I'd see clouds of cockatoos burst from all that green and silver, a broadside of white wings.

I was being driven by the Crosbys, he an historian of Australian children's literature. They were gentle people, amused and amusing, but belonged to that very large order of married couples who should not be allowed to occupy the same car. Their disputes were mildly expressed but persistent, relating to every twist and turn of the journey. We arrived in the blue haze of our destination (caused, the haze, by droplets from the eucalypts) after disagreements that would have made perfect sense if they'd thought they were driving on different continents: and, once there, we made our way in a continuing atmosphere of mild contention from lookout to lookout, great crag to great crag, and to falls and cascades: both providing a name, but never the same name, for each of these marvellous spots. Against this background, Denis agreed that his talk of the difficulty the pioneers had had in getting through to the Blue Mountains and beyond, as if such things were in the past, was a little odd. Never mind, I said, as we set out on the problem-strewn return journey to Sydney: what more could a man ask than marital comedy combined with natural grandeur?

Another children's writer, appalled by the explosions in my chest, invited me to visit her and her husband on their farm three hundred miles from Sydney. The very great variety of children's writers never ceased to astonish me. The popular notion of a comfortable sort of woman is beside the mark: apart from her often being a man, the characteristic of comfortableness is not by any means to be depended upon. A children's writer may write, like any other, out of unease and horror. Margaret did so as consistently as anyone I'd read. The farm, reached in a little plane flying over country one wanted to brush energetically – but those white spots of dust were sheep – was out of the colonial adventure stories of my childhood. A long house in an orchard setting, standing on a terrace made for it eighty years earlier, it looked out of its pleasant windows at what resembled a fusion of Devon combes. Everything was mildly, if enlargedly, English, until your eye took in the silver of the trees – or the character of the wrens that flew from bush to bush on the terrace: she, of course, high-tailed, but ashy-breasted: and he appearing to have had the contents of a small tin of poster paint emptied over his head, a startling spill of pale blue.

I walked with Margaret along their river, which lay within the confines of this orderly farmland, but spoke in one way or another of a natural disorder only just compelled to obedience: such racing curves of water, under such prickly tangles of bush, such huge fragments of old trees, clones of the silver rocks they stood among. The landscape climbed and fell in what you saw was an altogether larger than English way: and everywhere was the still-standing silver of dead trees, killed by the economical system of giving each a single deep saw-cut.

All over the world nature requires only five minutes to resume its sway: here, I thought, it would need only five seconds.

I was driven fast to Canberra: the city whose site was chosen by parliamentary vote, and that has a curious pop-up quality. If from scratch you invented a capital city in an English-speaking country in the twentieth century, this would be it: this *was* it. Absurd, one recognised: tolerable cities *grow*. Handsome, Canberra: such glass, such lawns and parks, such fountains: such a well-placed Henry Moore: so curiously boring.

And then I returned to Sydney, and to Bondi.

4

Jack lived with Cor in a garden flat. Cor, in full, was Cornelia, Dutch in background. Her parents had taught in the East Indies, and now she herself taught art and design in a Sydney school. 'It will be knee-deep in dust – everything all over the place! Cor is such a slut!' Jack murmured as we approached the flat. It turned out to be an affectionate inversion of the truth. Cor kept the flat in a state of decorative perfection: not so much in the spirit of an anxious housewife as in that of a compulsive maker of splendid arrangements. There was a long narrow sitting room, the wall towards the garden being glass: and everywhere fine sheers and straw blinds filtered and coloured the light. There was a fruity feel about it – it seemed sometimes that I was sitting inside an illuminated apricot or plum. Though much that hung or was mounted or stood on the shelves was worth looking at, a great deal of it from Java, Bali, Indonesia, Cor could turn a gewgaw into a thing of teasing beauty by the way she placed it. On my arrival she was on a sofa in the sitting room, looking through the bright gap that led to the kitchen: she had observed a blank patch of wall visible from this position, under a shelf, and had decided that an old grater, its three leaves opened out like a triptych, and nailed into place, would perfectly fill the blank.

There were times during my stay when I thought she was looking at me reflectively, and might be working out a better use to which I could be put than simply sitting there unplannedly laughing at Jack's stories.

To those stories there was always an edge of what might generally be called alarm. So we talked of Jack's beard, and of paternal views of beards. My father had regarded my own first beard, hurriedly grown soon after I'd left school, as an act as politically aggressive as if I'd raised the hammer and sickle over the roof of our semi-detached. 'This is not Moscow!' he'd growled. Jack's father, back in Upper Holloway (which Jack said he'd heard described in Sydney as a slum, so that he tended to say he'd come from Lower Highgate), had not been in favour of a beard, either, but had adopted another tactic. 'My mum saw the lady from over the road talking to my dad at the front gate. So she asked what they'd been talking about. And my dad said in a small weak voice that she'd come to ask who the little old man was we'd taken in as a lodger.'

Jack told this story like someone who was half-afraid his father's nudging little joke might have some truth in it: that in growing a beard he might indeed be acknowledging in himself some element of the little old man. 'You wouldn't say I was a little old man, would you, Cor?' Cor laughed hugely, but did not commit herself. Between his dread that he'd be swallowed up by his own comedy, and her fear that she would cease to be able to control her environment, they kept each other in order with the careful refusal to be completely reassuring about anything.

'You clown,' I'd called Jack from time to time at Stonehill

Street. I'd used the word as a schoolteacher does: meaning a child given to disruptive comedy. Now I realised that the word was more technically true than I'd thought. A teacher assumed that clowning was embraced for sheer delight in comic self-advertisement, and pleasure in blowing things apart. To be a clown at school was to be a little terrorist, using laughter in place of gunpowder. But true clowning, I thought, talking to Jack, might well be someone's way of balancing hostile qualities inside himself – or incompatible accounts of the nature of things. Well, I'd clowned during a disastrous first year at the grammar school. Finding that the simple view of life propounded by Barley Road, the image of social and intellectual existence it offered, could not be matched with the haughty complexities proposed by Queen's (all those gowned masters), I'd sought the only refuge I knew: a perilous sort of hilarity. 'This boy's behaviour is that of a silly child,' the headmaster had asserted, on my end-of-year report, 'and must improve.' The comment had the tone, I now think, of something completely inapposite. It was like remarking of Macbeth that his behaviour was that of a reckless murderer – and must change for the better. There would have been the same absence of inquiry into reasons why, coupled to the same meaningless demand for reform.

I remembered how one of Jack's habits had always been that of offering stage directions. So, bringing a piece of writing to my desk he'd murmur: 'If you feel like sneering, sir, please do so. Higgins and I expect it.' It was a self-protective form of comedy, and he was drawing on it now, teaching in difficult conditions in Sydney. When he'd read the part of a boy in a classroom drama in a falsetto voice, Greg Dancy had called out: 'Must have jumped on his horse too hard!' The comic moment, and Jack's relish of it (it was as if Greg Dancy had spoken for him), took some of the sting out of the doubt he had of his ability to teach at all. And the doubt was great, and struck at the heart of his belief in himself. I remembered how the early experience of teaching did this to you – made a question not only of your teaching but of your whole nature.

'Well, I do get sent up badly because I'm a Pom,' said Jack. 'What has most depressed me lately is that the hardest-working girl in my class tried to get moved to another one. That couldn't be arranged, and for a while she became very nasty. So I had a talk with her, and she said I was too soft to do her any good. She needed someone to push her along. I was a nice person, but I was too soft to be a teacher. And I find this demand that I should be a heavy disciplinarian very hard to cope with. I hated that sort of discipline from teachers when I was a kid. It made me uneasy. I think I know what needs to be done for that girl. I have to prove to her that her opinions on a book are as good as mine, so long as she can support them.

'But then I ask myself: how much can I do in two years with six periods a week?'

I could think only that, given his pleasant character, his profound wish to do well, and the experience in which he was now deeply engaged – of measuring his own nature in terms of its capacity to be of service to others, which he was also fervently occupied in measuring – given all this, everything he was doing wrong, he was doing right.

What I loved was walking a few hundred yards from the flat and finding myself above Bondi Beach. Such an extraordinary scene: as if some particularly marvellous stretch of the Pacific had anchored itself alongside Clacton-on-Sea. The ocean had snapped its jaws together and there it was, the great bite of the beach: and, behind it, man had carefully created a remarkable example of urban ugliness. There was nothing at all to be said for the scrum of shops and houses that crowded the mildly rising land in every direction.

Jack and I paused once on a side road leading to the never-failing astonishment of sand and sea and sky. Opposite, a pub: through its dun-coloured windows, the silhouettes of men some of whom, I knew, would be wearing shorts made of torn-off jeans: with, in some cases, tattoos climbing their legs of the sort I'd seen on the limbs of someone pointed out to me as a local bank manager – on one leg, a schooner reeling under the wind: on the other, a woman reeling in her underwear. The topmast in one case, the head in the other, continued under the man's shorts. A fat woman in black passed us, whirling her handbag round and round in what might have been some sort of greeting. Across the street a van drew up: it bore the slogan NIBBLE NOBBY'S NUTS. 'You can see why the ladies of Darling Point were horrified to think you were going to stay here,' said Jack. He'd run into one of them, he said, and she'd referred mysteriously to what was owed to 'a visitor of *that* calibre'. 'You made it up,' I said. 'No – honest!' said Jack. 'Well, it was a word that was always on our tongues at Stonehill Street.' He was clearly as pleased as if the word had fallen into his mischievous lap twenty years earlier. '*Calibre!*' I hadn't heard the last of it.

I thought of the politer suburbs where I might have been lodged, and the kindly propriety of the entertainment I'd have been offered there. I was at home in such places, of course, having decades of acquired politeness behind me: I hadn't actually gone howling through anyone's High Street, under the disapproving eye of any John Logan, for nearly half a century. Indeed, I much liked being polite. And Jack himself, I had to remember, had a record in this respect. A girl had demanded recently: 'Why are you so bloody polite? I *hate* it. I'm not used to it. Why can't you talk to us like other teachers? All this bloody please and thank you. I don't like it.' And when he'd lapsed into shouting at another girl, a quiet and conscientious creature, she'd come to him after the lesson. 'You don't have to say sorry,' she'd said. 'I'd rather be shouted at than spoken to. I wish you'd do it more often.' He said sorry again, about not shouting at her more often, and she'd become very annoyed. Jack had promised to yell at her at some moment in the fairly near future. 'Of course,' he said wistfully. ' I shan't do it.' So he and I were polite enough, even to a degree that gave us trouble: but Bondi was deeply more congenial to us than Darling Point. I thought what was at work in me was the resident of the council house in East Barton that had been our home, 1922–26. Did everyone perhaps experience the best sort of ease in an environment resembling the one in which they'd had their original brief sense of being naturally and securely situated in the world, before they grasped the unlikelihood that, on such a desperate planet, anyone was at home anywhere?

5

I'd been persuaded to fly to Adelaide, according to some vague plan that had filled my friends in Darling Point with alarm. It was, they said, a typical Australian scheme, in which some slave of a lecturer was given his air fare but might find he had to pay for his accommodation himself: as well as giving talks in ruinous sequence to anybody who was at hand – and some, he might find, who were not. 'You *will* tell Roy Evans if he's asking too much . . . but you won't, will you!' 'I daresay I shouldn't.' I knew I wouldn't. I liked Roy Evans, in charge of school libraries, who'd proposed the journey in a manner combining ruthlessness and ruefulness. 'We shall overload you,' he said. 'Ah.' 'I don't know if we shall recompense you.' 'Ah.' 'You'll come?' 'Ah,' I said, liking his dismayed approach to the whole venture. I thought the sub-Shakespearean truth about Macbeth might be that he'd offered Duncan just such an invitation to Glamis. 'The wife has her moods. It might be one of her bad nights.' 'Ah,' Duncan would have said.

And so here I was, stuttering and whining down to Adelaide. 'We're here,' said the man in the next seat. 'We are indeed,' I said, incurably English. 'Eh?' 'Yep,' I said.

Roy took me to the El Gaucho Motel: and then to his home: stressing on the way that Adelaide was different from Sydney. Of this city invented in a single bold stroke by a certain Colonel Light in 1836 (though the El Gaucho was not part of his original conception), a matter of streets meeting at right angles, a bold grid laid on the ground, I had no difficulty in believing it to be unlike that thrilling wedding of sea and land I'd left behind. I felt a ludicrous nostalgia for Sydney, as if I wasn't a stranger there, too. Together with a precise longing to be back home: which turned out to be Jack's and Cor's garden flat.

Roy's home had a curious feature: where anyone else, and especially someone in charge of libraries, might have had shelves of books, he had shelves of wine. His family were sitting in their living room – boys, girls, his wife, mostly on cushions, as if arranged by some stage director. They were deeply friendly, but seemed not to move much, if at all, from these positions. My enormous cough had returned and Roy found, somewhere along his alphabetical shelves of wine, a bottle of cough mixture that had belonged, he said, to his father. With this and a fag end of whisky, he returned me to the El Gaucho, on the way outlining my programme: too full, as he had warned. I re-entered my automated bedroom, which with its anonymous readiness to do anything for anybody filled me with terror, and found that every breath was painful. Was it disease? or, as experience had taught me was more likely, an over-reaction on the part of my physical self to the fact that my unphysical self felt a long way from home, over-burdened, and vastly over-interested. If only people, as one element in this overload, would consent to be dull, obvious, not worth wondering about! I thought of Roy's family sitting in their clearly fixed positions, and of those walls winking with bottles, and wondered. My fever growing, I lay coughing and wincing from the pain in my chest in this barren box on the fringe of a terrible and marvellous continent, and tried not to think of the three talks I had to give next day.

Instead I thought of Jack and Cor, and of a moment the day before when we'd been in a sort of pocket forest on the edge of a beach, and Cor had begun collecting wood. She had plans to add this to the other *objets trouvés* in the flat, claiming to have spotted a blank area on a wall. Jack denied that there was – or after the years Cor had lived there, could be – such a blank. In any case, he said, remember the experience of this latest guest of ours. Nice enough to say he loved the flat, but look what happened when he made some small gesture with his hand. In fact, I said, I'd flung my arm out violently, making some educational point or other: but it was true that even cramped gestures would bring some item of Cor's marvellous bric-à-brac tumbling. Anyway, said Jack, collecting wood from Australian forests, of whatever size, was against the law. 'But it is *dead!*' cried Cor. 'Oh Cor, that's like saying the Venus de Milo is *broken!*' wailed my old pupil.

But now I found myself wondering about Jack and Cor. Damn it, I wasn't bound for sleep, but was drifting feverishly in whatever was the other direction. A condition of hot, hateful wakefulness.

A College of Advanced Education: a random group of teachers: a hastily summoned, and startled, band of librarians. Roy said: 'This is *The Advertiser*. Will you have a word?' *The Advertiser* was an ill-read beard. It spoke of Enid Blyton. This was a name that flew to the otherwise empty lips of most reporters required to interview dying Englishmen introduced as authorities on children's literature. Roy said he was sorry about that. We returned to his home: where everyone was in the position occupied the previous evening. I thought I knew (and liked) Roy well enough to ask him about this, but couldn't frame the question. The Children's Book Circle gave me dinner in a restaurant, amazingly not requiring me to speak. At the tail-end, as I suspected, of a discussion about the problems of my funeral – would I be flown home or become yet another blot on Colonel Light's original geometry? – I was given valium. The El Gaucho processed me again, again without managing to provide me with satisfactory stretches of sleep, and I woke up for what might have been a College of Retarded Education: another random group of teachers: and suddenly, some children, agape. That evening an excellent writer laid on a party at which no one present was connected with the children's book world. She wrote both for children and adults: and her husband, a doctor, said in these situations he usually prescribed a powerful shot of elderliness. I suddenly found being fifty-five enormously curative.

It wasn't that children's literature was anything but a deeply important and serious arm of literature in general. It was rather that moving exclusively within its orbit was likely to make your back ache, after a time: because it did involve some element of bending, of making oneself smaller. There was a great tendency among those in the world of children's books to regard that as the world entire. The best children's writers I knew struggled against this invitation to become permanently crouched. Indeed, if a piece of writing for children is to be of useful stature, its creator must be given to standing, most of the time, fully erect. I thought it was like teaching, and remembered the warning Williams, our old English teacher, gave me when I began work at the Vale prep school: 'Whatever you do, cultivate the adult world: be sure you have a completely grown-up life.'

Roy announced a miracle: the next morning was to be free. His plan was to take me up the Barossa Valley, wine-tasting: but as things were, he said, I'd probably prefer to stay in bed. I found I abhorred the idea of allowing mere acute physical collapse to prevent me from a view of one of the great homes of Australian wine. And next morning I stood at the lip of the valley, looking back over the bright neatness of the city, aware of the sea and looking across at spreads of vine. It's a little Germany, the Valley, and full of churches from Central Europe, with their coloured steeples. The houses have the neatness of doilies, are laced – the lace often being that delicate ironwork found here as in Sydney.

'I would like my friend from London,' Roy would say, 'to taste' – and he'd name the château's best wine. But that, they usually said, should be approached by way of a succession of lesser wines: it wasn't possible otherwise to appreciate that the best was the best. So I sipped wine assiduously, good, better, best, amid a pleasant spinning of coloured steeples.

It was suddenly very late, and we hurtled back to the city. And there in the elegant City Hall I addressed the librarians of Adelaide: but had curiously little recollection of the event. It was one of those achievements that leave behind nothing quite so robust as a memory.

I'd met Roy's father now, and thanked him for the cough medicine he didn't know he'd lent me. He was a retired railwayman, who'd spent much of his life driving across the lower belly of the continent, from Perth to Sydney. He invited me to join him at a bar below the grandiose halls of Adelaide's main station, once a palace for the emperor Steam, and there I found myself in a little group of old men who had no conception of foreignness, or of the possibility that someone might be a stranger. So I was told, in the loudest of undertones (since I might well be deaf), that old Ben (pointed out, since I might well be blind) was, of course, asthmatic, and Jim, of course, had been with the railway since 1920: but I knew that, of course. And, *of course*, I'd have another midi of old?

After I'd discovered how impersonally to settle my impersonal account at the El Gaucho, and as the sun set, Roy drove me to the airport by way of Colonel Light's statue, overlooking the city he'd sketched out so elegantly at the foot of Mount Lofty. I thought of two different ways there'd been of scratching the human presence on this prodigious soil: the curved shapes of animals incised by aborigines in a rock above Bondi Beach, the urban rectangles of Adelaide. I had begun to sense an immense sadness in Australia, of which some of the conclusions of the conference had been signs. Here were children's writers attempting to make unity out of the aboriginal response to the continent and the newcomer's attempt, deliberate and wistful, at a response of his own. Perhaps, I thought unhappily, there'd be a real unity only when so much time had passed that the difference between an aborigine and a newcomer was meaningless.

It wasn't easy to believe we had as much time as that.

6

Back in Sydney, I went to see Stephen Jackson James.

He was the son of a neighbour in Barley Wood, and had been a playmate of my own son Tom. The crucial anecdote about Stephen Jackson (as he was mostly called) was of an occasion when, aged nine or ten, he suggested that Tom accompany him to a football match. Tom may have been under the influence of my semi-comic view, derived from the years I'd spent under the united thumbs of Percy Chew and John Logan, that being a sportsman was halfway to being a fascist. He said he'd go, out of friendship, but made no secret of his distaste. He came back apologetically, incredulously transformed. His passion for train-spotting remained, but *this* was a grand passion. It would last for ever! As (given the obvious problem of being certain about the ultimate stretch of such a prophecy) it had. At his most complex, when every other ordinariness was the object of Tom's revolutionary disdain, he remained the simplest of football fans. There were times when he'd be packing tumbrils with parents in the morning, and encouraging Manchester United in the afternoon.

He'd tried once, a year or so after his conversion, to enlist me as a Saturday companion, giving me for Christmas a wistful ticket to a First Division match on Boxing Day. We arrived early, frozen hours before the start of the game, Tom needing to find himself a place close behind the home team's goal. I didn't know why he had to occupy this position until, just before the whistle, I became aware of a tough-talking exchange between the internationally famous goalkeeper and someone in our neighbourhood: and looking round for this coarse member of the crowd, whose ribald intimacy with the goalie was clearly of long standing, I realised it was my own small, neat, decent son.

I tried very hard to like the experience of being there, but had small hope of doing so. I'd been to football matches when I was a little older than Tom then was: a retired colonial civil servant whose collection of *Magnets* and *Wizards* was irresistible used to take little mobs of us to see Arsenal, Spurs, an international or two. While these great clashes unfolded, he would stroke our bottoms, rather sketchily, very happily. It was years later that I realised his diffident caresses were not accidents, so my not being won to football had nothing to do with this feature of the experience. It was the coldness, on the whole, sometimes the weariness, and the having to stand so long, and the becoming absent-minded so you could not recall why you were there: and the gratitude that you *were* there, because you could boast about it, but the longing for the end to come. I knew that no one who had my feeling of boundless happiness when the final whistle blew could become a football fan.

And it was no better on that Boxing Day. I loved my small fanatic dearly, but knew I could not commit so many Saturdays to such discomfort.

That former child who'd had such an effect on Tom's existence now lived in a suburb of Sydney. When we met again in his front garden, the Harbour Bridge rising out of his shoulder like a wing, I remembered that he was not only called Stephen Jackson: he'd also been known as Young Stephen. That was particularly easy to remember because, 12,000 miles and twenty years from Barley Wood, he remained the young person I'd known: though with a moustache. But the title had not been a reference to his youth, which at the time wouldn't have seemed worth mentioning: it was designed to distinguish him from his father, also Stephen.

One of my earliest memories of Old Stephen followed the publication of my first book. Amid the conventional congratulations, Old Stephen struck a warning note. He hoped I knew that my book would have been accepted and printed only if it were politically harmless. Not having read it, he couldn't be certain *how* they'd have taken the radical guts out of its account of teaching in that down-at-heel corner of London: but that the guts would have been removed, he was certain. It might be wise for me to think over my exchanges with those lickspittles, my publishers, and to become aware of the castrating techniques they employed.

Old Stephen was a Marxist whose inflexibility was great and whose sense of humour was special. If he laughed, it was at the general condition of political innocence by which he was surrounded. He was enormously given to holding forth on the contrast between his understanding of our affairs, and of the way we were manipulated, and the ludicrous failure of such puppets as we were to perceive even the strings by means of which we were made to dance to those measures advantageous to our class enemies. The air was thick with strings, the air *was* strings, and we talked of everything else.

As it happened, while Old Stephen was all conviction, Young Stephen was all doubt. Except that, by one of those ironies that occur as between parents and children, he had something of Old Stephen's obstinacy. He was determinedly doubtful. When it came to refusing to stick his chin out, he stuck his chin out. Ultimately, he went to Australia – perhaps from an over-estimate of what was involved in getting out of earshot of Old Stephen.

I thought, simply remembering him without his moustache and replacing his ironwork-fronted house in Sydney with the old loose boxes in our garden at Barley Wood, of all the children who'd grown up with ours. Two or three breaths and a couple of rainstorms after they'd filled the loose boxes with the intense politics of childhood, they were gone, far and wide, lending their shoulders briefly to the business of keeping the sky in place.

Why was time in such a desperate hurry?

There'd been that occasion when Tom, teacher, had taken Nellie, doctor of medicine, into the loft above one of the boxes, and Dan, in electronics, had run them down. They'd given him sweets and told him to go away: and he'd rushed to James, banker, and to Michael, something to do with adventure playgrounds, and together with Jessie, educational psychologist, having consumed a pound of jellybabies at a speed that was a record even for them, they'd returned to the loft and demanded a further bribe: only to find that Nellie had been replaced by Cynthia, radiologist shading into housewife.

7

The more I went to look down on Bondi Beach – the more I walked on it – the simpler seemed to become the way I saw it. It was hugely the colour of sand: and blue and white: and rust, the long sweep of pavilion: and the silver of gulls, together with the bright red of their legs and bills. I loved the heart of Sydney, Circular Quay – 'Circular Square', as in my fatigue I named it to a bus conductor who thought it was what one would expect from an Englishman – and the Rocks where settlement had begun: even that first deep, dark road cut through the cruel stone, every inch of it seeming darker for the fate of the men who'd made it and who were not simply 12,000 miles from home but a year: and not simply a year, but forever. But I loved immoderately this pleasure-beach, and the walks by the sea on which Jack took me: once in the warmest darkness, when we paced an elaborately-lighted ship steaming away into the last varnished square inches in the bottom right-hand corner of the map that Miss Baker had unrolled for us at Barley Road, nearly half a century before.

Mr Salt, the lecturer who'd made teacher training memorable for me, used to say that every teacher of quality had had one unforgettable class 'where all was happiness and purpose'. The class of which Jack had been a member was such a class for me. Amid the general dismay of Stonehill Street, in the 1950s, these bright and witty boys had gathered. There'd been Higgins, who'd perhaps been the cause for their gathering, as the first class the school had ever known of boys volunteering to stay beyond the statutory leaving age. Higgins was a sort of clever innocent, who shouldn't have been with us at all – in the educational language of the time, he ought to have been selected for the grammar school. There'd been some simple, obvious error in the process: and a generally able boy found himself in a school which, for all the guilty theory, was designed for the generally unable. He was a boy, I thought now, not unlike Cor, who was enormously given to astonishment. In a school where language was strong, he made a strength out of a particularly weak adjective, then already out-of-date: he'd say an idea (often of the headmaster's) was '*blooming* silly'. 'Sir,' Jack would come to my desk to say, 'Higgins thinks your giving us this work to do is *blooming* silly. You will forgive the language. You know how foul-mouthed our friend is.' Our foul-mouthed friend would join Jack at my desk. 'What's he *blooming* well saying now, sir?' Brian Jones would look up frowning from the body of the class. He'd be reading Dostoevsky, shielding the book elaborately as if it were a comic. 'Sir, you're not letting things build up to a riot again?' he'd murmur with an affected frown. Any splutter from mild Higgins was defined as a riot. Jimmy Smith would laugh unnervingly, pretending not to be halfway through some rather difficult précis of his own choice. They were all more than a little under the influence of the Goons. The style of Milligan, Sellers and Secombe was brought to bear on a large amount of serious reading, and some ambitious writing. It was like finding, sewn into the middle of a copy of *Beano*, some of the better pages from the *New Statesman* of the day. Looking back, I thought it was perhaps the only way bright boys could blossom in the downbeat and desperate setting of Stonehill Street. When I talked of them at the time, as an illustration of the argument against severely selected secondary education, I knew I was suspected by some of inventing the group for polemical purposes. And here in Bondi, a quarter of a century later, I found myself the guest of one of my inventions, and delighted in his reality.

 That little group had gone their astonishingly various ways. The sharp-tongued one, Jones, had become a successful stage designer. 'He speaks cut glass and is sarcastic and vicious,' Jack had written to me soon after leaving school. 'Even his friends flinch from him.' Smith had become an architect with a busy practice. He, said Jack, switched off his mind if what you were saying was of no interest. 'I find this rather rude, but when I tell him so he never answers because his mind is switched off.' After Jack and Higgins had planned to ride to Naples on Jack's motorbike, Higgins had vanished, and had not been heard of again. 'He has perhaps gone to sow his wild oats,' Jack had written dolefully. 'People say that if you want to write you should do this. But it is not so easy when you have been brought up, as I have, to go after security.' A little later he had come down firmly on the side of instructive insecurity, and sailed for Australia. Landing breathless in Sydney he wrote: 'I had the same feeling about the trip as I had once when I climbed to the top board of the swimming bath, and when I looked down I was scared, but I could not retreat and retain any self-respect and so I made a poor dive, hurting myself. (I think that is the longest sentence I have ever written).'

We drove round Sydney in the darkness, which suited it so well – the Opera House a set of glowing gold shells, the bridge a blue hugeness with Luna Park absurd and bright under one end of it – and Jack looked for yet more ways of eating. We ate Brazilian, Egyptian, Vietnamese. We talked of my old colleague Mr Bedrock, who'd taught woodwork, and had brought to life in London a distraught puritanism with its roots in the Midlands. Caught between an imposed hatred of the senses, and a natural love of them, he'd been famous for his outrageous attempts to use teaching as a bridge between his incompatible selves. Jack said that more than one lesson in the woodwork centre had been devoted to the etiquette of the lavatory. There'd been a lecture on giving oneself a cleansing shake, and another that involved specific suggestions as to sheets of toilet paper. 'It was difficult,' said Jack. 'It was close to our sort of joke, but at the same time it missed it by a mile. Some of the dirtiest-minded boys in the class became very uptight about it. I think he may have undone a lot of perfectly good potty-training. Poor Mr Bedrock!'

And I thought sadly of that remarkable, unhappy colleague of mine, who ten years earlier had died (as I guessed) from the impossibility of enduring such contradictoriness within himself.

One evening Jack came back from a long afternoon with a boy to whom he'd taught English the previous year. 'He's a silly boy,' said Jack, dropping into one of Cor's beautiful cane chairs. In the evening sun the smoky sheers at the windows collected and created wonderful shadows. The sliding doors were open to the garden, and a small breeze shivered some of Cor's hanging bells. This rustling of leaves, I told myself, this faint tinkling, this blue sky, this late warmth, were all on the other side of the world. Cor said it was amazing that Jack had to teach silly boys. 'Well, I don't teach him now,' said Jack. 'But he latches on to me at tennis. And does he talk! It's all done so that I talk back at him. After two hours of it, my head aches. All this small chat about dogs, bikes, poofters, the dirty deeds of teachers, my limited abilities as a teacher of English. I said to him: "We *didn't* spend a whole term on metaphors!" "Bloody did!" he said. Well, of course, like most of them, he sees English as an authoritarian language. So you rebel against it. You mess it about. And in the process, of course, I get messed about, too.'

'It's amazing,' Cor cried. 'Jack, isn't it amazing!' She was startled by most things. 'It *is* amazing, Cor,' Jack would say sometimes, and then set out to discover what, at this moment, was the cause of amazement. I loved this refusal of Cor's ever to settle down complacently with any aspect of daily life whatever: and thought her cries were, anyway, generally suitable for the ears of someone in Australia for the first time. Inside me, during these weeks, someone had been exclaiming in much the same fashion. What I couldn't get over was the ease with which, having been here so briefly, I was plotting my way down town from Bondi, navigating through town in terms of fine decisions about going, or not going, through the park, through the mall, up that street or down the other. Life involved you so often in being prosaic in settings that murmured accusingly of the wild poetry you'd once known them to possess.

Australia, even if only a much-trampled corner of it, tamed in three weeks! Dreadful!

Though tame was not what Jack thought it to be. 'I am in daily touch with the wilder forms of life here.' He was marking essays in which his careful teaching was transformed into the extravagantly careless assertions of his pupils. 'India,' wrote one, 'is full of British writers, including Rudolph Kipling.' ('Amazing!' said Cor, looking over our shoulders). 'Am I responsible for that?' asked Jack. 'I think it must be said you are. But the misunderstandings are useful pointers, aren't they, to what you might do next?'

Jack groaned. Then he made a box yield wine. 'Have you ever seen wine in a box before? I don't suppose those ladies from Darling Point would ever serve you wine out of cardboard.' Well, said Cor, it was perhaps what they shouldn't do while I was there. 'To a man of sir's *calibre*, you mean,' said the exhausted Jack.

On my last day Jack and Cor took me across the Saturday afternoon harbour, scattered with the wings of little boats, to the Zoo. On the way to Circular Quay Jack pointed out a fruitologist, to be added to my collection of verbal inventions by Sydney shopkeepers: it seemed better than the previous best, a garage announcing itself as a lubricatorium. And from the Zoo on its small hill we looked back over the water, a sheet of dancing light: foreground, giraffes: far distance, the Opera House, the Bridge, the city's bright towers.

And on the way out, at the top of a sloping path, Jack caught sight of one of the metal prams that could be hired to take small children round the zoo. And, suddenly, Upper Holloway took over: he leaped upon it with a cry I'd not heard since I'd last stood in the Stonehill Street playground, and went hurtling to the bottom of the slope.

'It's amazing,' said Cor. 'Not, my dear,' I said, 'to me. But there was a time when it didn't just amaze me: it caused me terror.'

'You were terrified by Jack!' Cor exclaimed: clearly salting the information away for later domestic use among the hinged shadow puppets from Java, the fertility symbols and the Dutch plates with their puritanical captions.

8

On the homeward Jumbo I read a book Jack had given me: an account of Australian history post-1788 called *The Tyranny of Distance*. To my right a baby in his fourth or fifth month was in the process of covering the cruel distance in question in a day.

We moved with heavy smoothness towards London, my cough improving with every mile, and I heard Jack and Cor talking in my head. Cor had been telling him of a conversation she'd had with a friend, a doctor. 'She wants us to have babies and that,' said Cor. 'You have to have *that* and then babies, Cor,' Jack had said.

And in a toilet, trying to make myself look human for Kate, I thought of an unofficial game we used to play at Barley Road. In that game of Higher and Higher, I was now pissing Highest: spectacularly out-pissing Fred Wicks, Jack Withers, Bernard Slow, Jimmy Soper. I wished I was able to inform Jimmy of this fact, but thought he might have frowned rather than smiled.

PART THREE

1

'If it follows the usual pattern, you, Edward, will die first, and then you, Kate . . .'

Our friend and solicitor, Norman Lock, beamed at us. A man who believed that human existence was a gross and sprawling illegality on someone's part, his approval was more or less reserved for tidying-up operations: and making a will was a very great tidiness indeed. We had discovered that our existing will, in which fifteen years earlier Norman had swept us and our affairs into a neat heap ready for the grave, made provisions now quite inappropriate: neither of our sons would be pleased by the appointment of guardians, and with inflation some small dignified bequests had become tiny ludicrous bequests. 'I approve, of course, of updating,' Norman had said. 'But with a bit of luck this new one should last you out.' It didn't seem as exact a statement as we expected from him: but there was no doubt about his satisfaction. He had nothing about him remotely ghoulish: but for an early-evening chore in the office, you felt, give him a reasonably straightforward will. And if he had a pleasant personal relationship with the makers of this melancholy document, all the better.

As we made our way through our fifties, the mere arithmetic became less and less easy to shrug off. Recently in a Bush House lift a producer had said: 'Well, I don't think you look your age. I'd have said you were . . . no more than 53.' It was like being lured into a shop by the offer of sensational reductions and finding the discount they had in mind was 1%. The producer himself had the careless sheen of the mid-thirties: the pigment hadn't begun to drain out of his hair, the skin fitted over his jawbone like a well-chosen kid glove. There was no obvious way of testing the elasticity of his knees, but I was certain they responded so obediently that he barely knew he had them. I had knees that had become averse to the theatre or the concert hall. As my mind became more engaged by drama or music, so my knees became more disengaged from the whole occasion. They cried out for me to stand up, walk up and down: at worst, they begged me to bend them as they could not be bent, in the opposite direction to the way they were hinged. And there were days when my back was rusty beyond belief, and would have nothing to do with the attempt to put my socks on.

I was also putting into reverse the phrase about every fat man containing a thin man trying to get out. I'd been the very spirit of thinness for fifty years, and now this bulky stranger was forcing himself into my flesh. At times I felt my thin self and this new enlarged self standing with obstinate unfriendliness side by side, crammed into the same skin. At the same time, especially in summer, when the physical world itself was wholly fresh and young, you caught yourself supposing you might be alone in resisting all tendencies to ageing. You were sad for your contemporaries, who were wearing so badly: but in the sunshine *you* were immortally supple.

Until you did a weekend's gardening: which I did soon after my return from Australia.

I had this calamitous pain in my chest. It would not go. Every breath hurt. I thought this was the cruel finale of that music there'd been in my lungs even as I walked happily across Bondi Beach. I went to see our doctor, a friend as well as this informed spectator of our decay. Had I, she asked, done anything unusual lately, of a physical kind. I had gardened at the weekend, vigorously, I said. Well, that was it.

I'd torn a muscle in my chest.

Thank God, I cried. Now I could abandon the scenarios I'd been composing in my head on my way to the surgery. And what were those? Well, among other things I'd been saying to my friends: Look after Kate.

She laughed hugely. Good Lord. Kate, she was certain, would deplore my passing. But she would make an admirable widow. An independent-minded woman with an unshakeable interest in people and events. And I realised, with relief and only a small twinge of disappointment, that this was true. Kate would make a most sensible survivor.

Kate frowned when I told her. The image didn't please her. Who could tell, she asked. She might be more fragile than she seemed. In any case, why take it for granted that I would go first? There was such a thing as the occasional widower.

We'd catch ourselves at such absurd discussions, and laugh and sigh at once. The sad wrinkles of things were the absurd wrinkles of things, too. We confessed to being preoccupied sometimes in the middle of the night with the massive arithmetic of ageing. Since going to the grammar school, 47 years: since leaving it, 39. Thirty-seven years since being jilted by Jean Hopkins. Thirty years since teaching at The Vale. Since I stopped being a teacher, 17 years. When my father was my present age, I was 29. And so, gloomily, on.

I thought often of my father, who'd detested all neighbours, and had recently been overthrown by the ultimate neighbour, Death. He looked out at me from my eyes in the morning mirror. I saw him reflected in shop windows as I passed. My hands sought and clasped each other across my chest, in an unwilled copy of one of his most familiar poses. He inhabited my laughter. Kate said when I was angry she was afraid, not of me, but of my father's face possessing mine. Anger had been his essential mood.

In Kate's own face, her grandmother (who'd lived to be 101) and her mother came and went. She tried to keep her mother at bay; but Dorothy was like my father, an irresistible invader. Kate was alarmed, being essentially different from her mother as I had been from my father. What did it mean that Dorothy's negative eyes looked out through her positive ones? Dorothy had been profoundly negative, with a great dread of almost every form of action. Kate had once been about to go to Canada, to visit my cousins Bobbie and Jane, and her mother made a desperate speech: 'But Kate, you don't want to go all that way! You don't want to go alone! You don't want to fly!' Kate, who was eager to do all these things, said it had always been like that: 'You don't want to go to a party! You don't want to wear pretty shoes! You don't want to go out with *him!*' When I'd called to take Kate out, thirty years earlier, I was always instructed as to the need for a virtually instant return. It never sounded as if it was worth going out at all. At moments when we didn't care if we never slept again, Dorothy was urgent in the matter of sleep, from an early hour, being the major human delight. She'd clearly have been happy if, at the very door, I'd changed my mind. 'Don't let's go! You don't want to go! I don't want to take you!' 'I think you're being very sensible,' Dorothy would have said. Throughout these opening passages of my relationship with Kate, our failure to obey such beseechments had caused her to eye me sorrowfully. It should be possible to lay me under an injunction: the association might continue if I did not take Kate out, ring her up, or cause her to have notions of varying her condition in one respect or another.

Our crumpling skins were being infiltrated by bulkier selves, parents, a grandparent or two . . .

And now I couldn't read without glasses. To the fact that my skull, if I went in for the sort of self-disposal that resulted in skulls, would exhibit a disfiguring lack of teeth, must be added the thought that, cast up on a desert island with the British Library but without spectacles, I should be unable to read a line.

A writer who'd started one of his novels with a painfully accurate account of ageing, Christopher Isherwood, came to be interviewed. Good Lord, he said. My eyebrows soared as remarkably as his slumped. He'd broken his glasses. I wanted him to read a passage from his new book. He borrowed my glasses, but they were no good. My producer's were more helpful. As we waited for the green light, it struck me that one of his problems might be that the passage I'd asked him to read required him to turn a page. 'Would you like me to turn over for you?' I whispered urgently. His eyebrows slumped further, he grinned his charming dog's grin. 'Oh come!' he said.

'In memory of a good laugh', he signed my copy of his book. It was not the earnest inscription I'd have expected when I first read *Lions and Shadows*. That was forty years ago, when my father was thirteen years younger than I was now.

And so on.

2

A time of jubilation and dismay. That is, in terms of the private life. Public affairs continued to have the aspect of history as nightmare. The talk at nuclear inquiries was of possibilities of meltdown. It sometimes seemed that human affairs had reached this condition: we were on the edge of an ultimate calamity caused by the fusion of those great qualities of ours, so dreadful when brought together, our enormous cleverness and our enormous stupidity.

But meanwhile being in one's fifties provided this experience of seeming alternately on the edge of collapse, and about to enter upon some kind of immensely improved youth. And, mixed in with the sensations of being young in some way that was distinctly an advance on one's original careworn and unconfident immaturity, was the pleasure of contemplating the early adulthood of one's own children.

Dan, our younger son, was about to make us grandparents, and was reporting familiar anxieties, amusingly but sometimes alarmingly exploited by his dreams. Well, said Dan, in the latest of these his child, a stern creature, had grumbled about the name he'd been given. What a name to give anyone! Had his father-not-yet-his-father considered what it would be like to go through life burdened with such a name?

What *was* the name? we asked.

Dan said he didn't know. The dream had not revealed it. He was simply left with a general alarm about names. Later in the dream he'd been trying to dislodge his child from under the bed, where it had taken refuge. What was *that* about?

It was, we thought, about the essential shock of imminent parenthood. There was, after all, amid much else, a strong reminder of *Frankenstein* in the business of having created a new human being. The ingredients that had gone into the making of Dan's child were joy and desire, but at no time could a potential parent close his or her mind altogether to thoughts of the thunder and electrical crackle that had presided over the birth of Frankenstein's unhappy artefact. Such an easy power, that which produces children: and at the bottom of our souls, in the region from which dreams draw their curiously-cobbled scripts, there must be alarm at the prodigious consequences of such a rapid act.

Perhaps, I thought, this uncertainty as to the outcome of making love was partly what lay behind the old phrase: *Post coitum triste*. After we have coupled, we are sad.

I'd first met the phrase in one of the books John Logan had lent me, under Percy Chew's potentially indignant nose. That was Aldous Huxley's *Eyeless in Gaza*. At the time I regarded what I read, especially from the imprints of such publishers as Faber & Faber, Jonathan Cape and Chatto & Windus, as a series of instructions as to the correct conduct of things; and so assumed that, once the ecstasy was out of the way, one was obliged to feel this dejection. It happened to be a wretchedly long time before I subjected the theory to practical test – my adolescence being prolonged and largely compounded of notions derived in this fashion from literature. I'd thought recently, drawn back by the encounter with John Logan to my memories of the 1930s, of the ludicrously academic approach I'd brought, for example, to my encounters with my music teacher, Mrs Needle.

She was unhappily married, but it was the unhappiness of exasperation rather than tragedy. She'd made a simple, though large, mistake. Mr Needle disliked music. He didn't merely shrink from it, he despised it. I sometimes tried to imagine the courtship in which it had not emerged – or, having emerged, had seemed unimportant – that Mr Needle held music to be unnecessary, and the cause of foolish conduct on the part of those who admired and professed it. He thought the giving of concerts a particular absurdity. Affected people organised and attended and took part in them, to the neglect of their families. It seemed to be his general conviction, as reported by his scornful wife, that music flourished at the expense of people's domestic comfort.

All of this Mrs Needle told me while feigning to steer me through the opening bars of the Moonlight Sonata.

I think Mr Needle simply did not like Mrs Needle going out. In defiance of him ('He mustn't think he can have his way in everything') she took me to concerts, and I wonder all these years later at the sense of conspiracy that accompanied this simple cultural activity. I met her at some distance from her home, and she would drive me into London by what felt like a circuitous route. She can't have been shaking off pursuers, and yet her manner suggested that she was doing so. And there we'd be, listening to Moiseiwitsch or Pouishnoff – it was always a piano concerto that we homed in on – : and I'd never have been surprised to see Mr Needle enter the hall with his legal advisers and bring the performance to a sudden halt. Moiseiwitsch – or Pouishnoff – would, to begin with, be deeply vexed by this interruption: but would calm down when it was explained that a married woman was present in the audience without the permission of her husband, and in the company of an inwardly immoral schoolboy.

Though I have to say that, had he burst into the Queen's Hall, my only way of recognising Mr Needle would have been in terms of his conduct as the deceived husband. I never, as it happened, met him. His being always a fuming background figure intensified the feeling of awe he caused in me. The word for going with a married woman to concerts of classical music without her husband's permission, I believed, was cuckolding: and what I felt was that I was cuckolding Anon. Poor Mr Needle was a sort of Unknown Husband.

But, when it came to what I took to be adultery, I was not the first in Mrs Needle's book. That position was held by a shattered soldier of the First World War. I can't recall how Mrs Needle came to know him. But he was undergoing endless treatment at a famous hospital for those who'd lost limbs, and there she would visit him. I think now of the picture she drew of this sad hulk, and of the hopeless love between them: and of how her talk of him wove in and out of the discussion of the best way to play those opening bars of Beethoven's 14th piano sonata: and I wonder at the flat, banal touch it is possible to bring to fantasy. It can't have been much else – Mrs Needle's dream of escaping from the cruelly prosaic Mr Needle by way of an elopement with a ruined hero in a bathchair. I suppose, now, that his being handicapped was a condition of his being the proper material for Mrs Needle's fancies. I suspect she was bound deeply to Mr Needle – if by nothing else, then by her wish to be safely lodged in life. Hanging on to Mr Needle with secret tenacity, she pretended to fight free of him by way of a cripple and a shy schoolboy.

She proposed once that she drive me for the day to Oxford. To me, Oxford wasn't a place, it was life's ideal objective: if I could get there, academically, it would mean that I'd ceased to be the crazy presumptuous child my father held me to be, and had become, to a degree that might have made separation of identities difficult, Shelley or Matthew Arnold. I agreed to Mrs Needle's proposal with trembling enthusiasm. My parents offered no objection. I look back and wonder, not at my mother, who would not have believed that a music teacher could be untrustworthy, but at my father, who certainly must have sensed the frustrations that Mrs Needle was so anxious to be rid of. My father, I now know, was a specialist when it came to frustrated women. Perhaps he thought the experience, as he must have suspected it would turn out, would be exactly the shock this young prig needed to bring him to his senses.

I remember the drive to Oxford, in those 1930s that in recollection seem so naively airy. To make in imagination the return to that day means stripping away the world of motorways and removing most of today's traffic, slowing what's left to a dawdle. We bowled along: we breathed deeply: we were encased in a relative tortoise – Mrs Needle's Standard saloon, with the mileometer which she turned back, so she told me, after each of our illicit journeys. I walked with her round Oxford, until then unknown to me except from the pages of literature, as if I were a saint making a modest exploratory visit to Heaven. For some reason, my sharpest memory is of being in the kitchens at Christ Church. The suggestion of difference between what was served up by my mother in the ten foot by ten foot living room at Manor Road, Barton, and what was likely to be served up from these acres of butchers' tables, amounted to a promise of the entire change in my life that would occur when I came here as an undergraduate. From the dimensions of a semi-detached in Barton I would arrive at the dimensions of Wolsey's fatal folly: and unrecognisability would become my general character.

Mrs Needle, I remember, was much drawn to the notion of Wolsey as the doomed man. And I can see that, given some historical rearrangement, he might have represented as ideal a replacement for Mr Needle (whom Mrs Needle meant never to replace) as the limbless soldier or me. She would have met Wolsey on his last, fatal journey to London, and, confident that the block awaited him, would have discussed with him all sorts of future felicities of a kind particularly appropriate to a partnership between a disgraced Cardinal and an accredited teacher of the piano.

And, on the way home, she drew into a field, and proposed that we sit in the back of the car.

Poor lady! I must have appeared sexually useable, but wasn't. Not, that is, without boldnesses on her part that she'd never have embarked on. Perhaps the simple sensation of naughtiness was enough for her. If she'd ventured on a single straightforward audacity, my quaint honour would have gone up in something jollier than smoke. As it was, of all the ludicrous tableaux with which my adolescence is littered, this seems to me one of the most absurd. I must have sat with Mrs Needle in the back of her car in a field in the neighbourhood of Princes Risborough on that day in 1938 as if lined up opposite had been her parents (both still alive), my parents, and Mr Needle. She told a risqué story or two, and I laughed with academic appreciation. She referred to women's legs, I remember, saying she thought they were of interest to me: sitting inches away from hers, I said yes, of course they were, and chuckled formally.

And then I went home and wrote disparagingly of the way she was dressed, her figure and her wistful intentions. 'Her coat smelt of camphor, mingled with the tang of dried rain,' I alleged, according to my custom turning the day into an instant extract from a novel. 'The breasts straggled left and right under the jumper, and the thigh-bones made a ridge under the skirt horribly suggestive of dried flesh. The stockings were a high pink. She belonged prematurely to the dowagers, to the huge-bosomed, to the stiff right and left motion of ageing legs. She carried with her the disgrace of her imminent doom. Under her arm's grotesque caricature of embrace he smouldered angrily.'

'Ungallant' is hardly the word for it. Poor Mrs Needle took me out for the day, and chose Oxford knowing how the idea of Oxford fascinated me, and did this glowering schoolboy the honour of sketchily embracing him in a field in Buckinghamshire – and he went home and wrote about her in a particularly beastly fashion: which happened to be much influenced by his reading of the ill-natured novels of Wyndham Lewis. He held against her the facts that during the day she had been rained upon (but so had he), that her stockings were pink, and that her breasts were so arranged that one was to the left and the other to the right. His suggestion that they straggled is the sort of statement that brings guesswork into disrepute. He also seems to have found her guilty of being disgustingly old. She was, I think, about thirty.

But, of course, he wanted to be loved by Ellen Terry, Katherine Mansfield, Shakespeare's Beatrice, an early film star called Laura La Plante – Juliet. *Romeo and Mrs Needle* wasn't an imaginable title.

Oh, the sadness of reflecting that one might have read all the advanced writers of one's time and be so retarded! It was to be some years before I discovered that, left to me (and given my inadequacies as a Latinist), the phrase would have read: '*Post coitum* hurrah!'

3

Our other son, Tom, was now a teacher at the beginning, like Jack Seed: and, when he was under the stunning impact of a first term, I realised that I'd stayed on in similar circumstances only because I had a family to support. Tom was more stubborn: and was much moved by the plight of the awkward children he taught. The increase in so-called permissiveness, he said, had given them the language, but denied them the experience, of greater freedom. 'I've done so much covering of classes for absentee colleagues that I feel like a duvet,' he said. After a visit to Barley Wood he wrote apologising for any adolescent grumpiness he'd displayed: it would partly have been the strain of teaching, but perhaps the vapours of adolescence hung about his old room. I had to reply that if ever I achieved a few continuous days of adulthood I felt uneasily heroic.

And how edgy still, within whatever context of love, the relationship could be between ageing parents and children attempting to root themselves in life! The enormous anxiety of those years in which one is constantly auditioning for this role or that: when one's still in the midst of the vital chances and mischances: and so much has yet to be decided. Tom, on a visit, was at work once in the kitchen when Kate came in. 'What do *you* want!' Tom snapped: and they then danced round the room, howling with laughter. It was thereafter a phrase that, used by either of them, could act as a release. The fact being that, when twenty-six is elbow to elbow with fifty-six, all the affection in the world won't at times prevent this from being a deeply undesirable adjacency of young chalk and old cheese.

After the death of my old English teacher, Williams, I'd written to his widow, Em. Now I heard from his elder brother: Em had sent him a copy of my letter, he said, and he'd be glad if we could meet for lunch. So I joined him one day in the bar of a London hotel.

Hubert Williams was Willy made large and brisk – a successful business man in some fashion I wasn't clear about. John Logan had suggested it was a matter of fixing things up on a rather large scale, and making things rather immensely possible. His presence hinted at a great effectiveness, which certainly hadn't been one of his brother's qualities: but under it I sensed a more familiar sort of Williams, a man given to words (he was engaging already in random eloquence in my old teacher's fashion), someone who'd grown up in a world of literature and music: this element in him seeming oddly guilty, as if in the last resort he was ashamed of having chosen one family gift, of worldly competence, rather than the other, of disinterested ineptitude. I imagined this guilt was uppermost because Willy was the reason for our meeting.

The hotel provided a heavily draped setting for our encounter. Being in the bar was oddly like being in a coffin – such terminal comforts of curtain and carpet, and such a brassiness along and above the bar itself.

'You know,' said Hubert Williams, introducing me to a man sitting alongside him, 'Sir Richard Pickle?' I didn't know Sir Richard Pickle: and perhaps the alternative Williams inside him was struck by the thought that I was outside the convention of supposing that everyone here knew everyone else. 'He's a judge,' he said: and then, 'That's right – you're a judge, aren't you, Richard!' Sir Richard considered the question, and nodded. 'And our friend,' said Hubert, 'is an author. An author both prolific and distinguished.' Oh Lord yes, it *was* his brother's style of improvisatory eloquence, in which there was a tension between a wish to be exact and a wish not to be exact at all. This assertion, too, Sir Richard considered, and drank deep. I thought he had the air of a man who would need something other than merely being addressed by an acquaintance to force him into speech.

'Oh never, never!' cried Hubert now. Two men had appeared, I thought they were Arab, and were approaching him in a manner that suggested words were unnecessary: their very appearance amounted to the asking of some urgent question with which Williams was, perhaps, over-familiar. 'Gentlemen!' he cried. 'Another time? Truly inconvenient. Lunching a friend, you see.' They frowned. 'Forgive me,' he murmured. 'Tactless fellows. A moment only.' He withdrew a pace or two with them: there was agitation on their part: I heard mention of cement, and Williams said: 'Within a week. No difficulty in laying hands on such a quantity. Depend on me.' I thought there was nothing in the least shady about this. In such a setting, I was the most naive of spectators, in whose eyes any transaction easily appeared sinister: and, given Hubert's obvious wish that the lunch should be devoted to consideration of his brother's way of life, this evidence of his own very different daily pattern was probably not welcome. Thus, perhaps, the effect as of a world in which everything was done *sotto voce*, and in the darkest part of the room. 'Let's go in,' he said now. 'Take your drink with you. But let's recharge it first. George –' to the barman – 'another large whisky for my guest.' It was, I thought, my third: a style of providing drinks operated here that made normal prudent accountancy difficult. My head already felt unlike the rest of my body, constructed of another and much lighter material.

'Dear David,' said Hubert, once we were seated. 'I saw less of him, far far less than I should. It's partly why I was so moved by your account of him in your letter to Em. He was a first-class man, David. Family tradition, teaching, as you know. Began that way myself.'

And I remembered a story Willy had delighted in telling in class: of his brother's post at a Scottish prep school, and how he'd been asked if he'd take some music: and was on his way to the music room, his cello on his back, when he'd heard the skirling of bagpipes, and crept back to where he'd come from.

Williams's father, in later life a distinguished musician, had begun as a teacher of mathematics. There'd been this connection in the family between the power to make music and the power to calculate, and I wondered again if Hubert's present choice of profession resulted from the dominance of the second over the first. But why think in such a fashion at all? Oh, it was because in what Hubert was saying about his brother there was such an element of guilty panegyric. In writing to Em I'd mentioned the letters Willy had written to me when he was a holidaying teacher at home in Swansea and I was a lonely schoolboy with a longing to be a writer. 'You've brought them with you?' asked Hubert. I had done so, as he'd asked: and he read them with great attention, exclaiming as he did so, chuckling over one of his brother's characteristic phrases: sometimes sighing – as I guessed, when he came across some confident assertion about the literary future that, as it turned out, Willy was not to have.

We ate grouse, which I'd not had before: and we drank a powerful claret: and Hubert got me to talk simply of Williams as a teacher: and here was an enormous and splendid cigar. I spoke of a time when we knew, the whole class knew, that Williams was in love: he'd been observed, as we made our way through the School Certificate pages of *Julius Caesar*, to pick his teeth thoughtfully with a lady's hairpin. Later when I'd told Williams of this he'd said it must have been Em's. His previous love, hopelessly ill-chosen – she had no more appetite for literature than Mr Needle had for music – never used such a thing as a hairpin. He sighed a little as he told me this: he loved Em for needing hairpins, but had loved the other girl for not needing them, for having showering golden hair whose only comb or brooch – as he'd said in a poem he thought not wholly successful – was provided by her long white fingers. Em was all the other had not been, shy, a scholar, bespectacled, her tidy crop of brown hair needing to be made tidier still by hairpins. Willy had told me once how, on the coast near Swansea, he and the scholarly Em, neither at that moment particularly intent on scholarship, had suddenly realised they were in danger of being cut off by the tide: and had saved themselves only by climbing to safety to the top of a slide of rock – where they'd spent . . . I remembered how Williams had sighed and smiled and said no more. Except that a little later he'd invited me to agree that Shakespeare – consider the scene between Brutus and Portia – certainly knew how to write about love: to which proposition, having not yet reached even the erotic low point of the later stages of his association with Mrs Needle, Williams's experienced pupil assented.

And I thought, as I talked of this to Hubert, that Williams was then not much older than our son Tom was now, and must have been in the grip of the same anxieties as to the way life would settle down for him: and that he must often, as we poured into his room ready to disturb his thoughts of the girl with the white fingers, or of Em and her falling hairpins, have wished to cry: 'And what do *you* want!'

And then lunch was over, Hubert had to go off and transfer immense quantities of cement from one repository to another distant one: and we rose and left the hotel and crossed its courtyard, he saying he was grateful for this glimpse of his brother as a teacher ('Saw far far too little of him, one always knows these things too late, too late'), I aware of feeling as I'd not before felt at any time, the material out of which I was constructed now totally transformed. When I arrived, I remotely asked myself, had I been spinning in this fashion – had I been so extraordinarily like a child's top, to the very noise of one, the metallic whirr and then the sound of slowing down which meant that – ?

Which meant the top fell over, which I now did. 'Good Lord,' Hubert Williams was saying, somewhere over at the other end of London, 'yes, please, do give me a hand, excellent fellow, seemed perfectly well till a moment ago, *very* nice man, sudden collapse!' I was in a lift, I was being held upright by my old dead teacher's old living brother: he was saying, again from some position of the most curiously distant proximity: 'Have booked a room. Lie down. Take it very easy. Don't pay for anything. Sleep. Will ring your wife. My dear chap!'

And several years later, when I was spinning only moderately and was almost able to see what was in front of me, I was collected by Kate: who, in her generous way, was ready to lay the blame squarely on the shoulders of Australia.

And then Em died. That was when I caught Percy Chew's glare across the church. She'd lived very briefly after the death of her dear miser. I was glad he wasn't there to see Em and her hairpins go off to be burned in her varnished box.

John Logan wrote a broken-hearted letter. It wasn't just that he loved Em, though he clearly did: it was that the landscape of his life was being levelled, detail by detail. He wrote again to say there was a sort of guest night every term at Savernake: would I come to the next?

I did: though it meant hiring a dress suit. I said I'd be glad among other things to clap eyes again on a book he'd memorably lent me c 1935: it was called *Hammersmith Hoy*, it was by Giles Playfair, and it was about his father Nigel's marvellous seasons at the Lyric, Hammersmith in the 1920s. I don't know why it had such an effect on me – and, in fact, I barely remembered a precise word of it: I think it was that several first experiences came together – of acting myself, of being lent a book by a teacher, of understanding that the world of theatrical London existed and was near at hand. When I arrived in John Logan's rooms at Savernake, *Hammersmith Hoy* lay on a table, waiting, in the middle of a stockade of books such as I remembered from his digs in Barton, forty years earlier. I exclaimed over it, admired it: and was then told it was not the copy I'd once borrowed. All Logan's books had been lost in an air raid: and all but half a dozen or so had, over the years, been painstakingly replaced.

Of course, I thought throughout that evening, here I was again with the dandified John Logan by whom I'd once been beaten for writing a bad poem. I could only pretend to be at ease among the dress-suited: in reality I expected my uncomfortable collar to turn completely into the noose it so nearly was. Through the ritual of toastings and teasings I was smiling like an insider: but in truth I was unconvinced, uncharitable in my observations – an outsider. Generations of Blishens from the back streets of West London peered through the windows of the dining hall, fingers to their noses. And, as if he had caught sight of them, here was John Logan saying: 'Oh dear! It sounds as if I was being snobbish . . . all I mean is that if you've been secure in youth – felt you knew where you belonged – then you can withstand the buffets – and a shipwreck or two – without being rocked off your feet. Well, what I certainly discovered was that you could adjust to severe loss of income and status without despair.'

He lifted a glass and I suddenly recognised the eyes, the whole face. I realised that when we'd met again after all those years I'd been baffled by the accidental affects of age: I'd seen him in terms of wrinkling and bagging and bloating. But now the 35-year-old face had emerged: and I winced again, quite sharply, from the whistle-strap, the occasional careless lash of his tongue. The marks of age had suggested something tamed, but I saw there was nothing tame about those eyes.

'Severe loss of income and status,' he said: relishing the phrase and the wine together.

But the next morning as we walked through the school I was reminded of his other use of his tongue. 'Ah, Your Grace!' he'd greet me in a grammar school corridor: 'on your splendid way, I'm sure, to the library, where you will be adding to your already astonishing grasp of literature past and present.' My friend Ray Bolton was known to him as 'My Lord Archbishop': this springing from a moment in the changing room after Rugger, when Ray was draped in a large towel: for Logan, enough to convert him into a successor of Thomas à Becket and other wearers of the grubby archiepiscopal bathrobe of Canterbury. He conferred titles on us, absurdly, but often inspiritingly. The slightly ridiculous drama of it would raise the whole level of a day: you'd been at rock bottom, trudging from class to class, and now you were walking on air – springheeled, like him.

Snob – sadist, perhaps – poseur, certainly: and a man who essentially believed that outside his dress-suited round, all was commonness and socialism: he was nevertheless an invigorator, and in a school staffed largely by grey men he'd been mercurial, a brilliance, a source of wonderfully suspect, quite unpredictable fun. Oh, how to the end I shrank from him, a little: and how to the end I was deeply grateful to him!

So that morning, as we walked from court to court, Savernake proved to be rich in elevated officeholders: Prime Ministers, members of several royal families, the odd President of the Royal Academy, an Astronomer Royal and, mysteriously, a President of the British Board of Film Censors.

'Percy Chew,' he said, lifting his crumpled hat to the tiniest of boys. 'I've been thinking again about him. You know, he had an awful time in the Great War. Was adrift at sea, after a sinking, on a plank of wood, not much more: nearly dead when, by the wildest chance, they found him. Think of that, my dear, sometimes, when you think of him!'

Of course: like my father and many of the adults among whom I grew up, Percy Chew was someone whose imagination must have been possessed at times by demons: part of his past being incommunicably horrible.

The crumpled hat was raised for me as I left him at the main gate. 'Love to the beautiful lady,' he cried: still, I saw, bouncing a little on his feet – a very little, but definitely bouncing. He was unable merely to stand. I'd thought of him often when, in *The Submarine God*, Rufus and I had written about the tricksy, sideways-posing, wing-footed Hermes.

'And apologies for the overnight accommodation,' he called after me: affecting, as always, that it was the other person who suffered from *folie de grandeur*. 'Sorry it wasn't Chatsworth!'

4

. . . and Rufus and I went to a house on the lip of a Yorkshire valley where, every week, two established writers met with sixteen unestablished ones: the object being described as evasively as possible. It was not to be teaching: it was to be a sort of encounter, and there was to be a sort of work. Persons would, so to speak, make themselves available.

It began, for Rufus and me, with the train journey north. There was something about Rufus's attitude to the journey that made it seem we were settling into the train: making it a deeply comfortable home, probably for some days. With Rufus the simplest Kings Cross-Leeds train became the trans-Siberian express. 'Oh good!' he'd cry, as we found our seats: and would spread out his possessions on the table in front of us. They'd include several novels, not one written after 1870: and the manuscript of the book he was working on at the moment. He reminded me of a prep school boy I'd once taught, who'd shown a curious relish for being in detention, arming himself for that punitive hour with a cushion, a heap of books to rest his feet on, and a complete picnic. Once seated in the train, Rufus would glow with comfort. Sometimes I thought I'd be firm, and make him discuss some current writer I'd been reading or interviewing, some poet still warm: but it wouldn't have been fair. In this aspect he reminded me of Michael Moorcock, who'd said in an interview: 'I don't read many modern novels – *not* because I'm not . . . ' – he'd caught himself being dishonest – 'because I'm *not* interested in them.' Rufus, so to speak, beamed with apathy upon much of the contemporary scene. Ten minutes out of Kings Cross we were talking, as ever, about Charles Dickens.

The house had been a millowner's: dark stone on a crest of fields that careered down to a river: a green cliff, steeper still, rising on the other side to a height that somehow astonished, for it was halfway to being a green cloud. You looked in one direction towards further cliffs – this was coastal scenery without a sea – and in the other to where the lumbs stood among the trees, seeming themselves to be trees of stone. They were the great chimneys of the former mills, marvels of masonry. Their silence, and the general deep silence of the valley, always caused a ghost clamour in my ears, the sound of the urgent activity that once filled the place, and that seemed the more audible for being now so absolutely of the past.

It was strange, strange, to be here at the latter end of the twentieth century, making this literary use of the house, looking upon that once hard-driven valley as a deep silence to walk in: surrounded by so much that had groaned with work and want and was now tidied, emptied of old stress, visited for leisure and pleasure.

We brought our own latterday stresses with us, of course. Here and there, among our sixteen, there was talent: but often in association with personal histories that had turned it from its natural function, which was simply to release itself, into an instrument in some private conflict. So a man might come here to draw attention to the existence of a gift his wife despised: though it was more often a woman whose coming was an unhappy rebuke to an insensible husband. Here were talents attended by a great variety of timidities. There was dread of the risk involved in the attempt to complete a piece of writing: sometimes an even greater dread of the attempt to be published. Some talents, small ones, protected themselves by inventing extraordinary rules for the game of writing, which made it impossible to play. There'd been someone on one of our visits who'd made himself believe that every feature of a story must be standing knee-deep in secondary meanings. In his work, no one ever merely lit a cigarette, sighed, or caught a train. He had written, in fact, about a train journey, and had a character in it clutching, at some point, at a strap – not to steady himself, but (he anxiously explained) to demonstrate the virility that at that moment in the story the character was in danger of being thought to lack. Sitting with us in Rufus's room overlooking the tumbling valley, the author was suddenly and horribly struck by the thought that in our trains there were no longer such straps. His story was hopelessly modern in setting. Must he not wearily rewrite it, taking it backwards in time until he'd reached a date at which it could be verified that such a strap might exist? His story having foundered, as he thought, on this infuriating historical error, it was now in danger, he cried, of foundering on his ignorance of research. How did one track down such an evasive detail? He must spend at least an hour, please, *please*, with Rufus, who'd surely mastered the skills of research, and might be imagined spending more time in the British Museum Reading Room than at his desk. I saw that Rufus, whose research was continuous and mostly unmethodical, and who'd never entered the Reading Room in his life, had turned pale. But look here, I said, if we were to take it that men customarily made gestures designed to assert their virility, then to say that for those riding in trains these must always take the form of a clutch at an overhanging strap meant that, for some years, men relying on this form of transport had been prevented from making such a signal at all. Rufus flung open a window, an act foreign to a man profoundly tolerant of fug, and thrust his head out of it. Our pupil (which was not how we should think of him) stared at me wildly. He was not in search of easement: he wanted to know how to make writing quite impossible for himself.

And there was the inevitable member of the course who, very simply, was intolerable. For him or her this was an occasion for punishing the established writers for being established. Sometimes this took the form of being almost, or completely, beyond anyone's understanding, in order to make the point that the success of the tutors followed from their being despicably comprehensible. 'I've been working on the proto-fascism of Virginia Woolf,' such a person would cry, 'and, as I don't suppose I have to say, this has brought me pretty close to the edge.' Rufus would look out of the window at the cliff opposite, and I knew that was an edge he'd like to take her pretty close to. 'I must admit that I was hoping you'd have spotted the influence of Musil and would want to comment on it at some length.' Nought out of ten, and less than nought to Rufus for having mentioned, good God, Jane Austen. 'I have to be frank and say . . . I feel some disappointment,' she'd add, focussing unmistakeably on Rufus's bow tie and smiling, mockingly. There was the woman who hurled herself, in general meetings and in private, against our assertion that the appearance of spontaneity was the result of hard work. The smallest correction or rearrangement of a sentence was an insincerity, she cried. A good book coming from the heart wrote itself. 'There's only one way out from the heart,' said Rufus, who habitually wrote from it, 'and that's through the head.' She wanted to lay the week waste with a campaign in favour of never having second thoughts about anything.

Among the rest, there'd be the shy gifted young man sheltering behind models: alarmed at the idea of being himself, wishing you to recognise that in this story he *was* James Joyce, and in that one differed in no respect from D. H. Lawrence. There was the mild teacher who wrote the cruellest of horror stories: and the wonderfully plain ageing woman, in a variety of torn and shapeless sweaters, who'd cultivated, as it were, a great untendedness in herself, wrote beautifully of the world of her childhood, and hid her face constantly behind huge scarred hands. There was the woman who, if the course had not confirmed her bitter disappointment with herself, would have been bitterly disappointed. There was the woman who made careful plans for her stories and was taken aback when they refused to follow those plans. She was, I thought, like someone who, bound for unknown territory, made a map before she set out, and then was appalled by the discovery that the land in which she found herself did not resemble the map. We were as tender with her as we could be: but reports said that when she left us she was in tears.

It wasn't easy, avoiding hurt. Keeping abreast of all the stories we were given to read (and, always, a novel or two) – that was hard enough. Then there was the need to submit good humouredly to being targets for those with a perfectly understandable hatred of anyone whose work had been published: and also to walk a sensible path between two forms of cruelty – over-encouragement, and under-encouragement.

Rufus and I always vowed we'd never return, and always returned. And there was no course without members who had something other than the wistful desire to be a writer, which made some happy and some wretched.

I'd remember how, when I was twenty or so, the mere shape of a sentence, or a sentence in which words had a particular thrilling existence, would make me dizzy with pleasure. The feeling, when I tried to recall and analyse it, was first one of excitement which sprang from the knowledge that there was no end to the effects, more lively than life, that could be created if you had luck and skill with words. And then there was a marvelling at how words could take fire from one another: and how four or five of them, five or six, could suddenly create something . . . well, yes, more alert and alive than the world itself.

And once, lying in my bed above the valley, which was as deeply silent as any place I'd slept in, a deep green grave, I wondered what had happened to Jess Bland, with whom round 1931 I'd embarked on the attempt to put P. C. Wren out of business.

5

I had this recurrent nightmare, which I imagine is a common one, about people I hadn't seen for years. Suddenly, in such a black dream, some old friend would seem to have been lost: as if indeed I had carelessly parted from him, or her, at some actual spot in the huge city of existence, and taken no care to ensure that we'd meet again. It was a nightmare, I guess, that sprang from dread of the unimaginably dense nature of the human traffic. How easily we are lost to one another! Beyond that was a sense of one's old selves, and one's old companions, being caught in the past as if by way of entombment: the past *was* a tomb. And *that* related again, I thought, to a terror in us that springs from our experience of how easily bad chance could do irremediable damage, and pass on, whistling. There'd been a particularly nasty murder, the discovery of a girl's mouldering body in a field, and I couldn't sleep for nights, thinking how casually irreversible her death had been: how her grave had been created out of thousands of the most stray sorts of accident, and how I couldn't alter one of them: could do nothing for her at all.

And where now was Jess Bland, for a year or more my dearest friend?

He was one of my two closest companions in the first year at grammar school, bound to me by the alphabet. In Haddock's class we'd sat alongside each other: Bland, Blishen, Browning. We had the warm amity of small boys – as physical as it's anything else: you tumble against each other, you race each other to exhaustion through the streets. We were puppies, not desperadoes, but John Logan must have thought ill of all three of us.

Bland was long and thin and had a tormenting stutter, about which masters in that generally cruel school tended to be cruel. 'Make up your mind what you're going to say, boy!' Haddock was a basically gentle, dull man, made irritable and unjust, I guess, by the absolute misery of teaching, as it was to him. The disapproval of the quick-footed John Logan must for this heavy old man have been simply another reason for sadness. I see him now, a distressed parcel in his tattered gown, constantly wrapping and rewrapping himself, and glaring at Jess Bland with the weariest hostility: 'Oh, *do* speak up, boy!' and Jess's stammer made heartbreakingly worse by Haddock's impatience. Hundreds of times I tried, and failed, to pray Jess out of his stammer!

He had three sisters, as long and thin as himself, with a kind of nervous prettiness: they weren't, but seemed to be, triplets, and I sensed that Jess ought to have been a fourth. He was made from the same temperamental and physical recipe, but had turned out uncomfortably to be a boy. We had literary longings in common, and spent much of our time rewriting *Beau Geste*. The fact that *Beau Geste* was already written didn't strike us as any reason not to write it all over again. Browning was much smaller than either of us, a square boy, with a blunt taste in jokes. In terms of electric wiring, I was the positive among us, Jess the negative, and Norman Browning was our earth. I think of him in the light, or the gloom, of a joke that secretly appalled me when he first offered it. 'What's a good way of making fire?' he asked. 'Don't know.' 'Rub my arse against your face!' I laughed, but wished he'd kept it to himself. It wasn't how I wished us to think of each other.

Then one day, in our second year at Queen's, I was suddenly seized with the idea of how strangely nice it would be if I turned our affection for each other into something else. Well, it sprang, I'm sure, from all that reading of romances in which *he* was estranged from *her*. They longed for each other, but were at odds: misunderstandings had driven them apart. In the unlikely environment of the grammar school I wanted to reproduce that situation, the staple element in so many films I saw at the Barton Cinema. The medium of disruption had, of course, to be literary. I wrote them a note announcing the end of our friendship. All was over. I can't recall that I invented a reason. It was, simply, done with, as the result of a huge change of heart on my part: some great sense I had of unspecific injury. I withdrew from all our accustomed encounters: wasn't there in the morning before school, was somewhere else at break, didn't walk home with Jess, mapping out the next chapter in our novel. The novel, which had been everything to us, died. We passed each other, speechless. I was now in one class, they in another. From time to time I refreshed the sensation of love withdrawn by means of some new letter, inventing new premises, emotionally imprecise, for the war between us.

The wonderful war! It thrilled me horribly, to be at odds with my old companions! It seemed much better than merely being friends with them, in the old style. As I try to understand it now, I see it as amounting to a passionate addiction to heartache. Being alienated from them offered the perpetual possibility of reconciliation. The time would come when we couldn't bear it any longer, we'd come together scarcely able to endure the delight of being reunited. It was the idea of that ultimate, but endlessly deferred, reunion that turned me on, I believe.

And I look back over the years and think what a perversity it was! How unlike the understood behaviour of small grammar school boys!

6

I seemed to choke very easily: there were a number of indications that the road from my mouth to my stomach might be in need of repair. After a melodrama or two in restaurants, Kate insisted I see the doctor, who said something might be wrong with my swallow. She'd arrange an X-ray.

I'd been under the eye of that machine before: it had offered reports on my duodenum, my lungs. This time the photography turned out to be amazingly difficult. You filled your mouth with barium porridge, and, at a signal from the radiographer, urgently passed on by the nurse, you swallowed. It was hoped that your swallow and his operation of the shutter would coincide. Mostly they didn't. He became furious, she became agitated: I swallowed with increasing despair. It looked as if I'd be swallowing for ever. It was where I'd ended up: swallowing a barium meal for a radiographer incapable of satisfaction.

At last, at his end of the room, he fell silent. She prowled around me unhappily, as I lay against the screen in my back-to-front nightshirt: which tended, given one over-bold movement, to bare the buttocks. At last she said: 'I think you can go now. I think it's all right.' I fled.

My behind again under wraps, I made my way out of the X-ray unit. In a corridor I passed the radiographer and the nurse. His eye fell coldly on me, and I heard him say:

'Ah nurse, I see you let the swallow go!'

I saw a specialist in swallows, who did a little writing himself. He told me of his latest attempt at a story, which involved a small problem of narrative, perhaps familiar to a professional like myself. It wasn't at all familiar, but I offered a suggestion or two.

This consultation over, he turned to the other.

I had an inconsecutiveness somewhere along the line of my swallow. I tried to understand the specialist's explanation. It seemed to be not unlike the problems that beset H. M. Stanley when he navigated the Congo. A matter of narrow gulleys, rockfalls, rapids. The food I ate went on journeys demanding very great intrepidity.

But an operation might make things worse. It was another of those points of wear and tear that occur along the way. Take reasonable care.

I'd met Jimmy Soper again recently in the High Street. His moustache bristling to counteract any impression of soft personal chatter, he asked me to imagine, if I could, that some vital organ of his, he was not specific, had slipped its moorings, and only after a rapid operation had been anchored afresh, though in a fairly unsuitable harbour. 'Happens to us all,' said Jimmy, drily, looking over my shoulder at a High Street full of persons with drifting innards.

7

If I couldn't tempt Jimmy Soper to dinner, I thought I might succeed with Georgie Owen. Between 1926 and 1936 Georgie had been part of the world as it was and always would be. We'd been side by side at Barley Road, and had gone together, scholarship boys, to the grammar school. In that curiously physical way in which, in childhood, you are conscious of your friends, Georgie was the proof that one might be fat and flushed, and still the best of fellows. He had an absurd, vulnerable inflatedness, his whole visible surface a matter of veins under stress. I think of him now, tenderly, in terms of his thighs which, turning faintly purple under the pressure of being a part of the machinery that made it possible for Georgie to sit, could be seen, anywhere before 1933, disappearing into his shorts. For some reason, in those days it was possible to have a straightforward view of the lining of one's shorts, stitched into place about an inch above the lowest point of the garment: and I think, now, of Georgie as largely a matter of purpling thighs and trouser lining. He was a good friend, but held that I was, in everything, excessive. I was over-enthusiastic about Harry Wharton & Co and books in general and the pleasantness of the fields round Barton and the beauty of the rather plain girls we were all drawn to: most of whom were contemporaries of Kate's at the girls' grammar school prudishly placed at the other end of town. 'Oh, you exaggerate', Georgie would say, when I'd outlined some feature of our common existence in what I thought was an inadequately vivid fashion. At the time, Georgie being such a damper was a cause of my love for him. Arriving at school to enthuse, and being met with Georgie's riot-squad's jet of cold water, was part of the pleasure of being alive. I loved Georgie for the very quality, belatedly identified as simple chilliness, for which, that evening in the mid-1970s, I was to despair of him.

Phoned, he said he would come. Could he bring his lady wife? Brought his lady wife. Arrived, huge, mottled: so generally purple that I was surprised to observe that he'd gone into long trousers. Thought Mrs Baker at Barley Road – though he had to say he could barely remember her – had been strict. A good, strict woman of the old order of teachers. Had difficulty in recalling Haddock. Percy Chew? Fine, fine man: had lifted the school into another league altogether. John Logan? Ah! Good games master, but Irish. One couldn't easily forget that he was Irish. It was distinctly against him. Only peripherally British.

Throughout the evening, Georgie referred to us as 'one': a usage perhaps intended to keep at bay the subversive implications of pronouns more personal. He clearly thought one's boyhood was a condition above which one had inevitably risen. One wasn't any longer the scholarship boy patronisingly adopted by one's betters. One's mother and father weren't around any more, making things awkward with their dropped aitches and general unease. One would have no eagerness to dwell on the social blackout from which one had emerged into sustained daylight.

When I recalled that in the Fifth we'd formed a Women-Haters' Club, he greeted the reminder of that small boys' vulgarity with the least possible smile. I produced the diary into which I'd stuck the scrap of paper recording our resolve to disband. 'The first period,' said the diary on January 18, 1935, in the booming prose I then favoured, 'brought forth a quiet finale to the Women-Haters' Club of Upper VS. All became singularly aware that this . . . was too great to give up; A. exuded a mysterious whisper of a particular philandering: R. H. – we all know about R. H.; G. was never earnest; S. is hopeful . . . and I – well, I ought to know.

'The actual dossier of conformity to this new attitude, hastily drawn up by R. H., and passed in a succession of grinning signatures, is herein preserved . . .'

With this forty-year-old dossier in front of him – I clearly thought that was the word for a document – I imagined Georgie might unbend. There were our childish signatures, extraordinarily ornate. Of the five of us, two had had less than a decade to live. A., who'd performed the feat of exuding that mysterious whisper, was Andrew Bell, a glimpse of whose genitals had sent Podge Smith into furtive ecstasies: in the summer of 1940 he was shot out of the sky over the Thames estuary. The bones of R. H. were somewhere at the bottom of the Atlantic.

On the facing page I'd copied a verbatim note I'd made of a lesson given by our Latin master, Knotty. 'Now, surely! One-two – three – four – five words. Surely you can translate that . . . Well! translate it literally to yourself . . . come on. There are half a dozen of you. Can't one of you . . .? I'm leaving you to do it by yourselves now . . . What case is *eius* . . .? If you had an inspector in, he'd think it a very funny thing that a School Certificate form didn't know the gender of *eius* . . . *ne adsidua* . . . now he's going into a list of reasons . . . *adsidua consuetudine* . . .? You see, the way that you are handicapped is in your vocabulary . . .' For nearly five years, by then, we had been victims of Knotty's teaching method: which was based on the techniques of nagging. It is doubtful if any of us was unaware of the gender of *eius*: but we had lost all sense of the possibility of responding to his ceaseless grumble. Merely reading the words, at this great distance of time, caused my eyes to close. I pointed this out to Georgie.

But he did not wish to be reminded of Knotty. He was peering indignantly at the scrap of paper on which the children we'd once been had announced our intention of returning to the pursuit of love.

'Torn out of one's exercise book,' he said sternly.

8

Enclosed with Jack Seed's letter was a newspaper article about Bondi Beach: which had gone topless. Photographs provided proof. 'Dear Kate,' Jack had written in a margin. 'This is where Edward spent day after day after day . . .'

Having written a term's reports he'd gone round saying sorry to those who filled the bottom places. 'I couldn't care less,' said one. 'How unprepared I am to teach!' cried Jack. He was worried, too, about surely unteacherly feelings he had in school corridors. There were girls with heavy hips who tended, he said, to make him take wrong turnings. An aspirant to teaching of the greatest seriousness, he found himself in the wrong wing of the school because a child had splendid buttocks. There were Greek girls, from families newly arrived in Australia, to whom to be at school was to become part of some erotic melodrama. One girl had not been able to stop giggling when he corrected her work. She had been apologetic. 'I'm sorry,' she'd said. 'I'm not used to men.'

Out-of-school activity had barely improved on this. He'd been taking an obligatory course on language. On the heels of a piece of work would come a questionnaire. Nothing, said Jack, was allowed simply to happen. Any Australian event whatever was followed by interrogation. 'This elective,' he'd recently been informed in this fashion, 'was designed to make you become aware of the value of selecting the *exact* word for each *specific* occasion. Was this aim achieved in your view?' He'd had, said Jack, the greatest difficulty in preventing himself from replying: Yes. Sort of.

I told him in my answering letter of a visit I'd paid to a local school. They'd clearly expected me to be in some difficulty, drafting class after class into a large hall, and hemming the occasion in with teachers, who took up positions of a riot-containment kind along the walls. I knew, in fact, that there'd be no problem: because, to begin with, this was my home ground. On the spot where the school now stood I'd once made palaces of hay – with Georgie Owen, among others: and, in more or less the neighbourhood of the woodwork centre, I'd many years before discovered that you couldn't build a fire in the fork of a tree without setting the tree on fire. In those days our model of a tyrant (I thought of him when Miss Baker told us of Napoleon) was the farmer, who'd stumped everywhere after us, was never more than a field away, but never quite caught up. I talked of our war with the farmer. I talked of the need I'd already felt of making stories of what happened. I spoke of the way we'd gathered, the children of the town, every Saturday at the Barton Cinema, to acquire more stories. The tales of everyday life, our own stories, became tangled with the tales told by the cinema. I thought Jean Rawlins, at Barley Road, *was* Laura La Plante. I talked about being a writer, besieged by stories, and about the difficulty of establishing whether Barton was a reality or an occasion for fiction, or perhaps a place like others where reality and fiction became muddled. I challenged them to disentangle their own personal fiction from their own personal fact. I knew I could talk them into listening, because it is deeply interesting to think of one's own neighbourhood and one's own life as a source of stories, and as having existed in some form other than its present one: and because the business of writing, which involves drawing on the sensations and dramas and disgraces of life, is irresistible subject-matter. Of course, I did not sell them short in the matter of disgraces. Children love to be at the edge of scandal and infamy. We are all scandalous and infamous, I thought, and spoke accordingly.

Afterwards (I told Jack to make him easier about being trapped in educational jargon) the deputy head had said: 'My goodness, you *held* them! You could even keep their attention with *sensitivity* . . .'

I didn't understand him until I worked it out that sensitivity was Sensitivity, a whole branch of teaching to be embarked upon with caution: and that it was the current educational term for talking about delicate topics. I was praised for grasping this nettle, as I thought, because I'd said a writer was always a writer, at the end of the world he'd be thinking of phrases, and I'd talked of being at my mother-in-law Dorothy's deathbed and being deeply moved, but also being quite excitedly observant, knowing I should write about it.

Jack said he felt he was constantly sliding into parody. In the classroom he found himself a parody of this or that teacher he'd known. 'Sometimes I am you. Sometimes, to my great alarm, I am Mr Bedrock.'

Lately, horribly, it had occurred to him that he was actually living a parody of somebody else's life. 'If you know this to be so, you *will* tell me, won't you!'

9

I'd talked at that local school about a problem that lay densely ahead of them, at some distance, but worth thinking about in any discussion of the attempt to pick out the lines of the story of one's life: that of simply distinguishing year from year. I thought the first nineteen years, certainly, had great separateness one from another: that was when one year of time equalled one year of experience, the measures were exact – no problem. Mostly what happened then was a first: was new: perfectly filled out the time it occupied. Later came repetitions, dullnesses, numbnesses, and experience shrank inside its container of time. And lately, trying to distinguish 1959 and 1958, I'd thought I might make a time-chart of the kind you see in primary school classrooms, a frieze to be pinned to the walls. A personal time-chart might do worse than indicate where you went for holidays. That idle hole in the year was, I thought, the best of mnemonics.

So it was when we went to Korcula . . . that was the year of the amazing summer.

Down the lane in Barley Wood one evening came a duck and her brood. The pond had failed. They entered our garden and settled grumblingly in the shelter of a berberis. We borrowed a child's inflatable paddling pool, blew it up, and filled it with water: but they stayed uneasily where they were. They knew what *wasn't* a pond when they saw it. Late in the night the lane quacked angrily: here came the drake, in search of his family. All night the gaps in the berberis were full of their uneasy eyes. We knew this because it was the summer when it was often too hot for sleep.

Korcula? That was blue water, golden town (simply a beautiful heap), silver mountains. One evening a walk ended in a tiny inexplicable marina: an old man reading on a balcony: the setting sun exploding in the water ahead of us and making ghosts of mountains and islands.

And suddenly everything out on our hotel verandah began clattering and flying: a great wind had come from nowhere: the mountains were sunk in cloud: the hotel lights went, and came again, and there was the rattle of rain and bang of wind. We fought our way to the harbour, where boats were heaving and drumming on the water: some small ones already sunk. An aluminium yacht from Boston, elegant, untended, was beating itself to pieces against the harbour wall, and townspeople were attempting to protect it in the context of a tremendous argument as to the best way of doing this. It seemed that deep points relating to the whole philosophy and technology of rescue were being debated, while the expensive toy, thrust up on amazingly sudden swells and dropped into amazingly sudden holes in the water, blunted more and more of its beautiful sharpnesses with horrible blows on stone.

That agreeable Adriatic had become cruel, distressed and distressing: it was wonderful to see, but at the same time told an alarming tale: that at any moment a calm life could become a life tormented like this hugely disturbed leaden water. I wondered again at how we ever imagined ourselves to be safe. An astonishing feature of human consciousness – that for large periods it invents a sensation of security!

Of all the memories one might long to grasp at on a deathbed, among the most desirable must be the recollection of having time to sit and stare with enormous attention at some glorious scene: as then, the storm over as if it had never been, and Kate noting that the sun did not make a continuous trail across the sea. We tried to put into words what it actually did. It struck spasmodic sparkles out of . . . the constantly-changing facets of the water? So it was a ribbon of inconstant bright dots? Deep, deep contentment: being involved in such an absurd pedantry of observation. It had been Kate's discovery long ago, anyway, in childhood, that if you gazed hard at a scene, and named its details over to yourself, it would become recallable. To that extent you could choose your memories.

We committed to heart, among other things, a solarium constructed by British soldiers stationed in Korcula between 1813 and 1815, a gift to the townspeople: who, in fact, had a habit of evading, not inviting, the sun. We imagined their courteous pretence of pleasure, offered this means of courting sunstroke in comfort. We liked it best – and would sit in it, staring across the blackened silver of the sea – under the moon: when, said Kate, it surely became a lunarium.

We were drawn by the offer of a three-day trip, a sort of wandering by boat. It was an old wooden smack: at night, tied up, it creaked. We slept in little warm coffins of cabins: there was an inefficient loo: a handsome skipper: simple, filling food: the sun: the sea. For those three days we travelled through a warm mistiness. The water was thickly glassy: the sky gleamed, and all was silver and pewter. A small boat looked like a fly on a pewter dish. Much of the time the silence was deep; when it was broken it was by some exchange of low voices: the splash of a swimmer: the small natural splashings of the sea: and the whine of flies, bright green or like travelling fragments of highly polished brass.

With an effect of immense decency, the captain undid a further button on Kate's shirt and gestured, in explanation, at the sun. He had a phrase or two of English, and employed one when patting Kate, in passing, on the bottom: 'Well done!' He brought us fresh figs: he sang in a low obstreperous voice. I thought he'd have fitted in perfectly with Fred Wicks, Jack Withers, Bernard Slow, Jimmy Soper and me, in Barton in 1929; and he and I would have been rivals for the love of Jean Rawlins. He'd have triumphed, of course, I having no command of Adriatic tricks with buttons.

The little islands we passed were like mossed-over whales – it was Kate's phrase. One had a particular perfection of shape: with a long low curved rise from a point, and a smaller curved fall to the further end: at the sharper end, the smallest bristle of trees standing above the general green. It was a perfect pubes of an island. There were patches on the water that made it look as if the sea had puddles in it.

Most of our fellow-travellers were German: one had the face of a 1920ish tennis star, eyes half-closed with good-naturedness: he lay about browning his big belly, took photos entirely at random with a ludicrously elaborate camera, and might well, I thought, with a little adjustment of time (and, on my part, of philosophy) have shot me. Or I might have shot him. And the benign sea around us, of course, was not only capable of conjuring sudden storms, but had been a theatre of death for many. It had been a buoyant arena for war.

It was odd, among all those Germans, not to understand the jokes, only the laughter. It was like being on a school outing, partly deaf.

Leaving the boat and returning to the trivial respectability of the hotel was a small dismay. We felt we were brown urchins, and longed to be back in a town where we'd stayed for a night, that had shrieked with house martens, and where we'd felt most ragged, most free of timetables and intentions. I longed again for a youth I'd never had, partly because of the timid conservatism that had been a consequence of being a scholarship boy at Queen's, partly because of the war: a wandering youth. Neither Kate nor I had been tramps, and the tramp in us sulked a little, absurdly, in the absurd context of that mild trip along the Dalmatian coast . . . Kate took to stealing figs from gardens we passed when walking. The island was stone, stone, white stone: and we found a causeway that ran from the town uphill to a village two kilometres away – the thought of the industry that made it, exhausting in itself. Two kilometres of packed stone, in places many feet deep. Kate was of the local colours, her skin burned golden, her hair silver. Toiling up to the village in mid-afternoon we stopped, I some way above her: the town below us, bleached and orange, piling itself up to its peak in the bell tower of the cathedral. We panted, laughed: and knew, as sometimes you do know, that it was a moment of the most extraordinary healthy happiness that we'd never forget.

'The 8.10 to Hitchford,' said the announcer at Finsbury Park, where the temperature was higher than it had been in Korcula, 'stopping at Grange Green and all stations, is cancelled.'

We were home.

Where people had begun to look rather unwell: at the mercy of a summer far more suitable for foreigners. My mother, then eighty-six, to whom every new-minted word was a cue for a new-minted malapropism, had been struck by the spectacle of a grand-daughter cooling off in her king bee. 'You know,' she said, as ever impatient with us for our appalling dependence on the dictionary, 'the little thing they wear on the beach.' Computers, traffic lights, signalling systems broke down: the surfaces of roads became liquid. Our son Tom, cooling off at Barley Wood after a term in which heat had compounded the natural exactions of teaching, looked out of a window and saw me writing in my diary: 'All lies! Subjective nonsense!' he shouted, before collapsing into the general condition of liquidity. At Bush House, even important BBC persons revealed that they had legs, chests, bosoms. In the polyglot lifts I hoped (was my hearing as good as I thought?) that my cries of admiration were all as inward as I intended. Kate and I and our little dog Sal, who'd become extremely odd – she couldn't sleep alone, was clearly living in fear: of what might leap out of the unresolved tensions of such a life, I thought, suspecting that she pointed to a fate we should, before the end, endure ourselves – walked one evening across a harvested field, having to tread with care because under the litter of chaff were immense cracks. Strange, strange year, with such cracks everywhere, and trees dying of thirst. Yellowed leaves falling already in August: forest fires: our rhododendron dying: a premature autumn: and no lawn cutting, there being no lawns to cut.

My producer at Bush House had overheard a phrase: 'as brown as a lawn.'

And, the clay beneath it a parched fraction of what it had been, our house broke.

10

Having a grandchild – the most pleasant possible way of beginning to die.

'A little, screwed-up fellow,' said Dan, who was present at the birth, 'with enormous genitals.' The point about the genitals being made clear to him by an amused doctor: who pointed out that, against the necessarily limited bulk of the rest of the newcomer's body, they always did seem assertive.

Strange – to observe a son with a son in his arms. And to smile at a daughter-in-law, both having noticed what cunning collage a new child's face presented: a teasing mixture of family traits from both sides: and sometimes, completely *them*: sometimes, completely *us*. I thought my view of childbirth had been influenced for forty years by our history master Sandy Spring's talk of some child smuggled into a royal bed in a warming pan. The point of birth was plainly susceptible to all kinds of rogueries. But added to human dishonesty was the trickiness of the newborn child itself. Who ever knew where he was with a creature of such fluid appearance, the scrap that between today and yesterday had grown through millenia?

From my first glimpse of Tim, whose existence had been determined by a myriad of accidents, among them the skein of chances that had brought and kept Kate and me together thirty years before, I went for a weekend with a group of high-flying educationists. They had been behind much that had happened in education during the past two or three decades: they were brightly intelligent, master navigators on the seas of public affairs, and all held or had retired from important positions. Looking round at the first meeting, sherry in the Oxford common room, I thought they had that look about them you see in paintings of historic gatherings: in a corner, the outline of the group, each head containing an identificatory number. I mentioned the idea to someone I thought might be Number 3. Just an informal gathering of friends, sharing ideas, he said. I thought, to my surprise, that there was something oppressive about such a group of powerful people. They were the arrangers – had the expectation of being in at the ordering of human affairs. Nothing wrong with that, surely? Were important human issues not best left in the hands of the strong and thoughtful? They were affable, modest, humane, hospitable. Yet one of the best and most characteristic of the minds present was, as it seemed to me, irrepressibly bossy. When its owner spoke, it was like being addressed in the kitchen by some bulky cultural mum, rapping knuckles with her wooden spoon. Admirable ideas: and one wanted to sneak away and do something disgraceful. I admired many of those present, and had a strong wish to shout rudely after them in the street. 'Yah! Arrangers!'

I thought of Mrs Needle: and how I'd come at last to Oxford: not actually to Wolsey's academic palace, but close:

and what a disappointment it had been, for all the apparent brilliance of the occasion.

When I next caught sight of Tim I thought what an illusion we had, in the presence of the newly born, of the freedom of growth possible to a human being. To think in terms of limiting the development of this tremendously plastic scrap – how absurd! All was possible! Though every resemblance to father or mother, uncle or aunt, even a remote cousin, is a mark of the confines within which this new creature must travel, still we look at him, or her, as having perfectly elastic possibilities. And the illusion is not entirely nonsensical since, against the background of the restrictions that have closed in already on a five-year-old, the plasticity of the absolutely new child is immense.

I thought of the arrangers among whom I'd spent the weekend, those excellent, well-intentioned persons, and I felt inside a little angry pulsing of the feeling Kate and I had had when on that boat on the Adriatic: resting, I guess, on some perennial notion that a human creature might escape being arranged: might, somehow, within whatever genetic limits, create himself.

My mother, speaking for my dead father, said – because (Dan and his wife opposed to all pretension) it was all Tim was to be called – 'Tim! That doesn't seem much of a name!' And she wondered what this great-uncle, this great-aunt might think of it.

After my father's death, my mother had shaken herself free of much: but she was still deeply subject to the web of family opinion, real or imagined – and much of it now had to be imagined, so many of the original gossips being dead – and, as she delighted in her first great-grandchild, she also listened for hostile whispers in the undergrowth by which, I now saw, my childhood had been beset. It was an undergrowth of, on the whole, ill-natured talk: no one in the family to be relied upon to speak well of any other member of it.

Well, for example, there was always talk of scrounging. That had been, for people on the whole desperately poor, an accepted, necessary way of life: but those who accepted it also reserved the right to scorn it. Of certain members of the family my father had a view entirely conditioned by the expectation that they would scrounge off him. 'My younger brother Will will be round any day now,' he'd say. He insisted curiously on the fact of a brother being younger or older than himself. 'And it won't be for my blue eyes!' His angry laugh. 'Hopes I'll have a shirt to give him! You can bet your life your mother will find something for him – a blouse for Hilda, something for the kids. Give the hair off her head if someone asked for it.' It was always his image for my mother's helplessly generous nature, which appalled him but at the same time was a matter of perverse pride. As a small child I'd waited with dread for the crisis of charity in which (by a process which I supposed intentions of an extremely altruistic kind made possible) she uprooted her hair and made a sacrifice of it. We had a dangerously large number of bald or balding relatives. Will would come, chatter, and leave with a parcel. 'They make me sick,' my father would say, having been extremely amiable the whole evening. 'Eyes everywhere, looking for something they can take away with them.' My mother had confided that she'd been greatly drawn to Uncle Will when she'd first met the seven Blishen boys: I wondered if she ever hoped she herself might be one of the objects Uncle Will would have liked to take away. His scorn for my father was as great as my father's scorn for him (as a child I was very much aware of this straightforward tournament of scorns, with my father and his brothers as the contestants), and was based largely on the fact that he was a practical vegetable gardener, and my father indulged himself with flowers. My cousin Jim, Will's elder son, had told me recently how he'd go home from visiting us and Uncle Will would ask: 'What was your uncle doing?' 'Pruning his roses,' Jim would say. 'Good God! *You can't eat roses!*' The progress that had taken my father into the Civil Service, and made a clerk out of a member of a family powerfully hostile to occupations of a settled and seated character, had led inevitably to this effeminacy: the waste of soil, time and care on the inedible rose.

Then there'd been the matter, which now interested me greatly, of its being accepted that no one in the family spoke, or expected to speak, or was expected to speak, accurately of any detail of the family history. It was taken for granted that one lied about these things. Extraordinarily, this did not result in general scepticism, or a plain refusal to believe anything that anybody said. I spent much of my childhood listening to my father and his brothers telling tales to each other of the truth of which I knew none of them was convinced. They nodded, smiled, assented to patent lies. And it was all based, I suppose, on an understanding that each of us has his own distortion of the truth to offer, and that anything else is beyond human reach. It was, now I thought of it, one of the important reasons for the unhappiness between my father and myself. I had gathered from literature (and from Williams and Logan) this notion that something like the truth was accessible to the powerful and earnest skills of human language: and my father knew that this was the ultimate madness. He'd given birth to a prig, who didn't know how to participate in the game of lies. 'It'll be an early grave for you,' my father would cry, setting out the worst, but only just the worst, of the fates he saw lying ahead for me. Damned boy! Who'd have thought the simple wish for the social advancement of one's children that had led my father to welcome my scholarship success would lead to this *refusal* of social advancement, this inclination to engage oneself in subversive scribbling!

My poor father! How could he know that the simple unpleasant life he had in mind for me could not be achieved by way of the obvious machinery, set up by the educational arrangers of the day? How could he know that the theory translated itself into Percy Chew, pretending to be what he wasn't, and John Logan, pretending to be what he was: and Williams, catching me up in the slipstream of his own doomed longing to be a writer: and my good friend Ben, brilliant schoolboy betrayed by the arrangements: and Kate, who'd been as cruelly let down by the system as anyone: having a gift the girls' grammar school had known little about, the gift of tenderness.

I looked at Tim, across whose face whole genealogies flickered in a second, and prayed, as a grandfather must do, for the well being of my beloved descendant.

11

I'd been invited to Canada – once again to talk about children's literature: and it seemed an opportunity to visit San Francisco – and Mae Gloucester Graham, who lived in one of its hilly suburbs. She wrote letters on her own scale: brief. Children's books arriving for review in boxfuls, she said, she'd been able lately to do only what was under her nose. I suggested that, as a matter of simple physical fact, there couldn't be much of that.

From another university in a part of the world about which I now had nightmares, my friend Robert arrived in London on leave. Through year after year of the Amin nightmare he'd managed to hang on in Kampala, watching over his students in so far as that was possible, disappearance and death having become quite arbitrary: and presiding over a staff that, for dreadful reasons, grew smaller and smaller. This term, he said, his deputy had come to him: returning from a lecture, he'd observed the familiar messengers, with their dark glasses and careless machinery of death, waiting outside his room. He'd managed to avoid being observed. He must go at once, said Robert, to Kenya. That was not possible, said his deputy: his students were sitting their exams, and he must stay to mark their papers. He could not be dissuaded, and was hidden in the university until all the papers were marked: when he was successfully smuggled over the border.

Robert described the deaths of friends. Laban, for having once written an historical play that had been represented to Amin as an attack on himself, had had his head beaten to a pulp by hammers. Jared, who'd been moved by the idea that linguistics might provide an approach to literary criticism, had been poisoned: and his wife, Lisa, poet and lecturer, had died in an extremely improbable road accident. These last deaths were, and promised to remain, impossible to digest. Jared and Lisa were young people of vivid promise. I thought of an evening, ten years before, in their house in Kampala, among their shy bright children: private-minded Jared marking papers as we talked: a thunderstorm, one of those East African storms that play in the air above you without practical results, cosmic vanities of thunder and lightning: and Lisa, in a coloured leaf of a dress, with her body that seemed to laugh without her needing to laugh, or to grow grave without any other need of gravity on her part, and always to enact her intentions a second or so before she became aware of them. She was always on her way into the garden or into the brilliance of her kitchen (did they never turn lights out, or was it their own excited brightness that made me remember a blazing house?), before she knew why she was going there.

The last time I'd ever seen them was in our living room at Barley Wood: a party, and their small daughters, the head of each of them a heap of the twigs and twirls of hair that back home I'd seen Lisa toiling over, made simple noises on the piano, under the captaincy of our son Tom: and Jared talked about the work he was doing at London University: and Lisa danced. And we were deeply relieved that my Uncle George had left the day before, having declared during his visit, on the arrival of a black messenger from the BBC: 'There's a wog coming up the path, Kate!' Uncle George's view of Africans was like the one held by my father: who'd regarded my connection with the BBC's African Service much as if he'd discovered me, forty years earlier, courting the company of boys from Higg's Lane, which ran at the bottom of the polite road in Barton in which we lived. Merely having one's home in Higg's Lane, my father believed, had a dire moral effect: leaving aside a tendency to harbour fleas. His never quite friendly view of Kate rested partly on her coming from Higg's Lane – the more sober end: but still Higg's Lane.

For Uncle George and my father, alas, Africa was the Higg's Lane of the world.

12

Oh, really, life did at times seem a particularly revolting soap opera, viewed in a distracted, intermittent fashion: so that suddenly you were made aware of the fate, or present condition, of someone you'd lost sight of several hundred instalments earlier. It was perhaps what Jack Seed had in mind when he talked of his fear of living a parody of someone else's life. Was one, perhaps, never much more than an understudy? How awful to go through so much and then to be made aware that, to this or that member of the now appallingly crowded cast of one's own corner of the drama, one might as well for the last decade or so – or much more – have confined oneself to muttering: 'Rhubarb rhubarb rhubarb.'

I ran at a dinner party into Rose-M, with whom I'd been disastrously in love five minutes earlier, as it seemed, when she was twenty-two. She was perfectly recognisable, but had the face, the body, the bearing of a fifty-two-year-old. It was astonishing, as if it had truly happened in a matter of minutes, this transformation of what had been so fresh, bright, rash, and had made my heart leap and plunge, into what was pleasant, experienced, and rather grave. It was odder still to know that, where I was once as uncertain and wretched as I'd ever been, I was now at my ease. I had an unexpected heady sense of returning powerfully to an old weak position, followed by a sudden longing for that very weakness.

Kate had known her, too, and had once been a fairly close friend. We talked of old days; and in ourselves we felt growing a touchiness about what Rose-M remembered and failed to remember. Reminded of moments that had for us a sort of immortality, she looked blank. For her, entire persons, once known to us all, had never existed. And as the evening wore on, under the social ease that was a consequence of our being in our fifties and not our twenties, another kind of unease made itself felt, for Kate and me.

As we agreed afterwards, it is not possible to be wholly comfortable with someone who had been perfectly content to live without you.

'Canada,' said Gary Bunce, apparently from the North Pole, 'is the end! Avoid it, Eddy!'

'Oh Gary!' I groaned.

PART FOUR

1

Oh, this unnatural business of ripping oneself away at an enormous rate from one's usual setting! Here one moment I was in Barton High Street, and the next I was in Vancouver Airport, in what as far as I was concerned was the middle of the night. I presented myself at the immigration counter and, in answer to a question, announced with tired pride that I was a guest of the University of British Columbia under their Distinguished Visitors scheme. I didn't absolutely expect to be carried shoulder-high out of the building, but wouldn't have been surprised by some doffing of caps.

The man frowned horribly, read my passport very slowly as if it had been a displeasing novel of some length: looked at me, frowned: looked at the back cover of the passport, upside down, and frowned: and vanished at last without a word into a screened area in the centre of the space behind the counter. Time passed, and then passed again. Nothing happened. No one appeared. As a result of some message I'd managed to miss, human affairs had been suspended until further notice. It had been announced (and again I'd missed it) that eternity would be given a trial run.

I had never experienced such a pure blankness, as to time, one's future prospects, the whole principle of one's having a future.

Then the immigration officer reappeared. He placed my passport on the counter and groaned. He looked me up and down and groaned. Then he spoke. I was, he said, virtually a prohibited immigrant. If I was going to lecture at the University of British Columbia, then I was proposing to enter employment on Canadian soil: and should, before leaving Britain, have obtained a special form of entry that permitted this. He fell silent, staring at me in a manner suggesting that I must have some intricate reply to offer, and that it would make no difference whatever to my position, which was that of someone who'd manoeuvred himself into a void. I was nowhere, nobody, forbidden, shunned, accursed.

I said the University might have been expected to advise me of this, and the fact that they had not done so . . . In my middle-of-the-night condition, I sought to suggest that it was absurd to think that a great intellectual institution, one of the glories of the immigration officer's own country, would not have thought of this nasty twist of the story, if indeed this nasty twist of the story –

I became confused and stared at him with indignant hopelessness.

He left me and re-entered the screened area. After another foretaste of eternity, he returned with a face profoundly puckered and wry: it was the expression of someone confronted with the last thing in impossible situations. He then produced an enormous form, pink, complex, which he said was a form of discretionary entry. There had been bitter debate, I gathered, behind the screens, and I had barely avoided the most ignominious return journey to London, perhaps in the care of an armed guard. He frowned, sniffed, scribbled on the form – looked through my passport – looked at me – folded the pink form and explosively stapled it inside the passport: and, with a sudden decline into total indifference, turned away.

I seemed to have been admitted to Canada.

My old friend James Lyme said they'd never had this trouble

before. A dyspeptic official, perhaps? He had his daughters with him. I'd known them as tiny creatures in England, and here they were, substantial creatures in Canada, grown as native as Canada geese. They took me to my hotel on English Bay, and James's daughter Kitty declared she'd forgotten how marvellous a hotel was. Oh look, she said, trying to take in my huge room at a glance, you won't know whether to lounge on that enormous sofa or sit all day writing at that beautiful desk. I might go to bed, I said. The bed was too much, said Kitty. With that sofa and that desk – and look here, this immense bathroom, where you could happily shower from morning to night – who wanted a bed?

I did, and would have slept in it for ever, except for the plumbing. This was in collusion with the immigration officer, and throughout the next twelve hours or so gurgled and thumped its intention of sending me back to Britain in elaborate disgrace.

And in the morning, the afternoon, the evening, whatever it was, Kitty came and reminded me, gently, of the route to take if one wanted to walk in Stanley Park.

It isn't really exactly as it was when Vancouver sailed in: but Stanley Park is less unlike the original site of Vancouver than anywhere else in that mountain-besotted city. The librarian who drove me every day into the University said it was for her one of life's inexplicable features, that the founding fathers of a community so profoundly materialistic should have agreed to leave so many acres of real estate to trees, little lakes, chipmunks and squirrels. Not a single Canada goose, she said satirically, had ever been known to pay its way on that great thumb of land: but the keen dealers of Vancouver had elected to smile with contentment at the affront to their essential philosophy. As an outsider, a visitor from a tiny, cramped and much-used island, I could only say that I was grateful for the simple existence of Stanley Park. It breathes, it is greatly green, it offers what must be one of the most splendid walks in the world, five kilometres with the best of the sea on one side, and the best of the land on the other: and I trod it, on that visit, with the surprised tread of someone who had been only precariously admitted to Canada at all. I was there on breathtaking sufferance. Kitty said I must not be silly about this: Canada could have no corporate intention of excluding me: and anyway, wasn't I grateful for that unbelievably large bathroom?

Kitty had no touch of whimsicality about her. To her, most of what happened was amazing, but she expected it to be whisked away before she'd been able to focus it. She was one of the most vulnerably eager persons I'd ever known. She reminded me of a general truth about lively adolescence: that you are most painfully in love, and that the object of your love is the world itself. There is nothing anywhere that doesn't make your heart leap – and that includes causes of dismay as well as causes of delight. Kitty's warmth would have embraced, as thoroughly as any other display life had to offer, the end of the world.

When she'd gone, I made my way through the city. This was my third visit, and I partly remembered the place as a setting for lectures. Here , nearly twenty years earlier, I'd talked about the teaching of English to students who were being reared on the notion that the language was a poor relation of mathematics. You numbered the parts of speech and made sentences out of the numbers. Four or five years earlier I'd been here with Rufus: his main talk had been about a story he'd always meant to write but had never written, and was hilariously about the question that for Rufus was more important than any other: When does a story work, and when does it not? For so long now I'd observed him with his ear to some tiny fragment of narration, a little exploratory piece of storytelling machinery, listening for the sound of ticking. Sometimes he'd raise it to my ear and I'd seem to detect a distinct tick. But Rufus would shake his head. It wasn't, he'd murmur, a tick that would last two hundred pages. In Vancouver he'd talked of blundering into this beautifully promising but unsuccessful story that had dogged him for so long. At moments when he felt particularly pleased with himself he'd be aware of it grinning nastily at him from some shadowy corner of his mind. Listening to him discussing it was like hearing Stradivarius talk of the one violin of his making from which he'd not been able to scrape a decent note. Though what I remembered as much as anything was Rufus's legs. Below the table at which he was standing I watched them behave like nerve-racked pipecleaners, anxiously twining. A lecturer has to work hard to prevent his legs from offering a counter-lecture, all about his inner tensions. I'd thought once of a five-minute film that might be made in which you *heard* someone giving a public address, but *saw* only the attempts of his legs to knot themselves together and bring him down.

My own main talk on that occasion had been at a lunch given by a municipality to whom one conference must have looked much like another, there never being fewer than half a dozen of them causing acclamatory flags to be flown on the city's bridges. It was a dry lunch. There was a provincial embargo on alcohol on public occasions, so that amazing improbabilities were to be glimpsed in terms of citizens of the most evident worldliness throwing back bumpers of orange juice. I'd been expected to be solemn, I imagine, but it struck me that on such an occasion the case against sobriety ought to be made, if possible: and I'd scribbled out a sort of poem, called *The Lecturer's Confession*: which I had with me in Vancouver on this latest visit, ready to use if need be, as someone on a dangerous mission might carry a suicide pill. It contained, as it happened, references to John Logan and Percy Chew: but also to various horses I'd known when very small, and had not otherwise been able to celebrate.

> I remember (it went), it was some barely credible year like 1929,
> Old Mrs Brown, only I suppose she wasn't as old as I thought –
> At that time I believed anyone discernibly over twenty was preparing for the dark –
> I remember how she read to us, always at the day's end:
> The marvellous day's end, with Arithmetic behind us,
> Transcription behind us – truly, in those days, we did something called Transcription,

And I have an old exercise book in which I've solemnly printed the word
At the top of pages that were clearly copyings from the board –
Fancy letting us into the secret that Transcription was the word for that! –
Well, with those behind us, and Spelling too, and what we called History,
Of which I mostly remember: *Battle of Barton, 1471* . . .
The school was in Barton, you see,
And we had the good luck to have this bit of history on the doorstep,
Which made the whole business slightly easier to believe in –

Though I confess it was years before I really believed it had taken place –
For a long time, for me, History was a story they'd hurriedly thought up to fill the gap before I arrived, in 1920 –

Anyway, at the marvellous day's end, when the gas was lit, and
Between me and mum and tea there was only the squabbling peril of the journey home,
Then it was that Mrs Brown read to us: *Black Beauty*, I remember.
Without the slightest intention of disrespect, I must say I thought Mrs Brown *was* Black Beauty.
Nothing terribly wrong about equating a teacher much-loved with a horse of such sensitivity . . .

Even now, as I think of it, the story gathers around me, I am inside it, I cannot tell myself apart from the story,
And that's how it is when we read with warmth, to children:
As Mrs Brown did, in her round, clear, comforting voice . . .

I remember seeing the words, as she read them, going together,
Coming together, making sentences, paragraphs, chapters.

I think Mrs Brown believed she taught us about sentences and paragraphs
At the other, less marvellous end of the day, when she waxed so solemn
About commas, full stops, and i before e, except after c,
And all those circular statements about the adjective,
Which described . . . because it described . . . because it described . . .
Which was all due to its being . . . a describing word.

She also read us *Jackanapes*, by Mrs Ewing.
After I'd got over the surprise of a writer being called Mrs,
Which, after all, made her just like my mum
And Mrs Brown, who'd never written a book in their lives –
I think I believed a teacher who wrote a book might have got into trouble for it –
It wasn't what she was there for –
Well, as I say,
After I'd got over that, I enjoyed so very much the strange Victorian
Air of the story, the little boy on his horse . . .
My goodness, we were reared on the horse, if you see what I mean.
But then, we actually had horses all round us in those days.
One of my earliest memories – the milkman telling my mum
'Your little boy's scared of my horse.' He was right.
I was worried by the way it would explode through its nostrils,
Make its entire and quite remarkably long body quiver,
And sometimes urinate with shameless vehemence.

But oh, all that reading: all that being read to!
I sometimes say the task of the teacher seems
Enormously simple. All that he has to do
(And by 'he' I mean 'she' – I suppose we *shall* solve that problem)
Is to share his feeling for books.
And reading aloud
Is one of the best of methods, and only requires

That one learn to read aloud well.
Oh, I remember
Discovering *that* when I went to teach in London,
In a battered corner of London, where few of my boys
Knew what a sentence was, or a paragraph.
I tried to make them easier about spelling by telling them that Keats
Couldn't spell: but it didn't help. They just didn't know
Who Keats was. Most of them would have said
They didn't know what Keats were . . .

We had a Head then, nice man, who regrettably held
That reading aloud was the softest of options for class and teacher.
You could read aloud on the very last day of term, but only
Then if the class had been almost unimaginably saintly.
A wandering head: he used to come and look
Through the glass panels in the classroom doors: would go away quite happy
If he saw what he wanted: boys glumly agog, or scribbling,
Teacher eloquent, or writing on the board,
Or peering over shoulders as *they* wrote . . .

It was there that I learned to read aloud without seeming to do so.
Thank you, old difficult sir.

It's really all that I know about reading and children.
It all depends on someone warmly reading,
Which in itself gives rise, quite naturally, to warm listening.

I had an Irish teacher once who threw a book in my lap
On his way to the platform for morning assembly.
'Sssh!' he said. 'Keep it quiet!' It was *Tess of the D'Urbervilles*,
And forty years too late to hush *that* up!
But what an agreeable sense of conspiracy!
He, and the boys he lent books to, against the world!
(And against the Head, who believed the English literary innings had ended with Kipling:
Nobody since had gone to the crease in whites:

D. H. Lawrence in his cloth cap, and Aldous Huxley
Who didn't even know how to hold the bat . . .)

It's really all I know about reading and children.
That warm sharing
And sense, perhaps, of conspiracy . . .

Sometimes I'm asked to talk about the young and their reading.
And golly, I amaze myself,
Stretching these few simple thoughts over as many as a couple of most solemn hours!

3

When I'd written in a book, once, about the comedy of going abroad to lecture, a reviewer had taken the opportunity to sigh over me, saying that sort of thing was always a vexation to the lecturer, who did it only to help pay his rates or finance a holiday in Greece. This, though I'd made it clear that I'd enjoyed even the exhaustions, and hadn't earned enough to finance a day's outing to Clacton.

It *is* an odd enterprise, inviting people from distant places to come and talk: and springs largely from a convention that any reputable institution is bound to have courses of lectures, and that the prestige of the most prestigious of these might rest on the lecturers having been uncomfortably summoned from the ends of the earth. My present hosts made no secret of the fact that some invitations under the Distinguished Visitors scheme had been disastrous. Lecturers had been inaudible, incomprehensible, and unreasonable as to the expenses they piled up at their hotels. They had made amazing demands, and some had been distinctly impolite. A few had found it difficult to get out of bed. I hoped to avoid these defects, but imagined I would have flaws of my own to offer. For example,

I lectured happily off the top of my head if I was given a suitably eager-looking audience seated in a casual way close at hand. I was less happy when talking to audiences that, before I opened my mouth, looked sorry that they'd come. I know that people can look like this, wear expressions of frozen distaste, frown disgustedly at the lecturer as they wait for him to rise to his feet, and yawn at his first words, and still be inwardly friendly, keen and deeply glad they chose to spend their time in this fashion. But appearances matter, and I depended on being enthusiastic in response to enthusiasm, embodied in bright faces and receptive postures. I've felt from time to time less like a lecturer appraising his audience than like a condemned man forming strong dislikes as to the features of members of the firing squad.

But most of the time I deeply enjoyed this odd undertaking. It seemed an opportunity to shake such ideas as you had into new combinations as a result of presenting them aloud to actual ears. It also made it possible to blunder into new ideas. It was only by lecturing to teachers that I'd discovered what essentially I thought about teaching: that it was a tension between method and improvisation: or that I believed good teaching occurred when you'd forgotten you were a teacher.

But, as I walked about the city, the fact that I was there to lecture was soon buried under the sensations that followed from being reminded that this was a city with seagulls. It was, like Sydney, a great city wedded to the sea. The air that blew up these glass-lined streets was ocean-air. I found my feet had taken me in a circle back to Stanley Park, to those fat tumblings of geese and ducks: and I looked across a lake from that world of birds to the towering nests of human beings, and thought that I came so far to lecture, of course, from being flattered by the invitation: and because, much of the time, I enjoyed public speaking: and also because I had affection for James Lyme, his daughters and his wife, – the last coming from Yorkshire and longing to be there still, but understanding how rapidly deep the roots had gone that this English family had put down, in the most tentative spirit, a decade before. This coast captivates. Mae Gloucester Graham, whom I was soon to visit in San Francisco, had travelled from

New York thirty years earlier, on a visit, and never for a moment wished to return.

I came lecturing, when I got to the bottom of it, to breathe this air, be momentarily among these glass towers, be encircled for a week or so by these mountains: from my hotel window to look out across English Bay to the horizon, where one evening, caught in the stark silver light of the sun's rays striking through clouds curiously purplish-brown, a whole regatta of minute sailing boats appeared, blanched ladybirds with their wings raised for unfolding.

What the programme called a colloquium, which I thought must be a discussion, turned out to be a soliloquy. Programme-makers aim at grandeur. Little meetings in back rooms are seminars. Casual engagements with individuals are interlocutions. Once again I began to be Dr Blishen. I'd met before this determination to give titles to lecturers: I'd been Dr and Professor, haphazardly, in various parts of North America and Africa, and on one occasion, on grounds never made clear, had been Dean. These are not imputations easy to resist: it seems oddly pretentious, fussy, even ungrateful, to say, however gently: 'I am not a Doctor, you know'. 'Really, I'm *not* a Dean!' I was among librarians-to-be, and was asked to talk to a group austerely concerned with cataloguing: much, I thought, as a belly-dancer might be brought great distances to a theological college, to give a glimpse of other things.

And I worried all the time about the official illegitimacy, or barest legitimacy, that had been laid upon me by the immigration officer. I had given him, for the date of my leaving Canada, the date when I'd be going to the States: forgetting I had to return to Canada to catch my plane home from Vancouver. There seemed a large possibility of discovering that I'd made the wrong move on that arbitrary board, and might find myself nobody, nowhere. What happened, I'd think in the middle of the night, if you couldn't return to the States, and could neither enter nor leave Canada?

My public lecture offered the environment I'm worst at: a

lofty platform, a reading stand, a distant audience, and a very long and wantonly eloquent introduction that made me feel an ass. No one was ever the sort of man described, and if he had existed no one could be forgiven for going to hear him. It was a relief to find myself, at the reception afterwards, talking to a former Briton who on my earlier visit with Rufus had sent us home with a message for Scotland Yard. There had been reports of corruption among the Metropolitan Police: which had been a grief to Britons trapped in alien corners of the earth. For God's sake, it was difficult enough keeping the flag flying there! 'Tell'em,' he urged me, 'to pull their socks up!' And, seeming to fear that, with all the savage regions of Canada to pass through, only one of us might make it home, he entrusted the message also to Rufus, but with a variation. 'Tell'em,' he said, 'to bloody well remember who they are!'

This time, his champagne glass aslant, he had a general message for the British people. 'Tell 'em Trudeau's *a bloody Frenchman!*'

4

Someone once told me that, statistically speaking, any one person on the face of the earth was connected with any other by an average of no more than six steps of acquaintance. I expect it's all nonsense: but wherever I went I found people who knew people I knew. I also, very simply, found people I knew. Everyone becomes aware that the overbrimming world is also a small world. At a road block in some extreme corner of Nepal our next-door neighbour in Barley Wood, who spent his life mapping extreme corners, had found his car alongside one driven by a young man who until a few weeks before had run our local off-licence. And, bound from London to Vancouver to lecture that week in the University of British Columbia, I'd discovered that my cousin Bobbie was bound to Vancouver from Toronto to lecture during the same week at the next-door University of Victoria.

But Coincidence might, as Bobbie had said, be our second name. People had a tendency, having bumped into him in the extreme north-west of Canada, where he was engaged part of the time in a study of an Indian community, to rush off at once to bump into me in the smallest and least-visited village in Suffolk. And there was the extraordinary story of my arrival for the first time in Vancouver nearly twenty years earlier.

Bobbie was then a teacher in the university: and, so that I could visit him, had traded my services as a lecturer in a department or two in return for my air ticket from Montreal. I was then, as it were, the university's Doubtfully Distinguished Visitor. I was largely known for being known to Bobbie. He'd picked me up at the airport and driven me home by way of his office, where he had papers to collect. He went in; leaving me to run a nervous eye over a noticeboard in the corridor. I had the old teacher's fear that, even 5,000 miles from home, any of the notices displayed in an educational institution might concern me, and might require that I take a class in almost any subject, almost at once.

What happened when Bobbie went into his office was that his secretary asked: 'Professor Blishen, have you a relative called Edward Blishen?'

It was, that day, more than thirty-four years since we'd last met. That had been in Southsea: Bobbie was a six-year-old in the uncomfortable home of his father, my Uncle George, who, on his way to producing eleven children, was also on his way to abandoning one marriage, and its eleven products, in favour of another, socially more splendid one. It was as a result of that dramatic moment of upward mobility for Uncle George, and downward and mostly tempestuous mobility for his children, that Bobbie had arrived in Canada. I was a six-year-old visitor to Southsea, bemused by that large household, run during the day virtually by the children. I barely knew Bobbie from his siblings, except by that physical simplification by which small children tend to identify one another: he was a short-sided square.

So it was reasonably startling that Bobbie's secretary

should choose *this* day to ask *that* question. Why had she asked it? Well, she said, she'd been reading a piece in the *Guardian Weekly* written by someone of that name: and since it was an unusual one, she'd wondered if there was some connection.

'Come in, Edward,' said Bobbie.

Which was where decent coincidence would halt. But the piece the secretary had been reading was an account of that unforgettable class of mine, the one Jack Seed belonged to and that existed, as a group of voluntary stayers-on, because of the gentle brightness of Peter Higgins. Professor Higgins, his friends called him: this being, as they understood it, the usual title for someone naively brilliant, for whom admiration was mercifully diluted with tolerant fondness. For the sketch in the *Guardian* I'd renamed him Crumb. This seemed as unlikely name as any. The piece was headed: PROFESSOR CRUMB & CO.

In the corner of the room in which the secretary was sitting was a door that led to the office of the head of another university department. On the door was his name: PROFESSOR CRUMB.

5

We met on a Saturday morning, the short-sided square and (Bobbie's parallel impression of fifty years before) the thin rectangle, and it was much like being in Southsea again. The resemblance came down to a childish sense of being free for the day. It was a good, blue day, and we meant simply to drift, talking, round Stanley Park. I told Bobbie, to start with, how I'd mentioned to the lecturer who drove me into the university every day that I intended to spend the weekend with him. What was he? Oh, he was a sociologist. Next day she was reproachful. She'd done what a trained librarian couldn't avoid doing: she'd looked him up. 'Your cousin,' she said 'is not just a sociologist! He's a distinguished sociologist!' The six-year-olds in us cackled. Bobbie said he had a pale sort of postscript for that story, anyway. He'd once rashly confessed to dismay about his reputation in the presence of his numerous daughters, on vacation from various universities. At one time he'd had some clout as a radical sort of social scientist, he said, but was horrified to find that students now regarded him as a pillar of the Establishment. He appealed to a random daughter. 'Is that how they think of me at Queen's, Sally?' 'I don't think they know about you at Queen's, dad,' said Sally. 'Oh *no*!' Bobbie said he felt like a man who, resigned to stepping into a puddle, had stumbled into a pond. 'Oh no, not *that*!' He'd turned to the tenderest of his offspring. 'Janie, do they know who I am at McGill?' 'No, dad,' said Janie. 'Who are you?'

Reputation, we agreed, was no subject for such a morning. To our right, as we began our walk, the watery way into the city: the boats and the tall towers seemed alike sailing things: their reflections bobbed together. Over there, the coastal mountains, for which my cousin never ceased to yearn, as the fringe of the monumental emptiness – and even unmappedness – where he'd spent the happiest days of his life, dispatched by Uncle George to make his future as far from home as possible. The expenses of exile had not fallen heavily on my uncle: an emigrant's ticket on the boat, and the coins in fifteen-year-old Bobbie's pocket, had amounted to ten pounds, at most. The trouble was that, being given the huge freedom of Canada at such an age, Bobbie had found the rest of his life, including the surprised ascent into distinction, a sort of further exile. As we walked by the water that morning, he spoke longingly of what lay beyond, of days passed without seeing another human being, of feeling some kind of immense healthy insignificance: a human insect crossing the great floors between mountains.

Alas, I said: and then remembered how I'd noticed that I used this word rather often when reviewing. If I had to say I didn't like a book or a part of it, I said alas. Sometimes you caught yourself using a word that pointed to something in you there was no hope of escaping. I'd no prospect of feeling anything but sorry if I had to speak badly of almost anyone. Oh, the apologisers! Suddenly I saw how many of us there were, people with a limited gift of severity. It *was* a weakness: how ridiculous to respond to what you thought to be a bad book with a cry of 'Boo, alas!' I confided the thought to Bobbie: and we imagined an apologetic devil, standing at the reception desk in Hell and welcoming newly arrived damned souls: '*Hallo, alas*!'

We were turning on the tip of the walk round Stanley Park, ready to exchange the view of the north shore for a view of the open sea, and then of the low land on which the university stood. I had now remembered the woman who'd written to me, having oddly elected to count the number of times I'd said 'in fact' in a series of discussion programmes. In the limited time occupied by those programmes I'd used 'in fact' more often than you'd think anyone would use it in a year. For weeks after she wrote to me I'd walked about barely speaking, for fear an 'in fact' should escape me. Even now I was subject to whole discharges of it. What deficiency in me required that I shore up whatever I said with this reach-me-down buttress of a phrase? Bobbie quoted Canon Chasuble: 'I myself am peculiarly susceptible to draughts.' Was it possible that Genghis Khan suffered agonies because of some tiny private weakness: for him, enough to neutralise his public strength? Oh Lord, everyone surely had this intimate, contemptuous knowledge of some trivial frailty in himself, or herself, that ruined everything! Bobbie said there was an Indian legend about that rock over there, but he'd forgotten it. His own weakness of this kind, more dismaying than his huger defects, was that, having all his life taken such conscious care to know as much as he could, he'd been the victim of a subconscious self that had thrown his knowledge away as fast as it was acquired. I knew the image for that: the little English husband in Tati's *M. Hulot's Holiday* who, following in the tracks of his bullying wife, took from her hand the pebbles she proffered with a cry of 'Beautiful!' and, without a glance at them, hurled them into the sea.

Among us, as we walked, cyclists and joggers. Most of

Vancouver was running or pedalling. We were passed by compact bottoms, a bobbing trimness of breasts, an endless rotation of slim legs, and felt ourselves, by comparison, simply physically untidy. Age made the parcel sprawl. But now we'd completed this beautiful noose of a walk on the north-western tip of the device provided by geography to enable Uncle George to lighten his load of children (Canada not having received Bobbie alone): and made our way to a hotel on English Bay for lunch.

And in the afternoon, walking along a street whose name I loved, it had a touch of such careless pioneering extravagance about it . . . walking along Georgia West, we were greeted from the other pavement with a cry of 'Hi!' It was another exiled Blishen, a sister of Bobbie's, unmet for years. The odds against three people with the same uncommon name, lodged in widely different parts of the world, running into one another on Georgia West on any Saturday afternoon whatever, must be immense. Only the fact that we had become hardened to coincidence made it possible for us to carry off the occasion with a sort of worldly grace: which would have amazed, and perhaps saddened, our selves of 1926.

6

The Canadian National Station on Main, not yet open – I'd arrived nervously early: but there was a dining-room full of the cheerfulness of railwaymen. It was a cavern in which jokes echoed. A pink-haired woman, bound for Portland, with teeth improbably regular, said she was English, too, wished she could afford to return: but then, who'd want to live in a London that was in the hands of the blacks? I said that wasn't true, but she didn't seem accustomed to discussion in which propositions were resisted: she smiled, and said perhaps she was better off in Vancouver. Everything she said was commonplace, and after ten minutes my mind ached.

Then I was in the lofty Amtrak train, at the upper level, and we were stirring backwards, through a tangle of rails. The city, its towers blinking, had suddenly gone, and the mountains on the skyline, where a slow apricot of sunrise was spreading, had lost their splendour. In that yawning dawn, everything, however actually huge, was diminished and made doubtful, and for a moment the mountains had the petty outlines of slag heaps.

And then we were going forwards: light had taken possession of the day, and the train was announcing its advance in a deep, remote, thrilling bay, as if the driver had access to a particularly fine organ-pipe. Outside, as we brayed and droned through the world of factories, dumps, sheds, yards brimming with industrial debris, all that could stiffen was stiff with ice. In the sky a corridor of pale blue separated solid leadenness, in one direction, from a sort of puckered pewter.

So far, I thought, so dreary, on such a frostily grey morning. Here came the sea, here came more mountains, but they didn't make up for the human muddle in the foreground. And here was the border, and another immigration officer. In his shack on the station he unfolded my enormous pink notice of discretionary entry to Canada, it was as if my passport contained a comic item of underwear, and asked how I thought I was going to fly home from Vancouver on the 26th if I had to leave Canada on the 15th. I thought he was far more likely to know the answer to such a question than I was: but I offered the idea that I should then only be in transit. I shouldn't legally be in Canada at all. He made no observation on this, but admitted me to America. I wondered if I might lose the form, so avoiding some abstruse squabble on my return, but decided that, in this game governed by such slippery rules, it might be better to keep it.

To one side of us, there was now continuous leaden sea. Seattle, said the car-attendant, was under snow. There'd been icy rain in Portland. 'Better go back to Vancouver.' His voice was an easy bass. We brayed without stop, a clamour from our bowels. And stray dots of snow in the towns, a wind-made white scribble on the streets, had turned into a steady fall. ADVENTURE IN MOVING, it said on the brows of abandoned removal vans. FOOD AND GAS – NEXT EXIT. How spare, as well as adipose, the American tongue could be. SNOHOMISH COUNTY. Indeed!

It was farming country, clapboard, silent machinery. PURINA CHOWS. WOLFKILL. Was it still snowing, or was there only this cloud of snow already fallen that we were flinging around us as we went? UNAUTHORISED CARS WILL BE IMPOUNDED. EBBTIDE FLOTATION MATTRESSES. VETERANS' HALL. Nothing but graveyards of cars, with bonnets yawning. SOPER TOWING MARYSVILLE. The snowy bones of boats in reeds among pools filled with logs, snow-white. BUT HE WAS WOUNDED FOR MY TRANSGRESSIONS – the whole verse on a huge billboard, in red and white. Suddenly, nothing but boatyards. Bleak – but a beautiful bleakness. It was all sorts of variations on a morose theme. Exhilaratingly sombre, actually, because so persistent and yet so various. A morning in America, I thought, made wonderfully silent by winter!

At home sometimes Kate would protest when I read out the signs, the hoardings, the shopnames as they flew past. But, unable anyway to resist words, I felt that places were spelling themselves out with this absurd accidental poetry of commercial and other assertions. The country muttered at you as you went by. And this, today, was a foreign mutter.

We stammered over an iron bridge, and I was amazed by the heavy way the water below made folds of itself until I looked back and saw the tug that was causing that oily quilting. Here, under bridge after iron bridge, a gathering of surely a high proportion of all the iron bridges in the world, the water was the colour of tar. With our low-spirited blare, we probed this dank land: and it struck me that all the five hundred hotels in Portland might be full, and that I should freeze to death, watched thoughtfully by assorted immigration officers.

How easy, I thought, to read. Settle back and sleep. But I

would never come this way again: I was being offered this daylong intimate view of other people's world. The people, at this moment, of Everette, Washington. A tall man in a blazer superbly red was superintending the brief ceremony of embarkation. An effect of being so high, on the upper level of the train, was that you thought the people on the platform would need stilts to get aboard. But now they were with us and we were away, moving alongside a tremendous bank whiskered with icicles. And the sea had reappeared, wintrily stagnant. Small birds seemed to be frozen into it. We were in a sudden hurry to get away from Everette, which went in for some gloomy form of manufacture involving immense containers, round and tubular. Vats?

And now, backwards down a road, on toboggans, came half a dozen children. Dressed in bright wool, they were merry, intent on creating disasters for one another. There was a furiously laughing spill, and legs waving out of a snowdrift. I had a sudden impression of the way children occupied their own world, which seemed to be ours, but wasn't. They existed inside some great bubble of excitement, and we'd long gone to live elsewhere.

Edmunds, which had a marvellous view of the sea: at the moment, resembling a huge plate of lead. The sky was of the same heavy metal, so that the exact line of the horizon was anyone's guess.

PLEASE PARK AND LOCK.

The conductor said: 'Columbus discovered America in 1492, and the old cars on this line were built in 1493.' Said a woman passenger: 'Suppose some of us on this train were to go home and tell our children what you've told us!' I thought in England it might be claimed the carriages were built in 1067. Not that I could imagine a guard on the line between Barley Wood and Kings Cross making such a joke.

The conductor of an Amtrak was a jester. He went in, I thought, for a tender sort of teasing that was perhaps specially American. Well, here was a girl coming towards him. He demanded: 'Where are you going?' She pointed nervously forward in the direction in which she was obviously travelling. 'There!' And he stood gravely aside: 'You'd got me worried!'

And Seattle. THE OLD SPAGHETTI FACTORY. Where they made old spaghetti? And a switch of train, which meant we were now on the COASTAL STARLIGHT, the twinkling train to Los Angeles, which would take four hours to reach Portland. We lumbered out of the station, passing THRIFT STORE, EASY UP SHELVING and FISHER BAG CO. A train went past in the other direction, and I noticed it had a DORM CAR, which clearly wasn't a sleeping car, because it had those too. What did you do in a dorm if you slept elsewhere?

LUSTER-GLO CLEANERS. Everything brimmed with grey water. Said a voice behind me: 'It's Puddle Park!'

At Tacoma it was raining great quantities of near-ice. I went to the snack bar, several cars back, and was served by a young man who thought it was marvellously sensible of me to be going to San Francisco. Suddenly, poignantly, I missed Kate. It was because I knew she'd enjoy the ham-and-cheese sandwich, and the pleasant box in which I carried it and my coffee back to my seat. She'd have enjoyed the doors you had to negotiate: which, where a handle might be, had a blank oblong marked PRESS: you pressed, and they sighed apart. It was the exotic character of the trivial differences between familiar ways of doing things and unfamiliar ones – it was *that* that made travel thrilling. An exoticism of the unimportant! I ridiculously wanted Kate to be here to make an Amtrak door open with a sigh.

The sea again. Misty pewter. FROG LEGS 3.98 SQUID SALAD 4.95. The sea was old copying ink. I settled down to study the sea, and at once we left it. I settled down to study the land, and the sea was there again. In it, a wooded island, a blur. Connected to where we were by an immense suspension bridge: the biggest *misty* suspension bridge I'd ever seen.

And now the sea was crowded, with swimming birds that appeared to be, simply, too small for it. A flat blurred silver was the edge of the Pacific: against it, the stark black of jetties was extraordinarily thrilling. I was thinking how totally black and grey and silver it all was, and at once we were running alongside a river that was pea-green. It was easy to see it as a river of soup. And the train entered woodland; it was like riding in an American train through Barley Woods. And here we were at a station improbably called Centralia. If I jumped straight down on to the platform, I'd break my neck.

The way people walk, I suddenly thought, was expressive of their environment. Well, I couldn't see how an American walking along a railway-platform could be mistaken for anyone but an American. It struck me that travelling gave you at times a faintly resentful sense of difference. How dared they insist on being Americans? It was a feeling I'd sometimes had when I was with Bobbie. There was a sense in which I resented his electing to be Canadian, and suspected that he resented my choosing to be English.

I'd learned by now not to make a generalisation: it instantly failed. So the country was more open: but at once it was less open. We were in woods again, ensnared in a dark net of trees. As that gave way at last, the conductor was back, making bird noises with a gadget he held in his hand. A number of little girls, whose mothers had subjected them throughout the journey to hygienic inquiries ('Do you have to go to the bathroom or not?'), were astonished. The conductor hoped they'd not brought any ducks on the train, it was absolutely not allowed: and at once he made duck noises with the gadget. As she advanced to declare that she was not deceived, I saw that one little girl was wearing a T-shirt announcing, in many colours: I'M A GREAT KID, NATURALLY.

I'd always think of this part of the world as the country of the piledriver. Over the years, forests of wood had been driven into the water, had supported jetties, quays, warehouses, boathouses, and had reverted to being stumps of wood growing out of water. It was as if a whole civilisation based on the pier and the jetty had vanished. This was country that had been enormously tinkered with, and in which they didn't just build a factory: for here now was the biggest factory building imaginable, and they'd multiplied it by twelve, and surrounded the entire thing with a fence. We took hours going past it: part of that time being passed ourselves by a goods train, brisk, everlasting. Long after I'd concluded that there was probably no end to it, it went, and the boundless factory was still there.

No, you couldn't say they tinkered with this land. They dug it hugely up, they flattened it, they made hills level and turned every level into a mound. Everywhere, great earth-shifting machines.

Two of the mothers in the car, known to each other for two hours, were already years old in acquaintance. At times their conversation suggested an encounter between two women's magazines. 'I should have worked for years before getting married.' And sudden, strong, not wholly agreeable shared laughter. One had a little girl, Tasha: named, the mother suddenly said, after the heroine of *War and Peace*. Tasha was not being amiable to the other woman's small daughter. Her mother said: 'Tasha! Tasha, be gentle!' Then: 'We like to be kind and gentle to our friends.' This was clearly not what Tasha liked, at all.

A big hook of green river, and whole ballets of seagulls being enacted above it – a flutter wild and white above this strong green flow. And then a wood in which every tree had fallen down. A pipeline perfectly occupied, in the manner of a sort of Athenaeum, by seagulls. A piledriver simply, and sufficiently, named AMERICAN. Another goods train: the trucks like some crazy gazeteer, shouting SOUTHERN PACIFIC, COTTON BELT, SANTA FE. A sudden, brief but stupendous grove of dogwood. A flotilla of swans, and another, and another. And the bad weather closing in, as inglorious as a dirty handkerchief.

For five minutes I was busy with my guide to Portland, and looked up to see, too late, the one photograph I might have taken that would have summed up the whole journey. A wide gunmetal river: black stumps of piers in the right hand bottom corner: a silvering to nothing at the top: and, over to the left, the long flat shape of a building, an amazing bright apricot in the mist.

And we were in Portland.

All I'd ever remember of Portland, Oregon, was that it rained.

7

Airborne, I found myself raging at the immaculacy of American men. Their clothes always looked amazed at finding themselves in use. They could allow themselves to be walked up and down the streets of Portland and still seem to be hanging in the shops from which they were purchased. As against this instant and enduring dapperness, I was crumpled and stained: here and there, unspeakable.

But now we were over immense amounts of snow-covered mountains, even more crumpled than I was. And that was the Pacific below, interrupted by tiny clusters of rock. Sallowed by sunshine, it looked like nothing so much as stagnant cream. And *that* must be San Francisco! It was, I saw at once, a very large silicon chip. More evidence for my theory that the extremely small, however recently devised, always resembled the extremely large, however well-established. And now I saw the Golden Gate Bridge. It looked as if it must be the longest straight red line in the world.

This, said Henry, was the city he was comfortable in. Mae chuckled. We were inside the silicon chip, on one of its ribs, driving towards infinite quantities of sky: and Henry was deeply happy, showing me the city in which he felt so tremendously at home.

He'd lived there for a great many years, but it wasn't simply that. It was, he said, grasping the exaggerated steering wheel of his overblown motorcar – he'd been interested in my sensation of being very much a Gulliver in very much a Brobdingnag – that San Francisco was remarkably accommodating to human beings. It had this grand scale, and it also had . . . a great variety of modest scales within it. Henry sketched out the edge of this idea, and abandoned it in favour of recommending this view, that view. *There* was the fairly new building that looked so much like a sharp stick up the arse that he'd decided to resort to euphemism, and called it the great suppository in the sky. And here, as we shed the grand city and sped into the grand suburbs, was Grape Valley. It was a sort of Californian Hampstead: you climbed above a centre where good books could be bought alongside good cheese, and parked unbelievably in a coil of a green helter-skelter to climb the one hundred and twenty steps to the wooden house that was Mae's and Henry's. In their back garden was a small mountain. The house smelt of oranges.

Of course, said Henry, whose life had been uneasy enough, it wasn't as idyllic as all that: and he took me round his shelves, full of books and tapes that were fruit of the discomfort of being a sceptical American in an age of Americans affecting the other posture. Henry, whose father came from Lithuania and whose mother came from Russia, had been wrongfooted by almost every important all-American attitude since the radical moment of the 1930s came to an end: but what moved me on, and from, my first evening in Grape Valley was the absolutely American character of Henry's wrongfootedness. His critical view of this experimental continent was squarely based on his profound love of it.

Well, love – it was always domestic, wasn't it? It was always, given, in the first place, to your backyard. And, if you lived in San Francisco or near it, your backyard was a somewhat astonishing one. Henry took me to a hilltop and we looked down on the dense spread of the white city, lying bright and busy on its fatal site. What price underpinning here! There were schools closed for earthquake proofing, though that might have been a cover-up for a simple need to close schools. Look, said Henry, not concealing the jubilation it caused him to have this immense scene to display to a dazzled newcomer, look at the sea, the way it shapes the city – which is really only a small intricate one surrounded on three sides by water, with a population of less than a million. Look at the hills stretching away over there, beyond the great bridge, like the rumps of many lions with their heads down and their tails coiled!

If you like reading the signs and slogans aloud as you go, do that, said Henry. Yes, they do speak of a place! CALIFORNIA'S MOST ADULT ADS. HAVE A PRIVATE TALK WITH A LIVE NAKED GIRL. SENSUOUS LIVE BURLESK. HOT WILD STRIPPERS. MAN AND WOMAN LOVE ACT. Well, yes, said Henry. Let's go to Muir Woods, where there is nothing to read at all.

Nothing in Muir Woods but the redwoods, most of them four thousand years old, unspeakably patient vegetables, and the transient bay trees that stretch long pale arms in and out of the shade of them, in search of light. I can't imagine that the sense of peace the woods offer is exceeded anywhere in the world: it's reinforced by the absence of birds, who'd be poisoned by the tannin in the bark of the redwoods. Though peace may not be the word: it is whatever emotion is created when we're in the presence of living things forty or fifty times as old as the oldest of us. Near the entrance there's the cross-section of a fallen tree, marked so that you can see where, quite deep in among the rings, 1066 is to be found: that profoundly American date. I thought, walking here, of Bobbie and his feeling as a boy at large in the Rockies of the essentially healthy character of his sensations of insignificance.

It struck me also what a simple dizziness it was, when you thought of it or saw it embodied in someone as vividly alive as Henry – that taking of old European patterns of thought and feeling to a continent that, for all the way that man has swarmed over it, has an essential remoteness from him. Here was Henry – Lithuania, Russia and briefly the East End of London – making his profound home at the edge of a land monstrously unEuropean! And, given that the meaning of the word 'safe' has been so enfeebled, it's nevertheless true that London in the valley of the Thames looks safer by far than New York between its rivers, infinitely safer than San Francisco, waiting for the next impersonal shudder of the rock below it.

Henry had paid a price for being a lively exile, shot through with affection for the land that had embraced him, and furiously at odds with much of its spirit. Brought to California from England as a child, he'd been dismayed by his father's hostility to the country that had received them. Well, it wasn't simple hostility: it was that a European radical couldn't, of course, settle down comfortably with the dominant American philosophy, which was one of believing that untramelled capitalism would provide the road to everlasting contentment. And from the tension between his wish to be at home in America, and his understanding that his father was not (then, at any rate) a man to be at home there, Henry developed a physical twitch, a tic that spoke for a child caught between worlds. And when he went on to be a radical in his father's pattern, a man in whom love was not possible if the right to be critical was excluded from it, he carried the twitch with him. The great thing about him, for me, was that this tic, occurring between one leg of a thought and the other, was purely and agreeably a feature of what Henry was: a man who never accommodated an idea without regard for its opposite. I don't mean he was a balanced man: I mean he had a natural sensation of a man's need, thinking of this, to think also of that.

He was a great storehouse of jokes, but hated the idea of introducing them as such: he gave much thought to steering the conversation in the direction of a joke, his navigation being such that he'd usually be on course for another, and another beyond that. I thought he had no habit of careless assent, and liked that: and also that he had a notable sense of fair play in discussion. He seemed never to forget the silent person in a room. But Mae had another view of this: on his best behaviour, he was wonderful, she agreed: but . . . he had his lapses. At their first meeting, at a dinner party, she'd said: 'You talk of nothing but yourself!' 'Oh,' said Henry. 'Then let's talk of you. What do you think of me?'

Mae said she'd burst into tears if I paid for anything. She even handed me money for my trip on the cable cars. A lean young man with a horsetail of hair flung himself subtly and heavily on the brake, at the very split second when this rocking bobbin of a tram needed it: the bell clanged and the overhead number changed with the selling of every ticket: we rose to the top of a hill to dip marvellously down its other side: one huge prospect was changed in a clanging fraction of a second for another. It's odd to be in a world where crossing oceans in aeroplanes of immoderate size has become a banality, and a ride of a mile or so in a jangling heap of nineteenth-century machinery remains a marvel.

I wished our grandson Tim was with me. He'd have fallen for Henry at once, there being a strong resemblance to a friend with a similar gravelly voice, and a face much like Henry's: which was the Californian landscape in miniature. Of our friend, Tim said: 'I want that man!' and, having him: 'Take off my shoes and socks but don't bite my toes.' We had not expected to have a grandson with the tastes of a decadent Roman Emperor.

We walked one evening on the campus at Berkeley, and, seeing it through my eyes, Henry said: 'This is surely more full of weirdies than anywhere in the world.' Then the twitch occurred and he said: 'But then, I suppose this is a rare sort of place where strange human beings feel perfectly free to declare that that's what they are.'

He'd been an actor and an anthropologist: but I thought, though he'd never been one, that he was of those people who are, really, uncovenanted teachers. Wherever he was, curiosity tended to start up, people began to wonder about this and that, cross-reference occurred, dictionaries appeared. And for nearly seventy years he'd been drifting into inquisitive conversation with strangers. I left him at the end of the Golden Gate Bridge while I walked across it for the first time, and when I came back he was surrounded by a sort of loose seminar: the title for it might have been, 'The Effects of the Horrors of Monetarism on the General Issue of Using a Pedal-Bike on the American West Coast, with a Glance at the Quality of Californian Cheese.'

There was nothing remotely solemn or deliberate about this: Henry was subject to curiosity, and deeply interested in the curiosities of others. It struck me that if the worst ideas about the end were well-founded, and we had to stand about naked waiting to be ill-treated by demons, I'd like to be fairly close to Henry. Whatever good questions could get out of the topic of one's being about to be terminally abused by devils, Henry's presence would ensure it was extracted. We'd burn, laughing.

With his rumble of a voice, he had the good teacher's habit of preceding remarks with a sort of fanfare, some equivalent of the barker's 'Roll up, roll up!' In his case, the phrase was 'I want to tell you . . .' or 'I'd like you to know . . .'

He couldn't climb the local mountain, too demanding on the breath: and a sad place, anyway, for brutal murders had occurred on its gentle slopes, it was a green little mountain become sinister and out of bounds. 'I'm useless!' Henry exclaimed, about not having the breath for it: and added: 'With a flair!'

The Canadian immigration officer looked at my licence for discretionary entry: raised a good-natured eyebrow: and removed it with the air of a doctor cutting out some harmless but tiresome polyp. I expected him to say 'This must have been troubling you!' How could immigration officers at opposite ends of a journey have eyebrows of such conflicting character?

The breakers along the coast had been scratches on blue glass. The sea seemed also to be flawed as glass may be, with white flaws. There'd been a brown scab of mountains, with roads running across them like lashings of handsome rope. And then we'd drilled our way, bumping, down to Vancouver, and the voices of other passengers were insect noises inside my deafness.

And now I was free simply to go home.

PART FIVE

1

The very small, malodorous creature who'd come to me for a cuddle, I reminded myself, was my descendant. He'd be my present age in the year 2034, when I should be 114. My father, if his angry existence had been prolonged, would then have been 141. Meanwhile, Tim sought to spread himself on my chest while he gained strength for another attempt to achieve his newest ambition: which was to commit suicide on our stairs. He was piecing together a world consisting eminently of windows, birds, other moving creatures impatiently defined as guck-gucks, and wee-wee. The latter he regarded as a term covering the major part of human entertainment. Taken away by Kate on one occasion, he'd been disturbed by the thought that I might need consolation for his absence, or some proposal as to how the time might be passed until his return. Head on one side, 'Wee-wee?' he'd suggested.

Across the floor, advancing on one another, heads ready for collision: a dinosaur large and bearded, my son Dan, and a dinosaur tiny and beardless, my grandson Tim.

'Hello, darling,' I'd said absently, passing him on my way to some other part of the house. 'Hello, darling,' he'd replied: acquiring at once any word that was offered. 'Antidisestablishmentarianism,' Kate had said, as a test. He'd floundered, but got the bulk of it.

'Damn it,' wrote John Logan, 'Do you realise that some of my old pupils – who spent less of their youth amid the groves of literature than yourself, and rather more among those groves we know as Barley Woods – are *great*-grandparents! I begin to feel very old!'

It was his 'lettre de château', he said: which I supposed to be (as it was) a letter offering thanks for overnight accommodation. He appeared to have forgiven us the thoughtless modernity of the setting in which we lived. 'My dears,' he said, an old crumpled man with brilliant eyes: and prepared to yield, by way of ingenious forms of refusal, to our offer of the madeira he adored. He'd talk of Yeats and AE and James Stephens, who'd been visitors at the Logan house in Dublin when he was a boy. And he'd talk of Williams, and his unachievement. 'I'd more or less pulled my socks up when he and I first met – but, if I hadn't, Willy would have made me do it, double quick. Oh, were ever a man's socks so down at his ankles, all his life long! A school play once – he'd clean forgotten to order the costumes and wigs! I knew a leading costumier in London – took Willy up there – swore the costumes would be back the day after the last performance – needed by others, you see! A week after school had packed up – urgent message – would I come and clear the stage! Horror upon horror! There were all the costumes, all the wigs, scattered everywhere! Willy – full of the joys of end-of-term – had buggered off to Swansea – Forgive the language, lovely lady!

'And that was his life! That, poor dear man, was his entire existence! All that he promised, all his gifts, left scattered around, while he buggered off – to Swansea, America, France, this place, that place! Dear bugger, for ever buggering off without a thought of the mess he left behind!

'Beautiful lady – once I'm gone you can forget you ever heard the word! – That lovely tight-fisted silly silly bugger, Willy!'

It wasn't the epitaph I'd ever imagined for my old hero and mentor. But it suddenly struck me it might be a thoroughly adequate verdict on most of us. I imagined whole graveyards, entire cathedrals: headstones and monuments bearing, uniformly, the affectionately despairing judgement of descendants: HERE LIES . . . SILLY SILLY BUGGER.

2

I'd hear my own cackle coming through the earphones, and wince. Why, meaning to laugh, did I make that startling noise? And why ask that question, out of all the possible questions? Why um and er as between this word and that, when either would have done? Why, having made my choice, then go for a third word, no better? Why had I always suffered from Roget's-Thesaurus-in-the-head? Why leap in when she was clearly just about to say something strong and surprising? Why mispronounce his name? Why make it clear, every question a caress, that I longed to leap across the studio table and take her in my arms? Why, to leave him with no doubt of my admiration, provide him with such a background of eager grunts and snorts that we might have been recording in a pigsty? Why, even though she was desperately shy, ask questions twice as long as her answers?

Feeling these dissatisfactions, I'd listen to what the producer had made of interviews, mine and those of others, and write an In and an Out for each. The In being a piece as brief as possible, introducing the author and the book and making clear any unexplained allusions in the interview itself. The Out saying, more or less, who and what that had been. All this done at some speed in an open office, in the midst of chatter, telephone calls, the ordinary traffic of such a place. And I'd think at times, with amusement, how at the age of eighteen I'd started work in a weekly newspaper office, and had not at first been able to write a word. I was like a Trappist monk suddenly required to supervise primary school dinners. I'd associated writing with isolation and silence. Nearly forty years later I was still astonished to find that you could put words together, and not unsatisfactorily, in the heart of a hubbub. Miss Baker at Barley Road wouldn't have believed it: her habit when we were writing being to go round her already deeply silent classroom crying 'Hush! *Hush!*' Miss Baker was the creator of the most dense silences I've ever known. The scratch of one's pen was an offence. I'd imagine her on the seventh floor at Bush House, handing out ferocious punishments to gossiping secretaries and producers uttering cries of despair as they attempted, from the endless tape flowing through their machines, to remove the ordinary aberrations of human speech. 'My God!' my producer would cry, perhaps of an interview I'd conducted up the line to Oxford with the world's leading expert on vernacular architecture: whose extremely special eminence had not preserved him from sensations of amazing dread when asked to say a word on radio. His attempts at answers to my questions had deteriorated again and again into high-pitched squeals of total terror. 'My God!' my producer could cry, 'I can't make more than 2′ 10″ of this!' Where the norm was between, say, 3′ 47″ and, say, 4′ 38″, 2′ 10″ was disaster! 'Hush! *Hush!*' would have been Miss Baker's scandalised murmur: and he'd have had this extramural task imposed on him of writing out a hundred times: *I must keep my professional despairs to myself.*

There were times when the prospect of an interview filled me with extraordinary and, at the same time, ridiculous excitement. It was so when I thought I was about to interview Margot Fonteyn, whom I'd first seen on January 2, 1935. On that day my friend Ray Bolton and I had gone to see *Hänsel and Gretel* at the Old Vic: our first opera, about which – owing to a foolishly extravagant gesture on my part as a young diarist – I have little to report. 'There is no need,' I wrote, 'for description of the great opera; I hope I shall see it yet again to describe its splendours in more mature language. The last sweeping note was . . . where an adjective?' Where, indeed, except on the pages where I describe the unexpected accompaniment to this first opera: our first ballet. It was *Uncle Remus*, music by Gordon Jacob. Ray and I were made impatient by the long wait for the curtain to rise: this was a convention not made familiar to us by the Barton Cinema, where the curtains came together only frantically to part again on the sensible grounds that the cinema was constantly filling with new spectators. Ray and I had had little experience of entertainment where the audience was a fixed and slowly assembling quantity of persons. 'At the half hour,' I wrote, 'when our waiting was beginning to pale the wonder to come, the lights aslant from the boxes faded, and the conductor rose to applause. His magic wand flicked, and a low, dull note filled the theatre; it seemed to strike me so forcibly, as if it had obtruded in an unconscious way upon my funny bone, and the culminative [sic] effect of the long wait and the expectant hush and our presence . . . made me laugh. It caught Ray up in a breathless giggle, forced him on, and then turned him into an indignant demon. The impossible prelude over, with much stringing [sic] of fiddles and blowing of French horns [at the time I had absolutely no real knowledge of the nationality of any horn] the curtain rose sibilantly on a scene impossibly meaningless . . .'

Thus, it has to be said – with giggling and wrathful goggling – Ray Bolton, later a man of the gravest reputation in the world of insurance, and I entered upon our cultural inheritance. We made none of those imaginative adjustments that ballet – offering so welcome a release from words – requires us to make. 'Grouped on the stage,' wrote that severe critic once myself, 'were a number of grotesque figures – dancers in quaint animal costumes: the recognisable Uncle Remus, and a young and unmistakeable girl' (ah, the austere indignation lying behind that word 'unmistakeable'!) 'dressed in assuming velvet' (I clearly believed the opposite of 'unassuming' was 'assuming': as I suppose it logically is) 'as the little boy to whom Remus relates his stories. This group stayed for an interminable number of uncertain bars without a quiver – then, with an impossible series of extraordinary bounds, the old man and the little boy who, for the sake of familiar flippancy which must needs be the keynote of this description, I will call by his true name, Susan, leapt to the side of the stage, exchanging confident reminiscences. A wait. Grizzly bars. Then – I refer to the programme and find: "Brer Rabbit gets stuck to the Tar Baby, to the satisfaction of Mr Fox, who has been watching. Mr Bear intervenes." Brer Rabbit . . . leapt with girlish gesture upon a black mass which presumably was the aforesaid Tar Baby, and rolled in sticky anguish on his – no, her - back, to the tune of anguished fiddles whilst Brer Fox (Joy Newton), a young lady habited in long check pants – I thought of the Palladium Girls and grinned – a stage nose, and a queer peaked cap surmounted by a star which reminded me of Mr Carter's drawings for the 'Golden Penny', freaked around in dreadful pain but considerable enjoyment – again according to programme. Mr Bear, however, a kindly monstrosity in a brown paper head, intervened. Young Joy seemed unnecessarily disturbed, and fled the stage, starred cap an' all. Whereupon Mr Bear executed a weird and unaccountable dance, ending with that elementary exercise, the forward roll. Enter a young yellow and green unknown, according to the programme Mr Tarrypin . . . Nadina Newhouse. The youthful Nadina capered with the speckled-nosed rabbits. More capers with more monstrosities . . . During each dance Ray and I exchanged doubtful and disgusted glances, and as the last dismal wail died away on the smoky air we both uttered a loud tick of annoyance.'

It was with this loud tick of annoyance that, I have to admit, Ray Bolton and I saluted the little company that was to become the Royal Ballet. And covered by this same tick, I have to presume, was the infinitely famous lady to whom I made my first written allusion on that childish page: in pursuance of my flippant design having given the speckled-nosed rabbits the names of those who danced them: Jill, Joy, Berenice ('Ow!' the diarist cried, Barton having been short on Berenices), Heather, Joan and Margot.

The erstwhile speckled-nosed rabbit, alas, was unable to make the interview at Bush House. But I had better luck with a notable person who, but for a number of historical inconsistencies, might well have been myself.

Sir John Gielgud had just published a volume of memoirs. He

had been a large element in my existence. At school forty years before I'd played Richard II, in *Richard of Bordeaux*, one of his great early successes. Williams had taken me to see his Hamlet: the only performance of the role in which, as I saw it, the burden of being Hamlet had been perfectly borne. Over the years thereafter it seemed to me that the first half of the play was often well-done: the second half, often ill-done. The trouble was that, when it came to the great climaxes of the play, ranting and rage were so commonly resorted to. I remember thinking that as the curtain went up in 1935 Gielgud had gathered precisely the right amount of air in his lungs, and had then used it perfectly over the long labour of the play, until the final silence.

For my programme I'd once interviewed Ben Kingsley, after a very private Hamlet of his in a curiously private setting at the Round House. The first half had worked, I thought, marvellously, being Kafkaesque: the castle at Elsinore was Kafka's castle: Hamlet was, as it were, H: the sense was tremendous of a small human being having to bear the weight of a grotesquely swollen human issue. Ben Kingsley said well, they *had* talked much of Kafka in rehearsal. He said also, memorably, that as an actor he'd been convinced by playing Hamlet that Shakespeare, too, was an actor: the pacing of the part being perfect, a rest provided exactly when exhaustion was imminent: the actor reappearing at precisely the moment when, if he'd not done so, he'd have lost his grip of the audience. What I did not think had gone so well in this production was the second half of the play, when private Elsinore becomes public Elsinore. Kafka may be well enough, I thought, for the swift early swelling of the drama: but, for the angry lancing of that great boil, it's not possible to do without a gift of huge speech that never becomes rhodomontade, never dissolves into heroic splutter.

As I remembered that schoolboy experience, not once had Gielgud spluttered.

And part of coming together for Kate and me, who'd met in the first place as members of a dramatic society, had lain in a difference of opinion about Gielgud. She was an Olivier woman, and thought Gielgud had mannerisms that prevailed in every part he played. I thought all great actors had mannerisms, and that one had to look beyond the invariable music and gestures to another quality, the great actor's power to use his familiar self in order to arrive at a creature entirely original. Of course I knew it was Gielgud being Hamlet, but I also knew that it was Hamlet: who was fed by Gielgud, but was not Gielgud.

The composition of this difference between Kate and me, the closing of (as it were) the Gielgud-Oliver rift, had been a little part of that general merger of ideas and feelings that makes marriage possible. So to me Gielgud was not only a great actor: he was a memorable domestic item in my own history. On top of which I recalled a moment when Williams and I had read, it must have been before the war, a letter of Gielgud's, somewhere reprinted. It had the easily warm character of an actor's letter, was loosely extravagant: and Williams made a face. 'Oh dear! Perhaps . . .' he said. I knew he meant that we had perhaps invested our admiration in an unsuitable object. I did not feel this: largely because the local newspaper, referring to a later performance of mine in a school play, had said that I suffered from the handicap of having 'a Gielgud profile'. I think this meant that I had a certain obtrusiveness of nose: but I was thrilled to think I was so inconvenienced. This splendid actor would need to write (and publish) astonishingly banal examples of his correspondence before I withdrew my respect for him.

Well, I'd simply admired him for over forty years when I went to a London bookshop to interview him. It was, in fact, 43 years since, following *Richard of Bordeaux*, we'd been taken to see Gielgud as Romeo, at the Golders Green Hippodrome. It had been the first Shakespeare I'd ever seen. There was this wonderful Romeo: and this exquisite Juliet, Peggy Ashcroft: and this marvellous Nurse, Edith Evans: and, when it was over, we'd disdained public transport as a way of returning home and had walked, Williams and his little buzzing group of schoolboys, for five miles talking of that extraordinary production. I arrived home long after midnight, and my father was angrily waiting for me. What had I been up to? Up to, I said, was no phrase for it. We'd simply elected to walk home, to talk about the play, to stretch the marvel out. He'd heard nothing like it, he said. What sort of teacher was it who'd keep his pupils up so late? And who could believe anyone could spend so long, so late at night, simply talking about a play? What *had* I been up to?

It had nothing much to do with Sir John, all this. That he was part of the texture of innumerable people's lives must have been something he'd accommodated himself to, like all great public performers. But when I went to talk to him that morning, in the bookshop where he was signing copies of his book, I went as to an encounter with an old crony. There was, in one respect, no other way in which I could think of him. What I'd not been prepared for was the carapace of fame in which someone so celebrated for so long was enclosed. He was totally courteous, of course: and, of course, totally remote. My illusion of an almost lifelong intimacy was, when I was face to face with him, neither here nor there. Of course.

But it was ridiculously like not being recognised by Hamlet, John Worthing, Macbeth, King Lear, Benedick and Prospero, simultaneously.

An ephemeral art, alas, he said. So soon forgotten. But not really so, I said. Well, I'd seen him myself many times over the years, and was only one of those who carried in their heads the memory of this or that piece of acting. Ah yes, he said, his deep velvet voice stirred to amusement: ah yes: but his experience was that if someone spoke of a piece of business, a great moment in one of his roles, more often than not it turned out that they'd got it wrong. He hadn't played that role. Or he had, but on this occasion it wasn't him. Uncommonly often, it was Richardson, or Olivier, they'd remembered . . .

3

Our house didn't merely split: it was also, during these years, subject to flood.

It had turned out that we lived at the district's lowest point. Our neighbours without exception stood on healthily higher ground. The preoccupations of many of them during this period were not ours. It was a moment in Barley Wood when an enormous desire to seem to be living in Buckingham Palace became apparent. For smallish houses (if compared to actual palaces), largeish railings were provided: and a strong impression was given that the sentry boxes (and the sentries) were merely subject to delay. In the spring, daffodils were drafted in military quantities, and disposed in military fashion. Fairly simple houses were subject to façade-lifting: modest doorways were given immodest porticoes. Perfectly good drives were ripped up and replaced with drives of various sorts of deep pink or charcoal or (in one case) glaring green composite. Feature by feature, such humility as was possessed by the architecture of the 1950s was rooted out, and replaced with items of a pompous kind. New occupants of a house were inclined to have its old, usually thoroughly satisfactory garden removed in favour of another, instant garden. It was like living among so many theatres, with everywhere new scenery dropping from the flies or trundled in from the wings. Providing such transformations, many prospered: sometimes making telephone calls at random to propose new windows, extensions, pools, parterres. Offers to supply me with these, at a cost to be assessed, were usually made when I was in the middle of a sentence.

But water was our problem.

Our house lay in a bottom: strictly speaking, Dead Man's

Bottom. The name was an old one, dating back to a battle that had occurred in the fields we faced: the Battle of Barton, 1471. Five hundred years earlier (yesterday) there had been this cursing, snapping of limbs and lopping of heads, in what was now partly the Barley Wood Association's playing fields. The annual sports day ('*Please* will those who are entered for the three-legged race go *at once* to the starting line') took place where – or very nearly where – Warwick the Kingmaker had made a false and fatal move. It seemed likely that the Duke of Gloucester, later Richard III, had hurried through our living room in a pincer movement that was based on the minimum of respect for the ailing potentilla (which we were inclined to call an impotentilla) close to our front door. Five hundred years after all that agony, the fields still mildly sloped down towards us: we lay in this ancient trough. It must always have flooded, once every ten or twenty years, when clouds sensationally burst, or rain continued for long periods. But now it was happening every year.

There was this stream that pervaded the district. Old maps showed a trailing network of ponds and little lakes: most of these had vanished, but the essential flow of water remained, in the form of Pymm's Brook. Finding ourselves the only householders in a lane facing Dead Man's Bottom, two of my friends and I had asked the local council if the lane might be known simply as Pymms. What we had in mind was that our houses would become Pymms No 1, 2 and 3. Our request was not granted. Instead we were allowed to name ourselves after a copse that lay ahead of us, an old gathering of trees which, small though it was, seemed to contain a continent of silence and secrecy. I'd sit there under a tree sometimes to write, as private as if I'd been in a monastic cell. Though there were times when I'd had to take my note book back home, finding the ancient space already occupied by a local (or, more often, unlocal) business man and his secretary, lunching.

Now every cloudburst, every furious thunderstorm, brought water pouring down from these gentle, though once murderous, slopes about us: heading for a culvert exactly ahead. The culvert was old, intended for a world less generally watery. What had happened, they said, was partly that there'd been more man-made attempts at drainage, which, in preventing lakes from forming in the fields, directed the flood at us. There was also, in some vague fashion, more water of a domestic kind. The experts who came to talk to us had that indefiniteness, that effect of being contentedly lost among spacious theories, that is often the mark of the specialist. Asked for an opinion, they said, they would not have advised us to build where we had built. In fact, asked fifteen years earlier for an opinion (their records were as vague as themselves) they'd offered no suggestion of a doubt. Of course we could build there. One generation of experts may lack all connection with the next generation of experts.

What happened was that this thick flood of water – always looking to me like Leonardo da Vinci's drawings of human musculature, those powerful knotted strings – arrived at the mouth of the culvert together with a great scavenging of bits of wood, agricultural debris of all kinds. The grille covering the mouth had been placed there long ago in the hope of dissuading local children from creeping a quarter of a mile to the point where the stream came again into the open. Against it, when there was flooding, the water simply pinned branches, straw, every sort of rubbish, until the grille was turned into a cork. Unable to enter the culvert, the water rose: and sought the lane as a means of escape. It turned our lawns into lakes: it lapped at our doorsteps. And at last it entered one of the houses – ours.

I would never have guessed the panic that wilful water may cause. It has an inexorable thrust: it does not at all mind what it does. As Canute demonstrated, it does not respond to appeals for moderation. When threatened by flood, one attempts seriously what Canute attempted ironically. 'Oh please go away, *please* go away!' Kate wept, as the water rose. And, when it entered the house, I found myself speaking to the books on the lower shelves. As I tried to remember how to unplug our loudspeakers, and then lugged them to a landing, I urged my books to be calm. 'I will come and deal with you in a moment,' I assured them.

Another expert was sent to calm us. Or rather, as it turned out, to convince us that agitation or calm were neither here nor there. 'We would,' he repeated, indifferent to documentation, 'have advised you not to build. I suppose you could, of course, make a sort of wall to prevent the water from entering.' 'It might prevent, for example, our cars from entering,' we said. 'Ah!' He was not surprised to learn that we found being flooded a psychological disaster out of all proportion to what it was: a few disgusting inches of water, spoiling floors, threatening books. 'We have observed,' he said cheerfully, 'that elderly persons sometimes do not live long after being flooded. Very curious, the effect of water.'

We thought this too.

I noticed how the emergency brought out the essential person in each of us. I'd fall flat on my face in the water, as a preface to falling backwards into it. I'd have stripped, of course, more or less, as we all did, in our blind panic. Afterwards we could scarcely believe that our respectable lane had been full of persons dashing here and there in underpants and knickers. Neighbours, both civil servants, he and she, in the agitation of the flood became more obviously civil servants. He suggested, in the manner of one composing a minute, what might be done: the roar of the water increasing moment by moment, and the jam of rubbish at the mouth of the culvert becoming more difficult to deal with. She, half-naked, breathing desperately, noted his proposal, but ventured to make a counter-proposal. His analysis of the situation was not without merit, but might it not be said to have overlooked this or that feature, apparently secondary, but perhaps, on closer inspection, of the essence?

The water roared about our knees, and I fell backwards and forwards in a matter of seconds.

The next day I interviewed Alan Ayckbourn. He had not, I thought, hit upon a flood as point of origin for his sense of domestic tragi-comedy? He had not, he said: but would bear the idea in mind.

Somebody from the water board turned out to be not so much an expert as a person with a practical flair. It struck him that a grille placed at a long shallow angle, rather than one bang up against the mouth of the culvert, might act as a filter, able to pluck the debris out of any flood before it could begin to turn itself into a plug.

He was allowed to have his way, and we were not flooded again.

4

And then, of course, among the forces that sought to make your brief and expiring stay on Earth less and less comfortable (all of us with documents of discretionary entry stapled into our passports, I'd think: and none particularly anxious to meet the ultimate immigration officer), there was fire. Human fire, that is.

Combustible. I sometimes thought that might be the most widely applicable word for a human being. Suddenly Kate was slamming doors. I'd think to myself that to slam doors was a particularly *low* way of quarrelling with the world. It was to level against it the most unanswerable of charges: since when it's expressed as a slammed door the accusation has a horribly vague general quality. Everything is at fault, indifferently. I'd remember my father, suddenly going through the house, tight-lipped and terse, sweeping up for the bonfire anyone's casual litter: for example, yesterday's newspaper, perhaps a whole succession of yesterday's newspapers, waiting for my mother to bring her gradual attention to bear on them. One of the reasons for my father's rages against my slow-reading mother was the nature of her interest in the news, always based on what had happened last week, last month. '*But he's been tried and hanged!*' he'd cry as she made some pitying reference to a murderer or his victim: or both, for she was as helplessly generous with her pity as with her pence. (Perhaps it was from my mother that I inherited that tendency to murmur: 'Alas!') My father had little patience with the latest murderer, in those days when the possibility that he might be hanged made him hideously interesting: with yesterday's stale murderer he had no patience at all. One of his strongest stances: that of a man to whom no murderer could come with any hope of being pampered. It would be all those newspapers, all those murders, that my father would gather up, together with stray comics or attempts at model-making of mine, when he was collecting for his bonfire: not, we knew, because he lacked appropriate material, garden cuttings, newspapers my mother had genuinely exhausted and herself had tossed aside: but because he was desperately angry, for reasons he had no intention of declaring. His little world turned pale, and each of us wretchedly examined the possibility that he or she might be the cause of this distemper.

My father, yielding to his combustibility: a sulking rage, that sought out the smallest reasons for discontent, and made of them as much as could be made, and more. Lips, thin: eyes, stony or burning. Fists clenched: knuckles, white. I'd sometimes thought that, if you could examine the other places where his bones were close to his skin, they'd have been white, too: kneecaps, elbows. His very shoulder-blades would have been terrifying.

Listening to Kate slamming doors, I'd think of the way my friends expressed anger. Ben's eyes narrowed: became slits in the pillbox of his head: became the glint of rifle or machine-gun. More often, machine-gun: the scorns he shot you with came in stunning quantity. Rufus, whose normal manner was *andante cantabile*, became suddenly *staccato*. 'What?' he'd cry. He would aim a stark 'Eh?' at your chin: a swingeing 'Pardon?' at the tip of your nose. My latest producer at the BBC would slowly tear something – almost anything – to pieces. Gaps in the documentation of our activities were usually to be traced to these angers. And I'd noticed the signals of strain between Jack and Cor: 'Don't *goad* me, Cor!' Jack would cry, at a moment mysterious to a third person. When Henry grunted, 'Forgive me for interrupting your interruption,' Mae would cross herself.

And Kate slammed doors. But then I did worse than that: in contrast to her healthy creation of noise, I created silence. At 10 a.m. I was happy and buoyant and talkative: at 10.01 a.m. a harmless remark had caused a precipitation of all my unacknowledged resentments, grudges, dissatisfactions, and I had fallen into such an ashen dumbness as made me fear I'd never discover the will to speak again. And how, out of the amiable lake that one was, did these monsters rise? How was it that from one moment to the next, having believed oneself the most equable of persons, one found oneself a glaring silent horror of quite unpacifiable discontent?

I thought of our acquaintances the Taylors. When angry, they'd communicate with one another as if across great distances. 'I think,' Tony would say, 'that children rather enjoy being frightened by fireworks.' 'Is that what Anthony believes?' Sue would cry, seeming to check up on some remote whisper. She'd look round helplessly. 'Do I understand that Anthony believes that children like being scared out of their wits? Will someone tell me if that is his opinion?' 'Those really weren't my words,' Tony would murmur. 'Followed by his usual denial?' Her manner would be that of one who for lack of information is on the very edge of derangement. 'I should have thought it was obvious.' Tony would be confident that the ceiling was of his mind. 'I don't suppose,' Susan would inform a petrified random guest, 'that Anthony has for one moment tried to imagine the feelings of his own children when subjected by his carelessness to *tremendous nerve-shattering explosions* for which he has made *no attempt to prepare them*.' Miserably Tony might try the effect of a direct appeal. 'Oh, come *on*, Susan!' She'd laugh with determined coarseness. 'And thinks' – she'd amuse the French windows with the idea – 'to get out of it by asking mummy to be kind to him.' 'No real harm done,' Mr Rogers from West Drive would say, having no instinct at all for a dangerous situation. 'His *cronies* everywhere!' Susan would open a cupboard door and shout this comment at the rows of porcelain. Mrs Rogers would try the effect of a non sequitur. 'I gather there is *not* to be a bus service in Barley Wood.' 'Changing the subject,' Susan would snap. And then Kate might say, gently: 'I was scared out of my life by a Catherine Wheel, once, when I was five, I suppose, but then I discovered that –' Susan would be thumbing blindly through a book taken from a shelf. 'Oh tactful Kate! Oh, three cheers for *diplomatic* Kate!'

From such a point, it was all downhill; and misery would spread from household to household.

As combustible as most, I'd always wrestled with the problem that I had my mother's wish that things would go well, rather than my father's appetite for their going ill: together with an immense dread of reproducing the atmosphere of our home in Barton when the war between my parents was raging, as so much of the time it did – my mother angrily defending her desire for an absence of anger, my father furiously in favour of being furious.

In my fifties, all I had learned to do in this department of our combustibility was to act upon myself, wherever I could, as an instant fireman. One thing seemed clear: any outburst could be allowed to set ablaze everything around it: anger being the very best kindling for anger. In no time the flames could be roaring through your world. There was nothing much to be said for the experience: it didn't assuage the eternal causes of dissatisfaction within you. Oblige yourself to offer a joke, a kiss, an apology, and the fire would fizzle out, at once. An evening saved, a weekend, an anniversary. And more than saved: for what a seedbed for tenderness the threat of a quarrel could be! How, in the heat of it, desire grew!

But I'd hear my father snorting in the background: he, poor man, I think, having some deeply unhappy need of fire.

5

Some of one's ghosts were living ghosts: but some were dead. Death had begun to seem the smallest step anyone could take if he, or she, was to disappear. One morning I'd heard of the discovery of a neighbour dead in bed: and as, fresh from this wholly improbable news, I walked down the railway platform at Barley Wood, I thought Alastair might step out from one of the arches in which he'd always hide, his fingers smoking: smile as he always did: and say, as he always said: 'Good morning, squire.' And then we'd talk, quite naturally, about his being dead. I had this foolish thought that it was news that would interest him very much: it would make him talk. It was also something I would want to show interest in. 'I hoped I would meet you, Alastair,' I'd say, 'to talk about your being dead.' 'How did you know?' he'd ask. 'Well, Jane rang Kate.' 'It must have been a shock for poor old Janey – finding me dead, like that.' 'A nasty thing to happen.' 'Very nasty, squire.' He would sigh and grin together, making clouds of melancholy smoke. The smoke had been part of it all: so much tobacco burnt had helped, in the end, to burn him. And, on that morning of his death, he'd not had the time to disappear. The step between his lying cold a few hundred yards away, and his being here to discuss the matter, was the very thinnest of distances. He'd have been ruefully interested in that, too. 'Any ideas about it, squire?' He'd always been amused by my having ideas about things. 'I expect you have an explanation for that.' I never had, of course, but I had the air of being in search of explanations, just as he had the air of being in despair of them. 'I'm a shallow man, you know,' he said to me once. He had an enormous love of birds, and knew the local population almost to the last feather. I'd catch him standing stockstill alongside a local hedge. 'That's the seventh year those blackbirds have nested there.' Some sadness at the heart of this companionable man sprang from a submerged belief that life was a deep matter, and his conviction that he had no depth in him at all. There were times when it made him less than companionable, and that's why he'd hide among the arches on the morning platform: and I'd always felt pleased that he'd come out of hiding for me. I thought it was because of this ridiculous illusion I offered that I was a deep fellow, combined with the evident fondness I had for him. For my part I thought only that I was shallow, and he was very deep, about blackbirds and magpies.

And Phil Perkins wrote to say he'd heard me on the radio, and was I still in any recognisable sense the 'Ted' with whom he'd dug ditches thirty years earlier, when we were both conscientious objectors?

I remembered Phil as the agricultural comrade whose comic gift had been entirely his own. We'd walked once under a tree full of birds celebrating the spring (that of 1943, difficult to celebrate if you were not a bird): and Phil had said, 'I wish they would get married quietly.' And one frozen morning we'd come back to a pipeline into which we now needed to tumble the clay we'd dug out of it: but it had been turned by the frost to iron. You'd have needed a blow torch to make it moveable. Phil said: 'I knew we shouldn't have left it out all night.'

Replying that I hoped I was still the man (or child, fitfully verging on man) he remembered, I spoke of this natural wit of his, that (for three or four of us) had a little lightened the miseries of war. Phil wrote back that he believed his jokes, if he'd ever made any, must have been borrowed from others. The idea that he'd been a comedian of distinct originality – and I could have composed to that effect the gravest sort of sworn statement – seemed to make him wriggle, rather. I remembered that one aspect of this comic dissident, who'd spent a year in Lewes Gaol, had consisted of an unlikely ambition: he'd wanted to be manager of the firm he'd worked for, one devoted to moving parcels from this end of the earth to some other. Phil said in his second letter that, in the postwar world, he'd achieved this ambition. However, there were circumstances that had prompted him to agree to early retirement . . .

Almost at once I had a letter from his widow. Mrs Perkins said that of late Phil had talked of me often, and she knew he'd have wanted her to inform me of his death following one in a series of heart-attacks: and would have hoped that from time to time I'd remember him. I recalled Mrs Perkins as the young wife on whose behalf, amid the ditches and copses of wartime agriculture, Phil had collected catkins: wild flowers of various kinds: and small parcels of leaf mould. Though these collections had also been made with a glance at the appetites of his tiny daughter: whose delight it was, on Phil's arrival home from our smoky fields, to unpack the carrier on his bicycle. There were sometimes pleasures intended specially for her: twigs of a strange conformation, old birds' nests. I'd thought at the time how like the father of Beauty in 'Beauty and the Beast' Phil was, commissioned when he went from home to return with tiny, surprising gifts. And now Beauty wrote to me: herself married to a farmer. And she'd not known at all, she said, until his death, that her father had been a conscientious objector, or had even worked on the land. It had clearly been an episode in his life that he'd wanted to keep secret. I was astonished that a man who at such cost to himself had demonstrated the intensity of his view of things should ever wish to conceal it: and even more that he should have been able to hide it from a plainly devoted daughter. But I remembered that bold joker's obstinate shyness. He'd enjoyed quarreling with me in the ditch about art, which he regarded as a monstrous attempt to justify the painting of naked women: and about the further slopes of literature, which simply gave itself to whisking any sort of veiling off anything that ought, according to a consensus of Phils, to be veiled. I thought his failure to speak of the five years of his life spent on the land might have sprung partly from a feeling that those were, so to speak, the private parts of his existence. But it might have sprung also from his ambition. The manager of this firm of parcellers would not, I guessed, ever have disavowed his wartime stance: but he might well have thought it unnecessary to make reference to it.

Oh, said his daughter, now she understood why, when he visited her husband's farm, Phil was so vaguely but strongly inclined to give advice, generally of an outdated kind. But she wished so much that he'd told her of his pacificism. In that, she seemed to be entirely her father's daughter. 'All my adult years, I have felt it wrong that man should kill or maim man in whatever cause. I'm sure now it was far more than a mere feminine viewpoint: more a great similarity of character.'

One of Phil's delights, as the largely self-educated man who reserved the right to draw profound amusement from the manners of the educated (among whom, not having encountered those confused educators, Percy Chew, John Logan and

Knotty, Phil counted me), was to pick on some item of educated vocabulary and hold it, squirming, by the tail, while he questioned the need for it. One wartime evening, as he was about to head for home on a bicycle that had grown a tail of wild flowers, I rashly said: 'And so – my valediction to you, Philip!' His bike wobbled and crashed on its side, and he looked up from the ground, writhing with laughter: 'Valediction! *Valediction!*' he howled. Then he picked himself up, picked up his bike, mourned for a ruined flower or two, and rode off: crying, 'Ta-ta, Ted!'

And my valediction to you, Phil, I thought obstinately, thirty years later.

6

It was not so much that I read books, as that books read me.

My mother had pointed out that the armchair in which my father had sat, on our prickly visits to their retirement bungalow on the south coast, was, disguised with new upholstery, the armchair in which I'd sat myself throughout the years of my adolescence. My father's references to that period were based on the conviction that I'd rarely risen from it. Its arms were always piled with books: I always had my nose in some volume the very title of which was capable of causing him apoplexy. Titles could curiously anger him. I remember his fury when he found me reading a then-new novel by H. G. Wells, *The Bulpington of Blup*. He hadn't toiled in the ungrateful bowels of the Civil Service in order to make it possible for a disturbingly sedentary adolescent to read a book called – his disgusted snort – *The Bulpington of Blup!* I felt at the time that I was crowded into a corner of our very small living room, with a little distinguished mob of cronies – Wells, D. H. Lawrence, Aldous Huxley, Katherine Mansfield, W. H. Auden – all of us under threat from my father's apoplexies. Poor man! I wonder now why, once my marriage to Kate had brought about his liberation, he hadn't ceremonially burnt the armchair! But perhaps the business of repossessing it, having it provided with new upholstery, reserving it as his own, was a more satisfactory form of revenge.

To my father, heaven was booklessness: and my turning out to be so damnably bookish intensified this sentiment in him. And now, as I read book after book for my programme and books accumulated everywhere about us, bringing anxieties as to their accommodation – so that at times it seemed we must have shelves on the outer as well as the inner walls – I thought how it would have gratified him to find me uneasy from such a cause. Sometimes, uttering the invariable opening words of the programme – announcing myself 'at the BBC in London with The World of Books' – I'd be tempted to give my father's ghost some pleasure by using a phrase of his own: so that I'd say I was 'at the BBC in London with the World of Bloody *Bloody* Books.'

Damn it – one's doomed from the beginning: my having kept those vast diaries made this, in my case, remarkably plain. By the end of 1934 I was already being read by books. In my resumé of the half-year to December, there I was writing that, 'There is some indecision as to the best book of this half of 1934. Many of the distinguished books are lost in the maze of diction.' (I meant it was too exhausting to go back over all those teeming pages, trying to isolate every literary reference.) There were, said this doomed fourteen-year-old, a dozen or so worth mentioning: they included *Chaytor's*, by Adrian Alington: *Second Innings*, by Country Vicar: *The Ugly Duchess*, by Leon Feuchtwanger: *When Thieves Fall Out*, by R. Austin Freeman: *The Golden Age*, by Kenneth Grahame: and *Chapter the Last*, by Knut Hamsen. Required to be an eclectic now, I appear to have been an eclectic then. Hardy's *The Trumpet Major*, one of the dozen, 'owes its place,' I declared, 'to that peculiarly homely feeling that Hardy always imparts. I like to forget his particular creed' (strongly condemned by Percy Chew, with whose influence I was not yet at war: 'The kind of self-indulgent grumbling, gentlemen, that a decent fellow grows out of after the age of sixteen!) 'and read lightly. He is like a – no, I should say his book is like one of those tall cocktails, which last long and betray a hundred hidden delicacies in their depth.' (An image based on total inexperience: it would be a dozen years before I so much as tasted a cocktail.)

It was one of my first spluttering ventures, I suppose, in what I was only too likely to have described as the great swimming bath of outside contributorship. Though forty years on, at Bush House, Penelope had suggested that another term might be considered. 'Sodding freelances!' she exclaimed on one occasion. This was because quite reasonably it seemed to her at that explosive moment that freelances tended to urge her to buy their uncommissioned interviews with uninteresting persons: or, positively invited to interview persons of interest, turned in interviews without it. I could, it occurred to me, delight Penelope and my father simultaneously with yet another variation of my self-announcement: 'This is a sodding freelance at the BBC in London with The World of Bloody *Bloody* Books.'

But, though the requirements of the programme grew over my life like a weed, part of me was delighted to be paid to read books and talk to their authors. A friend and neighbour, a member of the English Chamber Orchestra, driving me home from a concert, said of his oboe-playing: 'What an extraordinary way to earn a living! Well, both of us, in fact! How did we come to be paid for doing what we wanted to do!'

I imagine my fourteen-year-old self compiling in 1980 one of his solemn resumés ('The influence of Knut Hamsen is the greatest mark of this stage. His attention to detail, his calm strength in matters of importance, made a strong impression on me. Otherwise nothing remarkable has happened to revolutionise these notes'). He'd record, among his memories, interviewing . . . Richard Hughes: whom I'd first met when we were sent together by the British Council to talk in East Africa. A gently sharp man, helplessly tall (Dylan Thomas had suggested to Vernon Watkins that they might go together to a wedding in one of Hughes's dress suits), who'd written his mature work (*A High Wind in Jamaica*, *In Hazard*) in extreme youth, and in old age set out to write his young man's novels. There were to be three of these, one more to add to *Fox in the Attic* and *The Wooden Shepherdess*: but it seemed to him that he was slowing down by some sort of geometrical progression, so that his best prospect was of finishing the last on his 120th birthday. He showed me once a chapter of *The Wooden Shepherdess* that he'd written in two manners: the first, that he'd grown up with, being one in which the sexual life of his characters was described without a single word of description: and the second, the manner he was now free to use, one in which spades – though spades didn't very much come into it – could be called spades. Which was the better? I had little doubt, and I believe he had less: the manner he'd mastered, one of allusion, said far more of the passions he was concerned with than the other. We were equally certain that it wasn't the absolute superiority of one manner over the other that had been demonstrated: but the truth that if one had passionate purposes one could learn to express them veiled or open, as the atmosphere of the time might allow.

Hugely acclaimed for his work during the first of his literary lives, he found that the work of the second was given a mixed reception: and I treasure the memory of his mildly smiling show of sturdiness in the midst of this, for him, unfamiliar experience. The life of Richard Hughes, it seemed to me when it came to an end in 1976 – that of a man with a manner curiously redolent of the conventions of the humour of his youth, in which a joke might be made by simply beginning words with capital letters, but who inside this manner was all ferocious and deeply uncomfortable imagination – offered yet another example of the truth discovered in your fifties, as the full shape of the lives of your old friends began to declare itself: that, as much as anything, each of us was a toy of time. With Jimmy Soper, time stayed still: with Georgie Evans, time went backwards: with Richard Hughes, time made a great mature knot of itself, at the very beginning of his career: and diffidently uncoiled and offered itself for inspection at the end of it. No writer I've read offers a better account of the unspeakably disastrous illness that bore the name of Adolf Hitler: the disease of solipsism, of the failure to grow into the belief that others exist. The portrait of Hitler, in the tentative work of a man in his sixties, springs out of the confident work of a man in his twenties, *A High Wind in Jamaica*, which is one of the profoundest of all accounts of the inevitable solipsism of children and an appalled view (written before Hughes, who'd never been to Jamaica, had heard of Hitler) of the possible consequences of the condition in which you alone exist.

My fourteen-year-old self would record an interview with a deeply shy woman, Olivia Manning, which brought out the sympathetic shyness of the interviewer: so that here, generally speaking, was an interview of great elusiveness, perhaps relating to the author's *Balkan Trilogy*, but possibly to the recent accident to one of her cats, fallen out of a window in London. Or fallen, in one of the novels in the trilogy, out of a window in Bucharest? Writers invent books, but at times it seems that the compliment may be returned.

Here is Ernest Hemingway's widow, as she enters the studio beginning to shake the many bracelets off her arms: so that by the time she has reached the table where the interview is to take place she is ready to make towers of them: knowing that, left on her arms, they would strike the table with her every movement and provide the tape with a background like a drumroll.

And here's a famous person feverishly inscribing his name in your copy of his book, though you've not got round to asking him to do so, for fear that you might rush off at once and sell it: which you happened to have no intention of doing.

And I imagine the young diarist would have done his worst with two interviews dating from the days when the programme was concerned with the other arts, as well as literature. When, for example, it made it possible for him (the fourteen-year-old fitfully transformed into a man in his fifties) to interview Alfred Brendel about master-classes he'd just conducted. Tall, austere, and quite evidently a comedian (as I'd guessed from moments in his performances, and from a feeling that the drooping gravity of his presence on a platform barely prevented at times the emergence of a skipping jester), Brendel had said to one of his young pianists, of a passage in a Mozart concerto that to commonplace ears had seemed delectable: 'Too complicated! It sounds like a bird who has learned to twitter from a record!' When another played a passage of, my ears suggested, unimpeachable pianissimo, he cried: 'Do we really want . . . *Heathrow Airport!*' (She played the passage again, I thought as whisperingly as before, and Brendel expressed great satisfaction with the distance between one whisper and the other.) During the interview I asked him about a master-class as a performance. It required some heroism on the part of the young pianist? We are not, he said sternly, concerned with ourselves, we are concerned with the music. We are not here to provide any performance but a musical one. However, I said, he *had* been very funny, and together with the rest of the audience I *had* found it possible to enjoy both the musical content of the master-class and the extraordinarily entertaining nature of his contribution. He'd looked at me sharply – then taken my hands in his and squeezed them, grinning immensely: had then become austere again, and dismissed me.

And there was an encounter, in her flat in the London clouds, with Elizabeth Lutyens: black-shirted, black-trousered, considering wine to be an essential accompaniment of an interview: and (like Richard Hughes, I thought) seeming in her seventies to be arriving at the very point of her youth. Oh, she said, she'd written serially before she ever realised it was the advanced thing to do! Like Richard Hughes, she'd had an instant maturity, that now had to be taken to pieces and examined. Life had happened – it had been deeply engrossing: now one was recalling it with astonishment: for the first time able to appraise it, to notice some of the details and the quite unexpected general shape of it. One was young again, exclaiming over the life one had involuntarily, busily created. It was like listening to music about which, because one happened to have written it oneself, one was, in a very special way, ignorant!

7

Children from a primary school I'd visited sent me letters of inquiry. 'What are the mane problems of being an author?' asked one. 'The problem I am stuck with is that I am no good with my speling.' 'I would like to know,' wrote another, 'if it took you a long time to get so perfect.'

I thought of the complex and accelerating state of imperfection it had taken me nearly sixty years to reach. At times it seemed ridiculous that we were ever born as single persons. I could have kept a whole crowd of selves employed, and another crowd happily idle. That mountainous accumulation of experience! To deal with it, one would need to be a bulldozer. I was not much more than a lady's gardening fork. This huge business of being alive, and the small capacity most of us have to handle it!

Now that my mother, in her late eighties, was becoming less and less in touch with immediacies, I found I was missing particularly one of the qualities she'd brought to bear on things: her gift of being at times profoundly and stubbornly prosaic. When I was a boy, longing for her to devote especially the evening hours to the harp, I'd been distressed by that: now I would have welcomed it. Quite late in life, she'd told me once – well, she was nineteen or twenty – she was introduced for the first time to the sea. It was at St Leonard's, she thought. Given the excitement expressed about this element by some of her friends, she'd looked at it very hard. 'But I had to say it seemed to me a lot of water.' I think she'd have been unimpressed even by Doomsday. All that foolish noise, people (who weren't *quite* people) being silly with flames! She'd have sat grumpily unmoved amid the melodrama. I felt I had in myself a little, but not nearly enough, of this preservatively prosaic quality of hers. It was there, for example, when I considered the question: Why did I dream so often of falling off a cliff? I knew this was held to be an image for all manner of disturbances in myself, none related to cliffs. But I couldn't help suspecting that I dreamed so often of falling off a cliff because I was afraid of falling off a cliff.

Though, matter-of-fact as she could be, my mother's bizarre way with the language made her now and then the last person to whom one would look for guidance as to common-sense realities. One of my nieces was discovered at this time to have inflammation of the colon. 'What you have,' said my mother, as ever surrealistically explanatory, 'is information of the comma.' My niece nodded dumbly. Associating with my mother, you gave your assent hurriedly to the most amazing assertions. The semantic fate of anyone who took her up on such a matter could be dreadful.

The fact that she was fading meant she had few sustained dialogues with her great-grandson Tim, who, when it came to ingenious uses of the language, could almost have matched her. Of late he'd begun to employ the interrogative tails of sentences without the sentences themselves. So he'd ask: 'Will you?' 'Is it?' 'Can we?' He had also invented a formula that I thought the adult world could well do with. 'I don't want to like it,' he'd say.

My cousin Will came on a visit. We hadn't seen him since we'd met in Ireland and he'd made war on the accepted views of the origins of the passage tombs. Now he sat among us, dragging this or that scholar across his conversation by the scruff of his neck, and his head would characteristically sink, sadly, as he talked. Once Tim, who loved him, dropped to the floor and peered up at his face.

Uncle George, the prime cause of Will's sadness, had died. It happened when he was in the bath. Perhaps the most remarkable egotist I'd ever known, and responsible for much despair, Uncle George remained, to the last, curiously difficult to resist. Attacked by mortality on every front, undermined by cancers and lesser enemies, he'd carried on: and had even kept his fatal appetites going long after they'd signalled their intention to bring him down. He'd been forbidden ever to smoke again: but why, it was asked, was the soil of the garden slowly being replaced with the butts of small cigars? He couldn't imagine the answer to that, said Uncle George, smiling his way out of it, but never actually having been in it. He'd been born with a flair for instant self-exculpation. I thought, after study, that he'd simply lacked the gift of guilt. I remembered a postcard I'd seen, sent to my father somewhere about 1906, when Uncle George had been adopted, or fostered – the affair was always smudgily referred to – by a wealthy business man. 'Dear Dick,' it said, 'please bring round my fiddle.' Heaven knows who'd given him the fiddle: an uncommon possession for a sixteen-year-old slum-dweller.

It was all over now: but one noted that Death had been obliged to wait until he was in his bath. And had, I guessed, approached from behind, to avoid that self-excusing smile!

It was while we were particularly conscious that the list of dramatis personae was simultaneously narrowing and swelling, so that at times we suspected that a certain amount of doubling up of parts was going on, that Kate and I paid a visit that brought home the distance we'd moved in . . . perhaps twenty years? We found ourselves on a part of the Cornish coast where, as young parents, we'd caravanned with our sons. It had been a cheerful blot on a stretch of cliff, caravans spread over two fields and the top of a small hill: but we'd put aesthetic unease behind us, feeling part of a warm fantasy of idleness: turning brown: replacing the usual exhaustions with unusual ones – the delicious fatigue resulting from sunshine and foolish games and walking high above the huge sea: together with hours of simply watching the behaviour of water as it broke into, and crept out of, a small fissure at a spot that, looking back, I see as representing the whole summer.

The sea still thrust explodingly into that fissure and backed hissing out again. Kate and I sat where we'd all sat once, and watched it. Otherwise, most things were different. The caravans had been moved some way inland, and from the cliff were not visible at all. There was no one on the beach. It was like any stage when the performers have gone, curiously smaller than imagined.

Because it was a place we'd known so noisy and crowded, that was now so silent and empty, this was a sudden measure of the distance we'd come, and a moving one. Looking back to a moment when we'd been caught up in the toils of parenthood, we felt oddly unemployed. From remembered bustle to this tidy silence . . . it was a journey we'd made, without knowing it. Imperceptible change had suddenly been made perceptible.

And I thought that the suck and bang of the water in and out of the split in the rock would continue for hundreds of thousands of years before it so reshaped this fragment of coast that it ceased to happen. A background of change against which the alteration in our own affairs was scarcely change at all.

Now my son Tom, with whom all those years before I'd sat speechlessly above the exploding water, was my teasing adviser. I'd appeared lately on a television programme: and had been dismayed by this sudden view of myself. Was this really me? Tom said: 'You don't look like that, you don't sound like that.' 'Oh thank God!' I said. 'You've removed my only reason for alarm.' 'But,' said Tom mischievously, 'you do *think* like that.'

He was off, now, with his girl and perhaps a toothbrush, to Greece, where they would resume their observation of the behaviour of the sea. A little while ago, wearing a straw hat from Kenya and a waistcoat from Oxfam, he'd lost a chocolate watch he'd been wearing in a pocket of the waistcoat to one quick leap by our little dog, Sal. And several scene-changes back, it struck me, he and our other son, Dan, had spent an important part of several summers – including those Cornish ones – making themselves a scholarly point of reference as to seaside postcards. Arrived almost anywhere they would set off for the relevant shop, and hours later we'd discover them at their labour of academically assessing the general rudeness of things. I don't know why I am not the father of two Doctors of Philosophy whose major degrees have been earned in the field of seaside sauciness.

It was all, I was reminded from time to time, dreadfully ordinary. Having written about such things, I had it pointed out to me that my life was uneventful, pitifully so. One reviewer of a book I'd written indicated the level of eventfulness below which I had fallen: 'He hasn't even run away with another man's wife.' It seemed to me that if anything, in our time, was unremarkable, and close to a non-event, it was a man running away with someone else's wife. I had actually and melodramatically been married to the same woman for over thirty years. As against such an unlikely achievement, what price some mild exploit such as walking across the Sahara from east to west on foot?

Well, of course, I did see that some lives, by their involvement with events of a plainly desperate kind, were more thrilling than others. But I had to say I did not know what was meant by an uneventful life. Simply being alive seemed to me an event on a very large scale.

I myself, as long as I could remember, had been quite sensationally up to my neck in life: indeed, awash with it!

8

Tom said perhaps the worst thing that could be said about this decade, the seventies, was that it was the period when it began to seem that human affairs were truly unmanageable.

Three intent young men in our local. One of them plainly, from the conversation, a hard-nosed Marxist-Leninist, newly but thoroughly converted, and the others ready to throw in their lot with him. He'd been lending them books, and they had questions to put: which he answered to their satisfaction. 'That,' said one, 'is another contradiction of capitalism.' 'Which they cannot resolve,' said the second. 'And never will resolve,' said their mentor. They were enormously pleased: and drank silently and deeply in, I guess, celebration of yet another contradiction identified.

And I felt a useless, elderly sadness. Not because there is anything absurd in laying a finger on a contradiction in capitalism. It is not an economic system for which I have any affection, and that it's caught out being contradictory is never a surprise to me. Nor does my belief that contradictions are deeply written into all human thinking, and all our systems, mean that I regard the attempt to identify and deal with them as pointless. It was that precisely these crisp certainties of theirs had been fatal to so many. And that given power, and the belief that with them the tendency of human affairs to develop knots and tangles had come to a halt, they'd certainly not have left the Friar's Holt standing.

But then, along the road, in the Duke of Gloucester, a different story altogether. This was not so much a local as a place, geographically indefinite, that attracted junior executives. They talked of percentages and sales and shippings, and very much about their nervous view of their colleagues, and their deeply unfriendly view of their friends: and I'd observe their South American moustaches and their thrilling bonnets of hair, and how more than one of them was unable to contain his stout body in his stylish suit. A shirt would be hanging out at the back, flesh would be visible. They would begin to talk with their elbows, and you would know the subject had been changed.

You would also know how many had been sacrificed to their conviction that thus the world must go: that this was the way of it. That you must be dangerously irresponsible as to the fate of the human race, as those in the Friar's Holt had elected to be dangerously responsible for it.

And I'd remember an embarrassing moment in my personal history: when I'd said: 'Lenin was a sort of saint, I suppose.'

It was in the Home Guard HQ, in Barton: actually, the Odeon Garage. Williams at the time was defending the nation with a very small revolver, which he had demonstrated to Ben and me with notable vagueness. Each of us had privately resolved, if Barton were invaded during the next hour or so, to treat Williams as the major threat. Meanwhile, he and Ben (who was on leave from the Navy, and wore bellbottoms: which made me think of my old friend as a sort of maritime pierrot) exchanged opinions as to politics and the war in the chess-playing fashion they favoured. Or perhaps it was table tennis: at which Ben was a past – and present – master. There, ping, went a comment from Williams about the Labour Party: and there, ping-ping, went Ben's spinning reply. Compared with my friends, I was helplessly emotional about politics, given to grand ideas, powerful large theories based on nothing very much, and dramatic illusions founded entirely in my wish that human beings should turn out to be in sight of a worldly paradise. I was able then (partly, I believe, from my reading of H. G. Wells and my general appetite for utopias) to think even of the appalling existence of Hitler, and the dreadful fact of the war, as obstacles on the way to universal felicity. I can't remember what it was Ben and Williams were discussing that made me suddenly see Lenin as a saint: but I had this vision, and made this utterance.

Oh, I now think, ever to have been such an ass!

Ben and Williams, I believe, paused for a second, startled: and then continued with their opinionative ping-pong. At such moments, or a little afterwards, Williams would say to Ben: 'And what about our good friend here? What shall we do about him?' And they would look at me quizzically. Only slowly did I realise that my old teacher, from whom I thought I'd picked up the idea that to be unworldly was best, considered me quite disturbingly incapable of practical enterprise. I'd failed Higher School Certificate rather spectacularly: and been a silly dead-end sort of weekly newspaper reporter: and now was a conscientious objector: and to Williams' knowledge had been staggeringly inept in the field of love. A tiny man, as a result of an early illness, he seemed for years to tower over me: as it were, commandingly shorter than myself. 'My dear chap,' he'd say, 'to get through the world, you must look like the world! Hold on to your inner sense of the true value of things, and master the game – master the game!' And here I was, somewhere in 1941, acclaiming the saintliness of –

Lenin! I was awfully aware of Williams's scarcely suppressed sighs.

His belief in my incapacity to understand the machinery of worldliness, which in the end enabled you to be as unworldly as you wished, was never to vanish. When Kate and I were about to be modestly married, on a modest half-term in my years at the Vale prep school, Kate arranged for us to have a prefatory party. As it began I heard Williams saying to the producer of the amateur dramatic company in which Kate and I had met: 'Well, now, what do you make of this?' It was said in the tone in which, a dozen years earlier, he'd have asked the sports master if it was a good idea to put me in for the high jump. Notable tendency not to take off – at any rate, in an upward direction! Seemed confused as between high jump and long jump! 'Kate is a girl of character,' Williams had said to me, on arrival: he and Em handing me an immense glass flower bowl, which startled me at the time: it was Kate who pointed out that it was a wedding present. I knew what he meant about Kate. She was brave to the point where a better word might be foolhardy. 'You're a dreamer, still,' he said. I knew he thought the marriage wouldn't last five minutes. The fact of being married would simply slip my memory, and that would be that.

Least effectual of men, as John Logan had made finally clear, he'd elected to find me monstrously ineffectual. Oh, how life bristled with cruel paradox! In the end, I'd turned out, *mirabile dictu* (a phrase I'd learned from him), to be more worldly and more competent than my old mentor. I took no pleasure at all in this: simply was astonished by yet another example of life's capacity to invert so many of its original propositions. Stay around long enough, and anything was likely to become its opposite!

A similar thought had occurred to Jack Seed, writing from Bondi. A characteristic of the soap opera we were involved in was that the development of its characters was so coarsely surprising. He'd been thinking of his friends in my unforgettable class at Stonehill Street, and how they'd called themselves the Three ('or, actually, quite an elastic number of') Musketeers. 'Twenty years later . . . Porthos has opened a vegetarian restaurant; Aramis has joined a commune; Athos, having lost his job at Butlins, has become manager of a punk group; and D'Artagnan was last seen wearing kabuki make-up in a singles bar.' That, he thought, was the spirit of contemptibly random invention that lay behind the script.

He'd been on holiday to the Trobriands, which he'd found chaotic. He'd hated the sense of social and administrative muddle – 'and the bowing and scraping that went on.' But then there were the people. 'Beautiful bodies. To call them black you'd have to be myopic. They were ebony – or rich browns. They were highly intelligent or very strong personalities. Their emotions were very near the surface and so there was a good deal of touching and laughing . . .

'Getting back to Sydney was a culture shock. The cars went so fast. The air was foul. The sea was muddy.'

He'd celebrated an end-of-term by taking a party from his class to an Indonesian restaurant. 'I was alarmed to hear one of the girls repeating some of my classroom remarks about Islam. She seemed to think Mohammed was Chinese. They called me "Daddy" throughout the evening. A man at the next table said: "Are you really their father?" I was glad to think I didn't look like a teacher. That made up for the horror I'd gone through, writing those awful reports.

'Mind you, just as we were parting for the holidays, one particularly sweet-faced girl asked me: "Why are you being so shitty this year?"

'Though I still suffer from the other trouble. That is, if you don't throw your weight about in obvious ways, they take it that you're soft. Don't I remember your saying it was like that for you thirty years ago? And didn't Kate once threaten to go to the school and give a talk at assembly, making it disgracefully clear that you weren't soft? We'd have enjoyed that, little swine that we were. Perhaps I should ask Cor to go and show her bruises. (She is looking over my shoulder and thinks this is a very bad joke).'

Amazing things, including clumsy kinds of death, had happened to his Sydney circle of friends. 'As you once said, we are surrounded by all these stories which really should be set down.'

9

There was, late in this decade, what I think of as the ginger autumn. The seasonal colour was more brilliant than I'd ever seen it: and I could think of no other word for it. I couldn't believe 'ginger' had ever been a poetically dignified word. At Barley Road we'd shout it at any faintly red-haired human being. But that autumn was profoundly and variously ginger. It was the year when Kate became finally white-haired, and I think of the season also in terms of that whiteness in the midst of this generality of gold.

Except that I couldn't really think it was gold. It was ginger.

It was also when I had a letter from John Logan written, he said, in tears. Suddenly, having always seen the grammar school under Percy Chew in terms of its having risen briskly above its foundering 1920-ish self, he saw it as having alienated Ben and me and all those who'd not wished to become young executives. Perhaps remembering W. B. Yeats's finger on the Logan doorbell long ago, he'd seen that the school had paid a price for its increased crispness: it had become a philistine institution. Reading his letter, I was horrified: never having wished to overturn the comforting certainties of such a man. But I remembered suddenly what Williams had said of him: that he desperately wanted to understand everyone and everything, but had small gift for doing so.

Williams had said this when I'd fallen in love with the boy playing the queen to my king in the school play. I'd appealed for help to Williams: who told me later that Percy Chew, having noted (from some evidence of gender-disorder provided by my weekly essays) that I was on what at the time was regarded as the number one primrose path to the everlasting bonfire, had wished to call for medical assistance. (Oh Percy Chew! – given his head, he'd have had half the school lobotomised!) Instead, the Welshman Williams had called in aid the Irishman Logan. 'I have arranged for you to spend an evening with him and your ambiguous friend,' Williams wrote from Swansea, 'and I urge you to consider seriously on that occasion whether G – a charming fellow: I sympathise with your feelings – is really the creature of your imagination. I have not told John Logan what the background is. He is a loyal friend and will do as I ask him because I ask it. He is an excellent man, and we have our Celtishness in common: but he does not always understand what he sees. He will give you a good evening.'

Though he hadn't done so. My friend Ray Bolton, with whom Williams wished me to contrast the alluring G, refused to accompany me: having understood, I think, that he was to be the prose of the occasion, brought into play against the poetry. And G himself, an amiable fellow whose accidental beauty was brought to bear, as I hated to think, on the fascinations of the internal combustion engine, wrote to say he was committed on the evening proposed to stripping down an MG. I wrote to John Logan and said alas, none of us could come. Williams would have been furious, had he ever remembered that he'd set the occasion up.

I wrote now to Logan, saying that he'd given me, in my turn, reason to adjust my view of the grammar school and its effects. Of course he was right when he said the school probably didn't have staff of the quality needed if, in those days, a child was to be helped to leap to Oxford or Cambridge. It hadn't the links with the universities that then counted for so much. Percy Chew's foolish brand of conservatism, his bristling refusal of sympathy for all young excitements and enthusiasms – these were another matter. He had introduced into the school a disastrous note of social dishonesty. But the school *had* been under terrible handicaps.

'Anyway,' I wrote, 'it had Williams, and you, who weren't really in Percy's army at all. You lent us books, took us to theatres, made jokes sometimes of a blessedly risqué kind, and weren't ashamed of swaggering a bit, in some senses being the Pistol, the Nym, the Bardolph of the staff. Somehow I don't think you'll mind my saying that that's what, savingly, you were, part of the time. You had a bit of the academic freebooter in you, thank God!'

We talked on the phone – and he said his own personal choice among the ruffians would be Bardolph. 'My dear! Part I've always wanted to play! When we were trudging down our Via Dolorosa, you know, family theatricals flourished! Kept despondency at bay! Young John always cast as the juvenile lead! And always wished they'd let him play a desperado!'

You tell me this now, dear John Logan, I thought, nearly fifty years after you beat me for being a suspected desperado, aged ten!

'Dear Dedward,' his next letter began, in a large effortful version of his handwriting. He'd amended that: and gone on to say I was to be asked if I'd talk at Savernake. 'Love John', he painfully and hugely wrote: and there was another short message about a friend of his I'd been interviewing (whose name was practised twice before the attempt to get it right was abandoned): then 'More love John' and a last word: 'I did say I've had a small stroke?'

His housekeeper wrote and said it wasn't a small stroke, it was a dangerous one that affected the flow of blood, and he was *very* low and seemed to have little wish to live.

The Head rang me with the news of his death. 'But don't grieve too much,' he said. 'He was himself right to the end! I saw him half an hour before he died, and he greeted me as the Chinese Ambassador!'

10

When it came to being sixty, it was difficult not to conclude that a notable amount of ageing had occurred, and irreversible damage done to the visible frame and also to one's invisible assets. Brain cells, as an example of the latter. I had never quite recovered from reading of the accelerating loss of these cells that is a price paid for failing to remain young. The information left me feeling that I should be able to brush the fallen brain cells off my shoulders like dandruff.

My father would have liked to be present on an occasion in Frankfurt, where I was covering the Book Fair for my programme. Stunned by the sheer quantity of books in those dehydrated halls, full of the coarse shouts of publishers and the amplified bellowing of men of letters, I'd asked Kurt Vonnegut, in the course of an interview, if he was not a little affected by book-nausea. No, he said. No. But then he was accustomed to industrial products.

I'd observed that the effect of Frankfurt on my producer, Roger, was a reflection of the increasing difficulty felt by essentially pre-automated human beings in adjusting to the changing world. He'd found the mere train service into the centre disturbing. The trains ran crisply on time, bringing us to the promised second into a many-layered station in which, again, everything was dependable. Accustomed to British Rail, Roger was unnerved by this merciless reliability. Though in France recently, he said, in a station converted like this one to almost complete automation, he'd been cheered to discover an unmanned information kiosk that was announcing, in nervous neon: JE SUIS HORS DE SERVICE.

In Frankfurt it was not possible to imagine a machine

confessing, or needing to confess, to its own fallibility.

Using what remained of my brain cells, those billions that hung on despite the autumnal storms in my head, I was continuing to lard reviews with alases. This was an activity my friend Maurice Lee, professor of education, had recently been on the point of abandoning. Exquisitely careful, he'd begun a review: 'No one will get nothing from this book.' From the proof that arrived it was clear that it had been through the hands of a sub-editor able to accommodate a perfectly desolate view of the literacy of professors of education. 'No one,' she had corrected Maurice, 'will get anything from this book.'

Trying to decide if at this stage they'd give my grandson Tim wonderful delight or dreadful alarm, I'd paid a visit to the distorting mirrors at Madame Tussaud's. And had remembered being there before, in 1939, when Tess Grayson and I had stood among those astonishing fatnesses and thinnesses, unbelievable squatnesses and tallnesses. Even on the gravest of citizens, the usual effect is to cause laughter. It caused us none.

I looked at Tess, a young woman of some beauty, reduced at that moment to an ovoid broadside on, standing on a couple of inches of very stout legs: and she'd gazed at me, a sort of premature late Giacometti, whose features fought in vain to remain in position on a face monstrously elongated and narrowed (his hair rising far above it in a cascading parody of his quiff): and we were beyond being amused. Our relationship had reached such a point that we could not even respond to the obvious opportunities for insult those reflections offered. Later I was to write a quite appallingly happy sonnet for Tess, beginning: Beloved ovoid, o my dearest egg! But I would have been amazed, as we stood there, to be told I should ever write a sonnet again.

The cause of our disagreement was absurd enough: I'd accused her of plagiarism. I'd discovered that a lengthy passage in one of her early letters, which had laced the disgraceful feelings she caused me with feelings of very great respect, had been taken word for word from Olive Schreiner's *Story of an African Farm*. I'd intended to be entirely forgiving about this: to say (along with much else: great parts of my waking life at the time being devoted to the composition of speeches, some an hour or more in length, intended for her fascinated ear) that, of course, by virtue of one's admiration of them, some words once read became almost one's own. There was a branch of this speech that came close to suggesting that the flow of literary theft might have been in the other direction, from Tess to Olive Schreiner. But, as I prepared to make what would have been a statement drawing upon features from the several speeches I'd prepared, I realised that what I actually felt was quite different: very unfriendly, mean, not a little cruel. Something made me want to triumph over her for pretending that Olive Schreiner's words were hers. To make things worse, I had chosen to broach the matter as we passed through the doors of the exhibition: visiting which had been an eager plan of Tess's. 'I didn't go as a child,' she'd said. 'I'd love to go with you.'

How to cut the ground from under the distorting mirror as an apparently irresistible cause of hilarity!

It strikes me now how close the young lover always is to the assassin: and how difficult it was for some product of Percy Chew's grammar school to behave well when, free of it, he entered into the relationships of love: which had always been defined as means of making oneself scant of breath. Percy and his assistants had ensured that even those who'd resisted them had a great deal of guilt to shed in the form of cruelty before they had hope of behaving in the gentle and affirmative fashion that love itself proposes.

Though, of course, young love must always be difficult to handle, even where Percy Chew has not done his worst. Never thereafter are you so struck by the outrageous strangeness of another human being. There he or she is, complete and improbable: you are allowed startling intimacy with someone who is all the more shockingly unknown for the sudden illusion of being known that the relationship offers. If I was abominable to Tess all those years ago in the halls of Madame Tussaud's, a cruelty for which I see no prospect that I shall ever forgive myself, it was partly because the first beloved, in a fashion for which there is no remedy, makes an enormous offer of herself, or himself, without any power to make the offer real. It is a moment when such an offer is total, and true, and when you know perfectly well how little is your understanding of any other human being. Such a generosity as you'll never feel again walks hand in hand with the angriest hunger for the very meanest sort of reality.

Forty years on in that hall of distorting mirrors I was largely struck by the idea of such a mirror as an image for one's personal history. It is only, I thought (coming away from another encounter with Jimmy Soper), because time, in fact a reckless speedster, creates an illusion of leisureliness, that we don't all fall about helplessly, seeing ourselves and our contemporaries passing from one rapid and horribly amusing distortion to another in its malicious mirrors.

The underpinning seemed to have persuaded our house to stand still. Seasonal things happened of the kind we take for granted only because we have been here a long time: suddenly the world is bleakly emptied: just as suddenly, it fills again with birds and leaves. I did not at first understand how absurd it was to say, to a friend: 'I've been here so long, I can't remember a time when I wasn't here!' The price of the first class stamp moved irrepressibly upwards. I had increasingly a feeling that had made my son Tom impatient when he was younger: that most things – or perhaps all things – were too complex for one to be certain about anything. I was still, at times, appalled by the huge possibility there is of misunderstanding between any two human beings. It was why I had mixed feelings about dinner parties: there being in those precipitately intimate encounters between strangers the very strongest likelihood that they would get one another wildly wrong.

I thought that with increasing age, though not perhaps quite yet, I might become less tied to fixed activities, to regular programmes and remorseless occasions for writing this or that. I shall range freely, I rashly told Kate. Like an old hen, she said.

And I thought how horrified my father would be to see me without what he'd always regarded as the ultimate human anchor, a pension. When I was no more than ten he'd already been urging the need to think in terms of secure retirement. Himself, he'd been quite frantically inside. Perhaps that was why I'd been in retreat from securities, and enjoyed the thought of being an outside contributor.

And if so, how unfair, in at least one respect! My father's passion for safety had rested on a deeply unsafe childhood. I remembered my mother's memory of him, as she first knew him, in the desperate depths of Paddington early in the century. None of his clothes had originated with him. He was dressed in bits of brothers, cousins, uncles – bits of his father, too. He had, she recalled, this monstrously long overcoat. He was terribly dashing in it: but, as she told the story, only a boy of his arrogant good looks could have made a success out of a garment so unsuitable. One of the million services she'd done him was related to shortening his sleeves. She'd wanted anyway (she'd say, giggling) to hold his hand. So when my father had the chance of being an inside contributor, as a civil servant after the First World War, he'd taken it, and never let go. And he'd desperately wanted me to hang on behind him! And I'd refused, and gone outside, instead.

It must have hurt him, keenly: as if a policeman had seen his son, on the most apparently pompous of grounds, turn thief.

11

Gary Bunce was in Moscow, I thought he said, though it might have been Mesopotamia. Anyway, he was coming nearer home, to some place I couldn't catch the name of, and would be physically assaulting bosses less exotic than of late.

He had his usual regional warning to offer. 'Avoid New Zealand, Eddy!'

'I shall,' I said: but not without some unease.